UNDER BRIGHT LIGHTS

Difference Incorporated
Roderick A. Ferguson and Grace Kyungwon Hong, Series Editors

Under Bright Lights

GAY MANILA AND THE GLOBAL SCENE

Bobby Benedicto

Difference Incorporated

University of Minnesota Press
Minneapolis
London

Portions of several chapters were previously published as "The Third World Queer," in *Queer Futures,* ed. Elahe Haschemi Yekani, Eveline Kilian, and Beatrice Michaelis (Farnham, U.K.: Ashgate, 2013), 117–30. Copyright 2013; reprinted by permission of Ashgate Publishing. An earlier version of chapter 3 was previously published as "The Haunting of Gay Manila: Global Space-time and the Specter of *Kabaklaan,*" *GLQ: A Journal of Lesbian and Gay Studies* 14, nos. 2–3, special issue on Queer/Migration (2008): 317–38. Reprinted by permission of Duke University Press. An earlier version of chapter 4 was previously published as "Shared Spaces of Transnational Transit: Filipino Gay Tourists, Labor Migrants, and the Borders of Class Difference," *Asian Studies Review* 33, no. 3 (2009): 289–301.

Published by the University of Minnesota Press
111 Third Avenue South, Suite 290
Minneapolis, MN 55401–2520
http://www.upress.umn.edu

Library of Congress Cataloging-in-Publication Data

Benedicto, Bobby.
　Under bright lights: gay Manila and the global scene / Bobby Benedicto.
　　(Difference Incorporated)
　Includes bibliographical references and index.
　ISBN 978-0-8166-9107-4 (hc: alk. paper)—ISBN 978-0-8166-9108-1
(pb: alk. paper)
　1. Gay men—Philippines—Manila.　2. Male homosexuality—Philippines—Manila.　3. Gay community—Philippines—Manila.　4. Gay business enterprises—Philippines—Manila.　I. Title.
　HQ76.2.P62M363 2014
　306.76'60959916—dc23　　　　　　　　　　　　　　　　2014005525

Printed in the United States of America on acid-free paper

The University of Minnesota is an equal-opportunity educator and employer.

20　19　18　17　16　15　14　　　　　　　　10　9　8　7　6　5　4　3　2　1

CONTENTS

City of Contradictions

When I think of gay life under the bright lights of Metro Manila, I think of nights spent standing outside the dance clubs, and especially of the quieter moments during unusually slow Friday or Saturday nights, when I found myself out on the street trading stories and smoking cigarettes with other gay men who were taking breaks from the music or from dancing. It was during those moments that I heard many of the stories I recall in these pages—stories about everyday life, nights on the town, images stuck in people's minds, adventures and misadventures over the years, and travels in and around Manila and to cities thousands of miles away. Some of the stories I heard during those nights were told with humor and interrupted by fits of laughter, others with the mild seriousness of embarrassing confessions. There were stories shared in snippets and ones revealed in long conversations rich with detail, at times fleshed out, little by little, over the course of several encounters. Looking back on all the stories I heard then, I know that each of them was, in many ways, singular and distinct; and yet, even as I recall their differences, a kind of sameness quickly sets in. For all the tales about gay life under the bright lights of the city that were shared during those weekend nights—including my own—emerge out of older, classed narratives of privilege, violence, colonialism, mobility and desire, and of emplacement and displacement in times of rapid change. They float up from stories about Manila that are not often told, the ones kept in the background of personal and collective memories or hidden in plain sight, in spaces like the streets outside dance clubs, where fantastic sites of privilege and metropolitan dreams collide with the disorder and squalor of the city.

In my memories, the streets outside dance clubs are sites of urban contradictions; they are spaces where fast lives appear subtended by the drama of life in a third-world city. I remember spells cast from DJ booths slipping out through the gaps underneath the doors of clubs, keeping us under their charms even as we stood beneath drooping electrical wires, on sidewalks cracked by the monsoons that came in the middle of each year. I remember how, when the rains came, sewage rose out of shallow, uncovered man-holes and gutters turned into streams full of cigarette butts and bits of garbage. I remember the sound of dance music merging with the cacoph-ony on the streets, with the horns of luxury cars and SUVs and of rickety jeepneys and run-down taxis; the touch of air-conditioning making way for the sticky feel of urban, tropical airs; the sweat from dancing mixing with sweat from humidity. In my mind's eye, the image of bodies dancing quickly fades into the image of a group of men standing in a circle outside a club, trading stories in perfect American English, and then to the awkward silence caused by the sudden appearance of a middle-aged woman in tat-tered clothes, a baby strapped to her chest, a hand stretched out for loose change. I remember other nights, other men, and other street dwellers: vagrants of all kinds, a gang of street children that arrived every Saturday night, and men raised on stories about how the money you give to beggars goes to bottles of glue or to the greedy hands of criminal syndicates.

When I remember life in gay Manila, faded details come to me of other scenes of privilege, threat, and abjection, held together, tenuously, in a blurry, nostalgic mix. There was the New Year's morning when I found myself sitting on a concrete bench jutting out from the exterior wall of one of the clubs, sandwiched between a group of gay men with their eyes half open and an emaciated homeless man with a smile plastered on his soot-covered face. I remember how we all just sat silently and watched the sky lighten to reveal the gray haze left behind by cheap fireworks launched from side streets, backyards, and the rooftops of buildings. There was the night I heard an argument about the price of Marlboro Lights break out between a man who had stepped out of the clubs and the ten-year-old girl who, every Saturday night, looked after the makeshift cigarette stall out-side while her mother slept soundly next to her on sheets of cardboard. There were the groups of men who patrolled the streets and who charged forty pesos (one U.S. dollar) to "watch" cars and the vague, unspoken threat of having tires slashed and side mirrors stolen. I remember how, before dawn broke on Sunday mornings, an old *taho* vendor would walk past one of the clubs, how the faces of the gay men standing on the street would light up as they rushed to him, and how the sight of them brought me back, always, to childhood images of bicycles and gated villages. I remember wondering if, despite the indifference on his face, the old ven-dor was shocked to find that his first customers were no longer small children ready for church but men built like athletes, dressed in tight

T-shirts and jeans, heading home at sunrise with alcohol on their breaths and other men on their arms.

My memories snap from these encounters on the street to images from inside the clubs: the T-shirts hanging from waistbands, the bottles of water carried around by those on drugs, the views from walkways overlooking dance floors, the lights. I remember one man's story about how he used to be an "angel," a dancer for the now defunct New York club Heaven and how he dreamt of moving back; another man's claim that he could identify all the men dancing on the ledge by the screen names they used on a popular personal ads website; plans made to travel overseas to attend circuit parties; and small talk about bad first dates, bad sex, television, a new bar that opened on the other side of town, an upcoming sale at a favorite shop. My memories drift back and forth between these images and stories—these fragments of the new banalities of privileged gay life in the city—and the scenes of contradiction that mark the streets. I remember the walls of the clubs as charged borders crossed and recrossed by those inured to the squalor of Manila and yet privy to moments of reprieve and frivolity and to circuits of capital and desire. I remember the clubs, and other pockets of privilege, as dreamworlds that were set apart from urban turbulence but constantly spilled out onto the street, where they came into contact with scenes of abjection and with the reality of a city in a state of permanent crisis.

At times, I remember life lived in Manila's sea of contradictions, and especially the movement back and forth, in and out of the clubs, as the stuff of travelers' tales about skyscrapers towering over marketplaces and shantytowns, the fascinating and horrifying feeling of seeing poverty and wealth standing side by side, of passing by a family living on a traffic island on the way to a bar featured in the *New York Times*. More often, all of this comes to me as a picture of extremes that possesses no shock value, of "zones of compromised ordinariness" that can be greeted with little more than a passing glance, with looks of radical indifference crafted over time.[1] In my memories, urban contradictions are ordinary parts of the landscape of the city; they define the shared backdrop, the common ground, of the stories we like to tell.

The stories I recall in this book are set in the first decade of the twenty-first century—a decade I cannot help but remember first as one marked by personal journeys. It was the year 2004 when I moved from Manila to Toronto, Canada, and the year my interest in social theory began to converge, unexpectedly, with my memories of the urban gay culture and the world of privilege I had only just left behind. In 2005, I returned to Manila and found myself even more fully immersed in club culture than I had previously been, and I began to see this culture and the city as a whole with the schizophrenic eye of one who is both a "researcher" and an "insider." In 2006, I left for Melbourne, Australia, to begin working on what would become *Under Bright Lights*, and the years that followed were years spent flying to and from Manila so often that words and phrases like "coming home," "going away," and "fieldwork" began to seem meaningless.

I remember this decade too in much the same way I imagine other Filipinos do, as the decade when Manileños once again marched the streets to oust a president, the Americans returned to fight "terrorists" in the south, groups of young soldiers invaded two upmarket hotels in the hopes of inspiring mass rebellions, Gloria Macapagal-Arroyo fought off protest after protest, Corazon Aquino died, and epic floods left Manila in ruins. And yet, though I was there on the streets the day actor-turned-president Joseph Estrada was forced to leave the Palace in 2001, and though my eyes were glued to television and laptop screens during the other historic moments that marked this decade, my memories barely resemble the picture of outrage and unrest that emerges when one pieces together the headlines. For the spectacles of failure and disorder that took place during the years I cover here occurred alongside other, minor spectacles that were, to me, just as compelling, animated as they were by the seductive force of progress, dreams of excess, and fantasy-desires for lives lived in wombs of luxury.

There were the new malls rising from reclaimed lands and on the sites of retired power plants; the sleek restaurants, bars, and clubs emerging in rapid succession; and the upmarket condominiums that promised "sanctuaries in the city," "lifespaces surrounded by everything plush," and "cosmopolitan living" for those who were part of "fashionable Manila." Throughout this decade, there was growing cynicism about the future of the city, but fervent efforts were also placed on the building of safe enclaves where "lifestyles" could surge forward, unhindered by the daily sightings and constant news of maldevelopment that inundated those living in Manila and those who observed it from afar. There was talk of lost foreign direct investment, but there was also a continuous influx of high-end designer brands. There were fears of growing poverty, but the number of expensive cars on Manila's pothole-ridden roads also appeared to be increasing. Bombs would explode in the basements of malls and people would return the following day to enact scenes of "normalcy." Newspapers were covering spectacular scenes of desperation, like stampedes erupting during the filming of game shows and dumpsites overflowing and burying scavengers alive, but they were also more frequently reporting scandals involving those who inhabited the first world in the third world, like the lifestyle columnist who came under heavy fire for complaining about having to share a flight to Greece with overseas domestic workers or socialites photographed snorting cocaine off the tips of car keys in the restrooms of dance clubs.

This is how Manila appeared to me over the course of my many departures and returns in the 2000s: a world of enchantment and disenchantment, where scenes of trauma worked like minor eruptions, giving pause to (but never stopping) the aspirational march of those on the winning end of "neoliberalism," "commodity culture," "globalization," and "empire."[2] My memories of Manila, in other words, are of a life speeding up, acquiring all the trappings of modernity, but also of a life embedded in the painful realities of a city unable to stay on the path of progress.

In some ways, the privileged gay life that I offer a glimpse of here can be seen as but another instance in the ongoing drama of a city that takes two steps back with every step forward. In other ways, however, this decade was, for many gay men, more momentous, more saturated with transformations that appear to constitute a sea change.

Once during the summer of 2008, I found myself standing outside a club on a major thoroughfare of the Makati Central Business District (CBD) with Arthur, a man in his late twenties whom I had met several years earlier.[3] Surveying the large crowd gathered that night, he began to reminisce in a tone that was, at once, mocking and prideful: "Look at these kids," he was saying. "Catty. Loud. Overconfident. Tossing drinks and snappy one-liners, owning the ledge and the dance floor, kissing in the dark corners. We used to rush from our cars to the old gay bars in Malate with our heads bowed down, afraid that someone we knew might see us. Now these kids stand in the middle of the road, in full view of everyone." Arthur's nostalgia did not take me by surprise. I knew him as someone who was prone to reminiscences, who made sweeping assessments about how life in the city had changed for gay men over the years, and who liked to talk about things that happened in the not-too-distant past as though they had taken place a lifetime ago. During the interview I conducted with him some time prior to that night in the clubs, he remembered gay life in the city as a blur of events. He remembered the night in 2003 when Manila's first "proper" gay club opened its doors and how we all gathered together in that tiny space and were buoyed by the thrill of newness, the intrigue when a rival club opened its doors the following year, the excitement over the first circuit parties held in Manila, the time when people began flying to other cities just to attend parties in foreign clubs, and the sudden waves of men coming out. He recalled the year gay events started acquiring corporate sponsors and glossy gay magazines began appearing on newsstands; the year international gym franchises began setting up shop all over the city, gay men began to look like bodybuilders, and started having sex in steam rooms; the year everyone migrated from anonymous text-based Internet chat rooms to a personal ads website called Guys4men, where photographs of faces and bare torsos were publicly displayed; and the year pirated copies of gay films and television programs from overseas began spreading through the city like wildfire.

Arthur saw himself as part of a generation that witnessed seismic transformations, the last generation given to hiding, and the generation that still remembered a time when there was nowhere to go but the bars that were ruled by a tightly knit set of older, moneyed queers and the comedy clubs where drag performers entertained a mostly straight audience. He knew, of course, that he was still young and, as he put it, lucky to see the gay scene emerge and evolve. Still, at twenty-eight, he had cultivated the air of a veteran and was treated like someone who had seen it all. That night, watching the people outside that club in Makati, he joked that he was the oldest person left in the scene. When I asked him where everyone else had gone, the men whom we used to see at the bars and clubs and who remembered what we remembered, he said that they had all "retired," were living "domestic" lives as couples, or had migrated overseas. "The old people now," he declared, "are all of us over the age of twenty-five." I laughed when he said that, though I was not sure if he was making fun of the ageism that plagued club culture or if he was merely pointing out that people grow old quickly in the face of rapid change.

For Arthur, the transformations that defined the decade were more than just examples of how the city had been taken over by what the *New York Times* called a "new confidence and energy" epitomized by "trendy, cosmopolitan" bars and "youth-obsessed nightclubs."[4] They were, for Arthur, part of a story of progress and struggle, of an ongoing search for recognition and acceptance. There were nights when Arthur would return to the studio apartment he kept in Makati and put his observations down in an online journal: "The new ones (at the clubs)," he wrote once, "revel in their freedom and their newfound sense of belonging. The older ones are more cautious and jaded, clucking their tongues and rolling their eyes, but also vicariously reliving what it meant to discover being gay and accepted and finally free."[5] He wanted to complain about how the "new ones"— men only a few years younger than he or I—could not remember gay life in the city before the transformations that followed the emergence of the gay clubs. But he kept himself in check, fearful of becoming that which he feared the most—a vicious queen—and instead extolled the virtue of having seen the transformations take place. He wrote of how "we had it hard," of "our depth of understanding," and how we had earned our candor with battle scars. He wrote of how "all of us used to feel that something was missing and that a real part of us was hidden," how "all of us were ashamed of what we felt" and "ashamed for the people who cared about us." He remembered how, as recently as the early 2000s, none of us were willing to post pictures of ourselves online in order to meet men to date or sleep with; how there was no club to frequent on weekend nights; how "there was no one to talk to" and how "no one seemed to understand."

He recalled how, after graduating from one of the top universities in the country, he had taken a job as a member of the editorial team of the city's "first decent gay lifestyle magazine." It wasn't easy, he said. He knew nothing about running a magazine and "barely understood what it meant to be gay." All the available local gay magazines then were pseudopornographic local titles sold on the sidewalks of the city's backstreets. Getting people to talk about their "hidden" lifestyle proved to be a challenge. Arthur spent most of his time calling the managers of celebrities to try to convince them to let their charges pose for photos and be interviewed. Most of them turned him down. The ones who said yes were those who managed female balladeers who already had gay followings or young actors desperate to catch a break. The major booksellers refused to sell the magazine, so Arthur called potential subscribers directly and hoped that word of mouth would be enough to generate attention and profit. After only a few issues, the publisher ran out of money and the magazine was discontinued. Disenchanted, Arthur went to work for one of the largest multinational corporations operating in Manila, where he kept his sexuality a secret, for fear of missing out on plum assignments.

Only a few years after the magazine where Arthur worked shut down, new, glossy gay magazines began appearing on the stands of major booksellers. I spoke to Arthur about these magazines soon after they came out and he told me that he knew the men who started them. He was, he said, proud that they were proving "the power of the pink peso." In his journal, he wrote about how, back when he was working for a similar publication, no such thing as a "pink peso" existed. "Back then, it was almost a joke," he recalled. "Top advertising people thought we would never get a decent advertiser. Now, my gym has a Gay Pride poster and nobody raises an eyebrow." At work, Arthur had begun to come out, prompted in part by the appearance one day of an intern who, after a week on the job, came out to the entire office. Arthur recalled, somewhat resentfully, how the intern's revelation sparked little more than a few minutes of water cooler talk and how he had to pull the intern aside to tell him, from behind clenched teeth, that their colleagues did not know that he, too, was gay.

Indeed, whenever Arthur recalled the changes that had affected him and other gay men he knew, he exuded a mixture of resentment and relief, satisfaction and nostalgia, and bitterness and a sense of accomplishment. The night we were out in the clubs, he told me, after criticizing the men standing on the street, that we should not begrudge them. "We have worked hard to be understood and respected," he said, another time. "And here they are. The fruits of our labors. In the gay clubs. In the magazines. In the circuit parties. Demanding recognition and gaining respect. Inch by inch by inch. We are now business entities."

I heard echoes of Arthur's stories when I spoke to magazine editors, club owners, DJs, and other gay men who, like Arthur, could not help but be astonished by the changes that have swept Manila during the early to mid-2000s. They told me that gay men were no longer creeping around in the dark and that gay life was beginning to take form, to emerge as a viable market. In some ways, I did not need to be told any of this, for the narrative of progress that the people I spoke to relayed—a narrative articulated in the language of capital—was also imprinted on the streets and in semi-public places like the clubs and malls that were multiplying all over the city.

When the clubs hosted large parties, their exterior walls were plastered with tarpaulin posters that featured the logos of corporate sponsors. The vendors of pirated DVDs were stocking numerous gay titles. Foreign liquor companies hoping to break into the local market were negotiating exclusive deals with the gay clubs. On major thoroughfares, local clothing companies had begun to put up large billboards featuring actors and models in their underwear, in shots that were, to the trained eye, unmistakably patterned after the covers of gay magazines and the invitations sent out by the organizers of gay events. The same companies were, in fact, taking out advertisements in gay magazines and sponsoring fashion shows in the clubs. Some of their shops were earning reputations as cruising spots.

There were also political changes afoot. In 2007, the activist group Ladlad, which attempted to run for Congress as a party-list organization, reportedly topped early surveys before being disqualified on the grounds that the group's application for accreditation "lacked merit."[6] The annual Pride marches were attracting up to two thousand people, a far cry from the first march in 1994, which, I was told, drew only sixty participants. For the most part, however, the world of activism and that of the parties and the clubs that I document here stayed separate, as groups like Ladlad pushed for working-class issues that seemed, on the surface at least, to be divorced from and of little interest to those who were immersed in surging worlds of private consumption.[7]

Once a year, however, at the large parties that followed the Pride marches, these two worlds overlapped. One of the few men I interviewed who was both involved in activist politics and a regular club goer said that he no longer enjoyed those parties. They had gotten too big, he said, and most of the people who went did not actually care about "*pride*." He made a point of drawing a distinction between those who knew what was being celebrated and those who did not, the ones who came as part of a cause and the ones who came only because of the size and scale of the party. When I asked him to elaborate, I expected him to speak of local struggles fought and won or to rail against processes of commodification, the way he had in our previous conversations. Instead, he looked at me with an expression of resignation and said, "Well, you know, the guys there now, they don't even know what Stonewall is." It was that offhand complaint that made it clear to me that though gay Manila was marked by many fractures and divisions, it was also held together, if tenuously, by notions of progress and history that were hinged on spatial imaginations that extended far beyond the city limits.

During the years I was conducting fieldwork in Manila, there was, among the gay men with whom I spent most of my time, a palpable feeling that things were changing, "that something was happening, that we were in something."[8] Something was happening next week, or next month, or six months from now, or whenever. A DJ from Los Angeles was due to arrive. The clubs were getting fitted with sound systems from France. Things were getting better; the scene was becoming more "world class." One night, I asked a club promoter if he thought the gay scene in Manila was comparable to those he had seen in other parts of Asia, Australia, Europe, and North America. "Not yet," he said, "but we're getting there. It's just a matter of time." I was struck, inspired even, by his confidence in the future, by his faith in things to come. Still, I could not help but think cynically of his (or our) attachment to that which was "not yet," for though I too was attuned to and moved by the spirit of acceleration and transformation that animated gay life then, it also seemed to me that whatever "progress" we envisioned would always be out of reach, forever encased by a force field made of local structures of violence and marked by the painful history of the city and the failure of older dreams of a coming modernity.

When Arthur recalls the Pride parties held in June of 2005, he remembers Tony, a wealthy gay man from an older generation, going up to people on the street outside one of the clubs and yelling, "Do you know M (a local socialite)? She's cheap! That's what she is! What does she know, anyway? She grew up on the wrong side of the tracks. She's over!" Arthur recalls this image disdainfully and says that it represents what "most people still think about gay men: stuck up, loud, gossip-mongering, discriminating, vicious and (with) no shame."

I do not know if Tony would actually object to being described in this way. He was a proud man who made no apologies for the wealth he inherited and the merciless way he wielded it to establish hierarchies where none were readily visible. The night I first met Tony, at an exclusive bar where several mutual friends of ours were having cocktails, he had had too much to drink and ended up making a scene when, in the middle of polite conversation, he pointed his finger straight at a man whom he had just met that night and, in a voice loud enough to silence everyone, declared, "I don't like you. You're cheap. Cheap. Cheap. Cheap." The man was stunned. He did not know how to react to Tony's insults and just sat quietly as Tony stared him down. It must have only taken a few minutes, but it felt like a long time before Tony's friends managed to pull Tony aside and convince him that he was already drunk and that it was time for him to head home. By the time Tony left, the other man was already gone. He had gotten up while Tony's friends intervened, bid the rest of us good night, and hurriedly walked out of the bar with his shoulders hunched and his eyes welling up with tears of embarrassment.

That was the first time I met Tony, but I saw him again several times afterward at some of the other upmarket bars and restaurants scattered throughout the city. He had, to my relief, taken something of a liking to me. He would sit me down and tell me stories about life in Manila during decades past and especially of the years prior to the fall of the Marcos dictatorship in 1986. Most Filipinos remember those years as years of violence and disappearance, of people being tortured and vanishing from the streets, and of signs of mass poverty erupting everywhere and quickly dropping out of sight like the shantytowns that were there one day and gone the next. For Tony, however, as for others who reaped the benefits of the hierarchies that congealed under the Marcos regime, those same years were years of grandeur, order, and beauty. They were years when nascent claims to globalness were gaining ground and dreams of modernity were being realized, concretized, for instance, in the magnificent modern structures that were rising from the streets, which heralded the arrival of the city in the world and of the world in the city.

Indeed, Tony's memories of the dictatorship and its modernist drive were marked not by images of violence but of glamour and excess. He remembered fêtes thrown in ballrooms and guests arriving from all over the world. He recalled attending extravagant parties thrown by friends of Imelda Marcos and spoke, fondly, of how she banned "ugliness" wherever she went. He remembered how people came to events dressed to the hilt, how they went on luxurious trips to Europe, and how everyone was "fabulous" and had "class." The stories he told of gay life in the city were likewise marked by excess. He and his friends would throw small parties at the five-star Manila Hotel and drive around the city to pick up rent boys—not like the ones you see on the street today, he said, but attractive ones from good universities who, for one reason or another, just happened to need extra cash. They would spend their weekend nights at a gay bar in the old City of Manila: a converted, rustic two-story apartment on a quiet street that somehow became the epicenter of Manila's nightlife, earning such a reputation for decadence that the whole of Manila "society," not only gay men, could sometimes be seen pushing through its doors. At that bar, I was told, socialites would pass out routinely on cushioned bleachers and just lay there until sunrise. Hosts walked around putting Quaaludes on patrons' tongues. Manileños were able to rub shoulders with barons and viscounts and mingle with Hollywood celebrities like Francis Ford Coppola, who once brought with him the cast of *Apocalypse Now*, and Lynda Carter (Wonder Woman), who supposedly wore a T-shirt from the bar's souvenir shop on the cover of *Time* magazine.

Out of Tony's stories, a picture emerges of a gay life and a society that knew what it meant to be "world class." For him, Manila was once already global; the city was not in the thick of a story of progress but at the endpoint of a story of decline. This was not, as one might surmise, a popular account of the story of the city, but it was one that was echoed by others who stood on the winning end of the polarized ways of living that marked the Marcos years. Another man from Tony's generation, for instance, once told me that the reason the famous gay bar in the City of Manila did not need a sign was because "the whole world knew where it was." "And where are we now?" he asked. "Most people wouldn't be able to locate Manila on a map."

One night, over dinner, Tony told me that, contrary to popular opinion, he was not in fact a classist. The gay bar he and his friends frequented, he said, catered not only to "high society" but also to people like R (now a famous beautician) and others who came from humble backgrounds. They all got along despite their differences in status, he said, "because the really rich and the really poor are the only two kinds of people in the world who do not care about what others think of them." During the same dinner, I asked him why he thought things had changed, why the glamour and decadence he remembered so vividly seemed to have vanished from the city and was all but absent from the Manila of the 1990s and the 2000s that make up the bulk of my own personal memories. Perhaps predictably, he credited the decline of the city to the rise of a middle class that "tried too hard" and had come into power under the democratic reign of Corazon Aquino, a woman who, in Tony's terms, had "no appreciation for beauty." "Do you know how Ninoy really died?" he asked me, referring to Aquino's husband, the opposition senator who was shot as he stepped down from a plane and whose death inspired the 1986 People Power Revolution. "Marcos didn't have him killed. He had a gun in his pocket, slipped on the steps, and shot himself in the face."

It was comments such as these that made Arthur, among many others, resent Tony. They called him callous and *matapobre*.[9] They said that he was not as wealthy as he made himself out to be, that he, too, was "only middle class." At times, however, I found the disdain for Tony puzzling. After all, most, if not all, the men I spoke to and spent time with were also part of a world where class borders were quickly and routinely raised. The world we inhabited was a world where a surreptitious glance could determine someone's worth, a world where classed insults were passed around with ease by men who, like Tony, were always in search of the "right party" with the "right crowd" and in the "right address." Arthur himself spoke in the black-and-white language of a marketing executive. He described things, places, and people coolly and, at times, harshly as part of classes "A," "B," "C," "D," and "E."

To me, it seemed that not much separated Tony from those, like Arthur and me, whose points of comparison were a past when there was "nowhere to go" and a present that appeared to be moving forward. Not only were we, like Tony, able to benefit from the hierarchies that ordered Manila, but our dreams of a worldliness to come seemed to be mirrored in his nostalgia for a time when Manila was known to the world. The difference was that Tony saw failure where we saw promise. We looked to the future while he looked to the past. In either case, however, the present of the city served, primarily, as a point of departure; it was the vantage point from which all of us stood, looking out for better times.

I had a panoramic view of the city from the balcony of an apartment where I lived for a year. From there, you could see, off in the distance, the modest skyline of the Makati CBD, flanked on one side by the scattered buildings of the old City of Manila and, on the other, by the new structures of an upmarket development called the "Global City." You could also see, densely blanketing the city, houses and apartments that registered the extreme ways of living that define Manila. There were the large houses clustered together in gated subdivisions, modest townhouses, apartment buildings in various states of newness or dilapidation, and squatter shanties made of scrap wood and corrugated iron sheets, many of them topped with old tires or other weights that held roofs in place when the strong winds came during the typhoon season.

From that balcony, you could look straight down and watch a German shepherd sleeping in the manicured backyard of a rock star's house or, if you turned your head slightly to the right, a pack of skeletal mongrels running around a small junkyard, kicking up the dirt that surrounded a hill of discarded appliances and car parts. You could watch narrow roads fill up with small trucks and taxis, tricycles and jeepneys, all those vehicles that produced the black fumes that Alphonso Lingis once described as capable of defeating any quixotic idea of exploring Manila's streets.[10] You could watch people, too, but as in most of the city, the bodies that could be spied on the roads belonged, almost exclusively, to those who had to be on the ground like the vendors who made a living off the streets, the security guards of our building who protected us from unnamed threats, or the maids who were sent down to the corner store a block away to fetch cigarettes or bottles of Coke. From that balcony, you could see Manila for what it was, or at least the way I always picture it: as a space where the mundane effects of capitalist modernity were piled, a landscape of contradictions.

At night, however, the contradictions of Manila were barely visible eight stories above ground. The view from my apartment was dominated by the distant lights of Makati and the Global City. Some nights, pairs of giant spotlights would shoot up from those areas and dance around the sky like twin beacons. These lights came from upmarket commercial complexes, from dance clubs or other venues where large events were being held. They reminded me, always, of upturned lighthouses, of signs of life in a veiled sea of intermittence and turbulence, quarrel and racket. Like the beams that came from lighthouses, these shafts of lights bursting out of distant sites gave directions. They told us where to go and when. They brought safe havens into relief, detaching them from the general picture of disorder that I associated with the city. They indicated where "things were happening."

One night, I found myself standing on that balcony, watching the lights with one of my informants: "They don't look like lighthouses to me," he was saying. "They're more like Bat-Signals. They're telling us to put on our tights, jump in the car, and get out of here."

I laughed. "Is that actually where we're going?" I asked, gesturing at the light.

"I don't know. I suppose. Where else?"

"All right," I said, "but let's not leave 'til later. I'd rather wait for the roads to clear."

Making a Scene

A collective sensing out of what might be happening. A state of
alert saturated with the potentiality of things in the making in
a personal, political, and aesthetic ambit that has not yet found
its form but is always promising and threatening to take shape.
A perturbation or disturbance in the atmosphere animates a
composition. Something throws itself together. An event. A scene.
A daydream . . . A sensorium attuned to atmospherics grapples not
only with things or power, but with the world—a worlding.

—Kathleen Stewart, "Atmospheric Attunements"

If I were to map gay Manila as I recall it, it would appear not as an enclave
but as a series of privileged sites pieced together, vaguely cast against the
noise and squalor of the third-world city. This map would include not
only the gay clubs where my informants and I spent many weekend nights
and the homes where private parties were occasionally held but also bars,
clubs, and commercial developments that were not identified as "gay" and
yet served as routine destinations for gay men. The lines that link these
places and that we ourselves traced whenever we drove through the city
late at night reveal that shape of an urban world in the making, a scene
that can be imagined only as a flow of movements, a shuttling back and
forth between and among places similarly invested in the dream of a fast
life unencumbered by Manila's disorder. On this map, gay spaces are not,
strictly speaking, spaces for minoritized others. They are neither apart from
nor simply a part of a world of affluence that exists within (and that often
simultaneously rules and despises) the postcolonial metropolis. Rather, they
are emergent in the aspirations that animate the city streets: they are caught
in the classed desire to dress "third world places in first world drag"; in

the flood of images that offer glimpses of distant places, the imagined end-points of a model of modernity that remains teleological; in the will to speed up, to escape and "fall upwards," past the limits of the city.[1]

In this way, the places that constitute gay Manila form a joint space best understood topologically, as attenuated, squeezed, pliant, and labile-like textiles—continuous with both the failures of the metropolis and the global aspirations of its elites.[2] They are havens that come out of the cracks of the city and rise in the wake of travels that are real and vir-tual, protracted and deferred, desired and imagined. From a worm's-eye view, these spaces appear as scattered structures surrounded by urban decay. From high above, they might look, collectively, like a tiny dot reaching out, a glowing speck on a picture of the world at night, "where the *oecumene* appears, like an upside down sky, as an immense galaxy made of all the lights of the cities of the world."[3] Gay spaces under the bright lights of Manila appear as sites where dreams of globalness rub up against the invincible facticity of location. To navigate and narrate them, as I hope to do here, is to offer an account akin to what Paul Virilio once called a "tele-topological puzzle"—a composition of surfaces that hold together only provisionally, with strained relations to notions of proximity and with cracks running wild under a calm facade—or to do as Toni Morrison once did and paint a picture of a "place that dislo-cates everything."[4]

Like all ethnographic accounts, the story I present in these pages is necessarily partial and incomplete. This book is not about a discrete, con-tainable space defined by dimensions that can be exhaustively explained but about a world that resists straightforward mapping and that I refer to as the "bright lights scene" or, simply, the "scene." This is a world enmeshed in increasingly global processes such as the incorporation of gay men into consumer markets, the emergence of hybridized gay identities in globalization, the spread of "mainstream" gay representations, the legiti-mation of LGBT politics in "multicultural" democracies, and gay tourisms and migrations. At the same time, however, this is a world bound up in the local cultural politics of a city caught in the throes of global modernity and of the neoliberal order that sets its rules. It is a world that takes shape in what I have begun to describe as the landscape of contradictions that defines the experience of twenty-first-century Manila. Arising amid mul-tiple transformations that overlap and ignite one another, the story of the scene's emergence is, as I tell it, the story of the fabulation of a lifeworld, folded into larger narratives about mobility, aspiration, and the fashion-ing of a "global-metropolitan milieu" out of the "noisy matter" of urban life in a megapolitan environment.[5]

Under Bright Lights is thus, at its broadest, an effort to picture privileged gay life in Manila as a composition, an ongoing *poesis* imbricated
in the logics and contradictions of capitalist modernity that are manifested in the material and cultural landscape of the third-world city. It is
an investigation of how the world-making practices of gay men reproduce
the cultures of domination that govern present-day Manila and that are
predicated on categories such as gender, race, and especially class, which
themselves are being reconfigured by and channeled into new circuits of
exchange, dreams of mobility and speed, and the fantasy-desires that live
on in the postcolonial present. Here, the production of a world grounded
in a minoritized sexual identity appears animated by systems of privilege.
Gay life is sanctioned by the market and its attendant technologies and
circulations. New sexual subjectivities and sexualized spaces arise, incited
by the same, never-to-be-fulfilled promise of global belonging that has
long driven the transnationalizing moves of Manila's urban elites. Put
differently, this book attends to the problem of third-world queer complicities. Here, the story of struggle, injury, and resistance that stands as
the abbreviated account of gay life in Manila, and in other de-centered
places around the world, is reread with one eye trained on the convivial
relations that exist between gay men and the forces that keep the wheels
of the prevailing order of things turning.

Though this book draws attention to lived experiences of gay male
privilege, the unfinished world it refers to remains a space on the margins, not only because it is made by and for sexual others, but precisely
because it takes form in a "third-world city." I insist on using this term
here, albeit hesitantly, in order to stress the way Manila has been imagined and narrativized by those within and those without as a city that
stands on the beaten end of the present geopolitical order and that has
grown accustomed to the feelings of futility and failure that accompany
modernization.[6] At once about states of local privilege and emplacement
in a city defined by its global marginality, the story I tell opens gaps in
master narratives of "margin" and "center" by tracking shifting positions
in diagrams of power that operate across different spatial scales.[7] In this
story, the figuration of subjects as either "winners" or "losers," "oppres-
sors" or "oppressed," or "colonizers" or "colonized" becomes difficult,
if not impossible, to sustain; a picture emerges of a world where multiple
hierarchies intersperse to form "nervous systems" and subject positions
are always, necessarily, contingent and precarious.[8]

What I am calling the bright lights scene is, thus, unlike the bounded
culture imagined in classical ethnographic studies. It does not refer to an
anthropological place that exists, somewhere, fixed, a destination waiting

to be arrived at and represented through a list of abstracted traits, but to a tangle of potential connections, an assemblage that comes together when links are anxiously traced, felt, and made between spaces, forms, bodies, objects, dreams, trajectories, images, signs, styles, and other forceful and affecting elements.[9] This is an assemblage that is, at once, a part of the city and apart from it. It takes form as "real" spaces like bars and clubs that materialize the scene as a distinctively urban experience. It bursts into imagination when event organizers assert that the transformations in local club culture mark the entrance of Manila into a global network made up of cities such as New York, London, San Francisco, and Sydney, among others. It is made by bodies that inhabit Manila and that are, at the same time, plugged into tele-technologies that allow distant sites and virtual worlds to be glimpsed. It is in publications sitting on local news-stands; in pirated DVDs bought and sold in the basements of run-down shopping malls; and in parties and events set in gated villages, high-rise apartments, and rented venues. The bright lights scene is a world dense with circulating expressive forms that effect transnational belonging and a world textured by local historical forces such as unchecked urbanization, hardened class relations, received meanings, and the surges of moderniza-tion and technologization that have punctuated life in Manila over the past few decades.

A scene such as this is necessarily difficult, if not impossible, to repre-sent. It has no clear beginning or end and becomes apparent only partially and fleetingly, during instances when "collective sensibilities seem to pulse in plain sight" and in moments one suddenly feels immersed in "some-thing that feels like something."[10] Some of these moments take on the status of events like the night in 2003 when Manila's first gay dance club opened its doors, the emergence in 2004 of the city's first glossy gay mag-azine and of a rival club in another part of the city, the introduction of circuit parties in 2005, or the arrival of celebrity DJs and the birth of Internet portals during those same years. More often, the scene becomes apparent in quotidian moments. It takes form during nights when people drive around and seem to know exactly where to go, not because they have set plans but because they are able to sense the energy in the air and know how to follow it to places where "things are happening." It takes shape when looks are exchanged between strangers who recognize each other purely because they seem to always be in the same places at the same time. In moments such as these, something happens that produces the quality of being in a scene; things come together to reveal a world that exists within the city and yet leaks out through the "infinity of openings" that have made the city diffuse, porous, and "overexposed."[11]

Moments such as these speak to how, in spite of the elusiveness of its dimensions, the scene is nonetheless palpable as a thing; how it can be named and recognized even though its relationship to territory cannot be easily defined.[12] These are the moments when different circulations make an impact and give rise to the patterns of impulses and tones that Raymond Williams called "structures of feeling," the promise or threat that something is happening that Kathleen Stewart described as "affect," or what Michel Serres might have referred to as the sense of "living together" and of "relations made flesh" that accompany the bursts and circulations of messages and objects.[13] This sense that one is "in" something, that a scene in fact "exists," is, however, not simply the effect of an additive process. A world's acquisition of form is contingent not only on processes of articulation and interpellation but also on practices of bordering—that is, on efforts to push to the horizon those things, bodies, forces, and spaces that threaten the production and coherence of a lifeworld.[14]

At first glance, one could say that what animates the borders of the bright lights scene is sexual identification, that at the heart of its concrescence lies the universalized, commercialized, and mediatized sign of "gay." Indeed, sexual identity—taken as a property of both subjects and spaces—plays a critical part in the worlding of the scene, as evidenced, for instance, in the near total absence of women from the sites I describe in these pages. Still, gay identity, even in its most fluid formulation, cannot evoke all the logics involved in the production of the scene's charged borders. The scene fragments in gay bars, where layers upon layers of codes allow otherness to be quickly read in outward appearances and where whispers, jokes, glances, and untranslatable pejoratives establish the fault lines of belonging. The borders of the scene are, in other words, more than the slash that splits the homosexual/heterosexual divide. They are the invisible lines that emerge on the streets outside the gay clubs, the intangible cordon that surrounds a group of gay men as they stand on the road, talking about shared banalities while a beggar hovers around them with her hand stretched out. They operate in modes of attachment to particular places in the city, in the routes taken when driving from one pocket of privilege to another, and in the interplay of desire and disgust that turn the strip clubs in destitute districts into symbols of danger and a time gone by.

The borders of the bright lights scene, in other words, point to the varied ways gay men are implicated in emplaced hierarchies and to the way those hierarchies are redeployed and reconfigured in practices of mobility. It is, in turn, this interplay between movement and boundary-making that serves as the recurring theme in the chapters that follow. In each of the chapters, I examine a particular form of mobility, beginning with systems such as automobility that operate within the city and leading up to practices such as gay tourism that involve travels out of the city and into the world. In examining forms and practices of mobility, I pay particular attention to the instances when the dimensions of the scene become apparent, as well as to the times when they become threadbare, when the othered bodies and spaces that serve as the constitutive outside of the scene exert pressure, cause anxiety, and engender violent practices of bordering. In so doing, my first aim is to catch the scene at its points of material and affective emergence. More critically, however, I hope to shed light on how complicity operates in the age of multiple mobilities and in the context of a gay life carved out from a position of (local) privilege and (global) marginality.

In this way, this book also stands as a critique of the idealization of movement in the study of nonnormative sexualities. Indeed, the focus on transgression and resistance that I am breaking away from here and that is inscribed in the very term *queer* has long been hinged on tropes of mobility.[15] As Eve Sedgwick once noted, *queer* itself means *across*; it comes from the Indo-European root *twerkw,* from which other terms such as the German *quer* (transverse), the Latin *torquere* (to twist), and the English *athwart* also derive. "Queer" in "queer theory" thus comes to stand for "a continuing moment, movement, motive—recurrent, eddying, troublant."[16] It has sought, by definition, to indicate "unpredictable mobilities of bodies, desires, and practices"[17] and to name "cultures" that have "no locale."[18] In turn, much attention has been given to the way dominant orders are challenged by "queer" mobility practices, from movements into and within cities that enable the founding of places where "counterhegemonic" norms prevail, to the oscillation of individuals between "fluid" identity categories, to the traversal of cyberspace and the creation of queer virtual worlds, and to other "queer" movements.[19] Taken as a practice engaged in by queers, mobility has emerged as an integral part of the arsenal of strategies that can be employed to resist normative systems that are understood as mechanisms of stricture, constraint, and discipline—that is, as barriers to movement or forces of immobilization.[20] In this book, stories of mobility are brought together, not as examples of a primarily resistant queer culture, nor as authoritative representations of an organized cultural real but as inroads to an investigation of the yearning trajectory that directs gay life in Manila outward toward the global, forward toward modernity, and upward toward higher states of class privilege.

The Space of the Bright Lights Scene

In the accounts that follow, the bright lights scene takes form as bars and clubs equipped with state-of-the-art sound systems and manned by DJs who have traveled the world; as bodies moving through dance floors or driving through Manila's roads or shuttling through airports; as commodities like publications; and as fleeting and ephemeral events. In these narratives, the scene comes into being, too, through the work of immaterial architectures. It appears as a node in an imagined network composed of cities thousands of miles away; as a site of production and consumption of images and forms and styles that suggest globalness; and as the space effected by the invisible borders that rise within the walls of physical sites like dance clubs. The scene emerges in the stories I recall as a culturally imagined space that is part of a diffused and fragmented city. It stands as an example of how social life takes form when urban walls have been punctured by "ruptured enclosures" that simultaneously enable new connections and engender new urban divisions and forms of difference.[21] At once tied to and in excess of the city, the scene can be imagined as a space marked by what Virilio once described as the "perceptual disorder" of seeing something far away appear as it were within arm's reach and something or someone around the corner as part of an other world.[22]

The bright lights scene can, in this way, be seen as an "imaginative geography" that operates along different ontological registers and spatial scales or the space that takes form when mobile bodies and objects and circulating images and signs are "stabilized" in immaterial and material sites and imagined as part of a putatively unified whole.[23] This is the space eked out when connections are made between intraurban and transurban networks, real and virtual realms, and local and global space. It can be pictured, in Virilio's terms, as the constellation of destinations spied and approached through the use of various vehicles, including the "metabolic vehicle" of the body, "mechanical vehicles" such as cars and airplanes, and "audiovisual vehicles" such as screens.[24] More than just ways of getting around, these vehicles are vision machines that allow us to see certain things while making others disappear. In Manila, nighttime driving reduces the city streets to a blur and allows for high-speed shuttling between pockets of privilege. Flyovers hover over highways and enable aerial perspectives that miniaturize the disorder on the ground. Cybertechnologies make distant and imagined worlds appear proximate, and physical spaces such as upmarket clubs have begun to function like teleports, transporting its inhabitants out of the streets and into "global space," through, for instance, parties that mirror events held simultaneously overseas. Taking into account the interplay of appearance and disappearance that comes with forms of movement, the scene can be further described as the net spatial effect of the perspectives afforded by the vehicles that affect privileged gay life in the city. It is a means of naming the space that becomes apparent when one considers the limits and extensions of vision involved in the practice of multiple mobilities.[25]

To think of a slice of gay life in Manila in this way, as a form of life made intelligible by the perceptions afforded by a cast of vehicles, is to think of space as a *perspectival totality* made possible by the interplay of technologies of mobility, forms of circulation, built environments, and interpretive frames.[26] Indeed, it is this image of space as a "perspectival totality" that now proliferates in cultural analysis. One sees this, for instance, in attempts to conceptualize urban imaginaries as "sociosemiotic matrices" that allow cities to be grasped and nominalized;[27] in explorations of how circulating images are materialized momentarily in urban screens and are able to produce transient publics;[28] in efforts to trace how city routes engender spatial "rationality";[29] in attempts to track the "material and social processes of transmission, translation, transculturation, and transfiguration" and to rethink culture in terms of "contested processes of objectification and struggles over cultural forms set in motion."[30] In the spirit of what Will Straw has dubbed the "circulatory turn" in cultural theory, *Under Bright Lights* shifts the emphasis away from the now banal observation that flows and movements have penetrated most, if not all aspects of social life, toward an investigation of how flows and movements instantiate, reorganize, and create spaces and imaginative geographies. It is this emphasis that sits at the heart of the call made by Dilip Gaonkar and Elizabeth Povinelli for an "ethnography of forms"—a mapping of worlds that "can be carried out only within a set of circulatory fields populated by myriad forms, sometimes hierarchically arranged and laminated but mostly undulating as an ensemble, as a mélange."[31] Such an ethnography, they say, would track the "proliferating copresence" of varied cultural forms "in all their mobility and mutability."[32] It would be concerned less with the "fragile autonomy and specificity" of individual objects than with the quiet work of assemblages that provide the "outline" of things and their excesses.[33]

The bright lights scene can be seen as one such outline. It is a map of discontinuous elements that do not just *add up* but *stick* together to eke out the contours of a way of life. Understood as such, the scene makes it possible to see disparate elements of gay life in Manila as part of a (minimally) coherent world, which nonetheless remains inchoate, slippery, and messy. More important for me, as someone interested in the role of privilege in world-making, examining gay life in Manila through the lens of the scene means honing in on and evoking the patterns and points of resonance between and among practices, people, objects, and images that are separated in space and yet jointly animated by relations of power that are local and global. Put differently, the scene provides a way of understanding the significance of cultural processes of accumulation and selection (and, thus, exclusion) in ordering gay life. It sheds light on the connections, codes, and meanings that are obfuscated in images of worlds made up of flows and circulations but remain recognizable to those *in the know.*

It would, however, be too simple still to cast the scene as but the spatial effect of interconnected "cultures of circulation" set into "frames of stabilization."[34] If the scene can be said to be the appearance of a perspectival totality, then it must also be said that this appearance has grown to acquire its own representational feel. Like the city wherein it takes form, the scene is "pulsing, alive, polyrhythmical, contingently eventful, and inexorably spreading and thickening."[35] Processes of stabilization turn the scene into an object in its own right and imbue it with a kind of autonomy. In Manila, people speak of how the scene is "evolving"; how it "progresses"; and how it has "grown," "developed," and "become more modern." People describe it as "boring," "stale" and "deteriorating" or "happening," "crazy," and "alive and kicking." In "Aesthetics of Superfluity," Achille Mbembe writes of the "unconscious" of the postcolonial city.[36] By this he does not merely mean the collective unconscious of its people but the way in which memories, histories, and fantasies are inscribed onto spatial forms and how, in turn, such forms "come to life" and reproduce themselves over time. Following Mbembe's lead, I describe the scene as an autopoietic object, as a space that not only orders heterogeneous circulating forms but comes to possess its own force, its own obscure logics that generate forms. The styles, turns of phrase, indices of desirability, patterns of movement, consumption patterns, and images that might be employed as descriptors of the scene are, I suggest, also productive, incarnated rules. Think, for instance, of how "modern" club culture works to produce new forms of gay subjectivity, how it "members subjects and tells them how to recognize something as something else."[37] Or think of how the circulation of images and bodies in the city work hand in hand to make the emergence of gay spaces possible, but only in particular locations and in particular forms.

The bright lights scene, in other words, can and should be seen as "imagination given substance"; it works performatively, producing the very space it names and describes.[38] This is a space that possesses its own "forceful autonomy"; it is "something other than unambiguously social," "something more than unambiguously artefact" or an instrument of deliberation and will.[39] It exceeds that sum of its parts and has come to *mean* something more than the forms it envelopes. It is a generalized space that is also a value-bearing, "coordinating and figurating machine" that entails, demands, seduces, intoxicates, and materializes.[40] Correspondingly, to convey some of the "feel" and "force" of a space such as this, it is not enough to name things that might be seen as its constituent parts, to identify sites like bars and clubs, streets and districts, and websites and media networks. These sites need to be seen, not as items on a list, but as metonymic entry points into "something that feels like something."

Something like this was performed by Jean Baudrillard in his rendering of the space called "America." To write about this space, he traveled through the deserts of Nevada, the freeways of Los Angeles, the valleys and canyons of Arizona, the lights of New York, and to various other corners and worlds. In the face of the differences that mark these sites, however, he kept one eye trained on the fragile skins of interconnectivity that bind them together and make them intelligible as a singularity to both insiders and outsiders despite their overwhelming contradictions. He wrote of America, but he did not mean to simply make claims about the geographically bounded site we locate on a map, but to tap into an "unreal substance," into the "giant hologram" called "America" that is "neither dream nor reality."[41] Baudrillard's reference to "America" was not an attempt to homogenize disparate sites but rather a move that speaks to the material way that dissimilar spaces mirror one another (the way Los Angeles, for instance, mirrors the absences of the wilderness that surrounds it) in order to produce an emotionally charged landscape. The space of the bright lights scene is not as vast as America, but its contradictions are just as stark, if not more so, for this is a space that emerges in the midst of extremes, at the dark heart of the third-world city where the dimensions of difference are ill-captured by terms like *diversity* or *inequality* and can only be conveyed by re-presenting the drama of urban life. Indeed, the space of the scene is not the smooth surface suggested by terms like "community" that are readily deployed in the rhetorical games of minoritization. Rather, it is a space that is ostensibly coherent and yet marked by gaps, blind spots, ambiguities, and anomalies. To speak of a scene, in other words, is to take interest not only in how things get integrated into a perspectival totality but in how things that fall away function like snags on which the imagineering of space gets caught.

To write about the scene is to note how the city—the very platform for circulation that enables the scene—also provides the materials for its interruption. It is to draw attention, for instance, to those moments when circulatory systems are brought to a halt, as when gay men drive around at night to head to the clubs, but are suddenly caught in standstill traffic and come face-to-face with the vagrants on the road: the old blind men and women with their plastic cups stretched out and their walking sticks tapping lightly on wheels. It is to consider the resulting awkward moments in the car, the brief pauses when raucous conversations suddenly die and everyone stares blankly forward, waiting for the encounter to pass, and the sudden jolt precipitated by a light turning green and followed by the car leaping back into action. It is to think about how all the talk of traveling to "gay capitals" across the world is preceded by anxious moments at foreign embassies, where even the wealthiest of gay men must sit with prospective labor migrants and bear the suspicious looks of immigration officials and the humiliating possibility of denial. It is to take interest in how, after visas are approved and travels undertaken, such ordeals are forgotten and the scene gets storied with fantastic tales of gay spaces overseas; in how trips to gay bars and clubs in run-down parts of the city take on the character of touristic narratives; in the odd juxtapositions outside popular clubs, where the sound of dance music merges with the cacophony of the streets; and in mundane moments of arrest and deflation, like when gay men buy pirated copies of gay films and programs only to find when they get home that the copy freezes midway and is unwatchable from thereon.

Put more succinctly, to speak of a bright lights scene is to speak of a gay life in the third-world city emergent in cracks and fissures, as well as stabilizations, integrations, and order. Indeed, if the scene can be thought of as a totality, it is only as a localized totality—an emplaced whole given form by particular practices and discourses of separateness. Things outside and things within, however, are not so easily defined. Othered bodies and spaces are as much objects of desire as they are the objects of derision; they are the others within that rub up against the scene, puncture its bubble and yet, at the same time, give it its force of seduction. In chapter 3, for instance, I write of the classed and feminized figure of the *bakla*—a local sexual formation often read as a conflation of homosexuality, transvestitism, and lower-class status—as an other within, a specter linked to the past that the bright lights scene tries to exorcise but that keeps returning, not because it still exists as a tradition, but because the scene requires it, keeps it as a mirror that holds up an image of what gay life once "was," what it might still be, and what it might become again if the scene stumbles on the march toward "modernity" and fails to plug those lines of flight that steer it "backward." It is this figure, I suggest, that propels the onward movement of privileged gay life in the city. It is what keeps it *progressing*, circulating, and assembling those things that serve as the raw materials for its alchemic transformation into a site of *modernity* and *globalness*. This logic, one could say, extends to all the abject sites and figures that challenge the solidity of the scene's charged borders and that are, in fact, integral to the scene's constitution and continued operation.

The Third-World Queer

Like other imagined spaces, the bright lights scene presumes a *we*—the impacted subjects of a wild and twisting assemblage of influences—but the *we* it presumes has no fixed referent and is haunted by a difference that is "far more fluid than models of positioned subjects have been able to suggest."[42] This is a we that recalls the violences of class difference. It is a we that takes form under the bright lights and is hence brushed with the gloss of privilege, the thrill of a fast life, and the enchantments of commodity forms—all of which acquire a deeper shine here, against the backdrop of the third-world city. The sense of privilege in this we, however, is not something that can be traced back to static models of class or read-off indicators such as income levels or jobs. It is, like the bright lights scene itself, vague, unwieldy, and under perpetual construction.[43] Under the bright lights, wealthy gay men might come under fire for having attended the wrong schools. Former schoolmates get classed by the way they speak, the slips in their English that betray humble origins, or the intonations that reveal childhoods spent in rural provinces. At the clubs, even under the dimmest of lights, class is read in microscopic ways: in the way shirts are tucked into pants, in the way hair falls at the back of someone's head, in the tone of one's voice, or in the way the smell of cologne mixes with the odor of one's sweat. In the space of the scene, there is constant sifting through bodies for signs of class difference and no one is safe. Here, as John Frow has argued elsewhere, "there is no class essence and there are no unified class actors founded in the objectivity of social interest: there are (only) processes of class formation, without absolute origin or telos, with definite discursive conditions, and played out through . . . balances of power, through calculations and miscalculations, through desires and fears and fantasies."[44] The scene I describe, in other words, is a rigorously classed space, not because it is inhabited by bodies that are positioned within a stable class system, but because its emergence is contingent on and complicit in the nervous processes of class formation that are found elsewhere and everywhere in the city.

The *we* presumed by the bright lights scene is thus a *we* that remains provisional. One cannot know for sure whom it includes before coming into contact with the lines drawn by whispers, looks, accusations, insults, and other micropolitical interpretive moves that establish boundaries where none seem visible. The bright lights scene is a space that fragments even as it expands; it is at once the effect of the agglomeration of circulating forms, the attenuation of space, and incessant narrowing and ramification. It is, in this way, like many other spaces built on the unsteady grounds of same-sex desire. It appears, from afar, as a unified space bound together under the mast of nonnormative sexuality, but upon closer inspection, it becomes evident that its surface is riddled with cracks that are as deep, profound, and mean as those that cut through the city wherein it takes root.

Indeed, more and more it has become apparent that the *queer spaces* once celebrated as sites that rend the hegemonic heterosexing of space are as enmeshed in the demarcation of bodies and ways of life as they are in the politics of transgression.[45] Intersectional analyses have brought to the fore axes of difference that appear as thinly veiled hierarchical codes: class, gender, race, ethnicity, religion, able-bodiedness, and all those other things around which people are forcefully organized. The rise to prominence of a conservative sexual politics centered on principles of privacy, domesticity, and consumption—what Lisa Duggan calls "homonormativity"—has energized investigations into the collaborative work of queer place-making and neoliberal governance, as manifested, for instance, in the stabilization of capitalist inequalities in gay male enclaves and the subsequent equation of the "freedom to be gay" with the ability to spend.[46] As a result, the picture that emerges now of urban queer life is one that is less triumphant than somber and marked less by the romance of resistance than by the insidious ties between queers, states, and markets that trouble distinctions between oppressor and oppressed.[47]

Part of the task of this book is to further complicate the picture of queer spaces as spaces produced by the valiant struggles of those who are minoritized by shedding light on how privilege works even in the spaces inhabited by a figure like the *third-world queer*, a figure that, even at a moment in cultural analysis when it has become de rigueur to recognize subjects as multiply positioned, too often remains preserved as a "still radical figure," an embodiment of alterity that sits at the losing end of cultures of domination.[48] Indeed, much of the work on what might be termed *queer complicities* has focused on how gay white men (or conflated figures of gayness and whiteness) are implicated in practices of exclusion and embedded in market capitalism.[49] This is an important focus, but I am wary of how it leads, directly or indirectly, to the conjuration of a list of abstracted, othered figures: the queer of color, the third-world queer, the disabled queer, the working-class queer, and the like that are invested with the potential for transgression by virtue of their exclusion and on whom faith is placed for a still radical politics.[50] *Under Bright Lights* is an attempt to pull the figure of the third-world queer back from abstraction—to disarticulate its parts and see how they are plugged into systems of privilege that are intensely particular. Here, the third-world queer is not just the other but an other that makes its own others: "He" is at the center of the city and at the margins of the world. "He" is alternately the beneficiary of exclusionary protocols and its object, complicit in systems like capitalism that, at the same time, immiserate the city he calls home. "He" cannot be sure where he stands at any given moment, not even in the individual space of a club, for there, as I have already suggested, grounds of privilege like class that are central to the psychic life of the third-world city are under perpetual negotiation and are established precariously at points of encounter through abbreviated forms of recognition.

I am interested here, in other words, in the interpretive moves that simultaneously call into being the borders of the bright lights scene and flesh out the social codes that make the amorphous we of the scene real and intelligible. Here, axes of difference do not resemble overlapping grids on which subjects can be placed; rather, they acquire meaning, if always provisionally, by reference to interlocked cultures of circulation. Think of how, for instance, in the virtual space of a gay personal ads website, a seemingly innocuous question like "Do you drive?" takes on the dark valence of coded class difference, or how bars and clubs might emerge in sites where there is no access to public transportation. Or think of the stories of transnational travel and how they reify networks of privilege by establishing common destinations and itineraries. Or think of how conversations swerve to topics that are accessible only to those who inhabit certain media circuits; how access to those circuits is linked to other markers such as style, education, and English language proficiency; and how those circuits function as alternative forms of travel, as means of gaining knowledge about the distant sites to which the bright lights scene is articulated and is imagined as having ideational proximity.

Here, and throughout the chapters that follow, class appears, not as a categorical property of subjects who are locked in place, but as variegated relationships to forms of mobility.[51] I would suggest, moreover, that other axes of difference such as gender and race, which shape exclusionary protocols, are also informed and transformed by these relationships. Think of how the use of *swardspeak,* the vernacular language of the *bakla,* might allow someone to be marked not only as feminine and lower class but also as local and immobile. Or think of how symbolic systems of race are transmitted by floating representations; how such representations become things that people act to; and how whiteness, in turn, might be performed through complex mimetic practices.[52] The axes of difference that define the boundaries of the scene, in other words, are only constituted in use and are dynamically transfigured across circulatory matrices. Correspondingly, in this book, I do not investigate complicity by simply identifying sets of dominant actors and excluded others. Instead, I try to track how the meaning of difference is produced in circulation, how forms of mobility bear upon conventional markers of difference such as wealth and appearance, and how subjects inhabit interlocked circuits of mobility, from urban networks to the flows of signs and images to the global circulation of bodies.

A Space of Desire

The *we* that is presumed by the bright lights scene is thus a we that resembles a *mobile class* or *speed class*—that is, a class formation that possesses a kind of mastery over forms of mobility and that is able to move faster than others.[53] This is a class formation, however, that can only remain in the realm of imagination. It can be seen as an ideal form—the subjective equivalent of the dream of free circulation that gives the scene its force of seduction. It is akin to what Gayatri Spivak called a "universal": it is something "we cannot not want" even though it can never be actualized.[54] Indeed, no such class formation can come into existence in the space of the bright lights scene, for this is a space that must contend with the materiality of third-world infrastructure, the nitty-gritty of the city, and the reality check of odd juxtapositions. This is, in other words, not the space of unfettered mobility thought to be inhabited by a speed class, but a space of desire that takes form in an economy of stasis and circulation, of fits and starts and friction.

For Walter Benjamin, the space of desire is the distance between a subject and an object that possesses an intoxicating aura—a distance marked by an insatiable exchange, by a sense of fascination, wonder, reverence, and mystery derived from the unattainable status of the object.[55] In Benjamin's account, modernity encourages the eradication of the object's aura and, in that way, produces a state of mourning and nostalgia.[56] In a city like Manila, however, it might be said that modernity itself stands as the object of desire, the "something" glimpsed from a distance that is "so real and powerful that the forces that constructed it fade to the point of invisibility."[57] The bright lights scene is fully imbricated in this desire. The circulations and frames of stabilization it involves are not aimless; they are incited by a picture of gay life that remains inseparable from the compelling narratives of progress proffered by universalized accounts of modernity. The movements of the bright lights scene are, in this way, undergirded by the logic of pursuit: they speed up in the hopes of shaking loose the grip of the city, stretch outward to images and spaces coded as gay/modern, and double back to effect transformations on the gay cityscape to bridge the gap between "here" and "there" or to reconcile the disjuncture between what is immediately perceptible and what is projected as "a vision of unrealized desire."[58]

The third-world city here becomes both the drag that weighs the scene down, as it marches forward and outward, and an object of desire itself, a thing that must be transformed in order to fulfill, if partially, the promise of modernity. It is crucial to note, however, that the third-world city is not a passive foil to the ambitions and desires of the scene or a space that can be socially reconstructed at will. It is, rather, a material complex teeming with objects and spaces that exhibit inertia and that demonstrate a kind of agency themselves. Upmarket clubs drive or appear to drive subjects closer and closer to modern life. Flyovers literally lift subjects out of the pandemonium of Manila. Traffic jams freeze them in their tracks and confront them, time and again, with the shocking fact of their place in the world. Transit spaces like airports force differently classed bodies to collide and signs and images plastered on walls evoke feelings of fascination and wanderlust, as well as fear, resignation, and disgust. Put differently, the objects and spaces that compose the third-world city alternately and actively abet modernist aspirations and put them into crisis. They act as "instruments of encounter" that cue particular desires and modes of subjectivity to operate as "ordering devices" that "direct us here and there" and as "imperatives" that "orient" us and force us to adopt particular postures.[59] Throughout this book, the city appears as a meshwork of forces and intensities or a hybrid space of distributed agency that sustains and troubles the desire for, and the march toward, an always elusive modernity.[60]

This book situates the bright lights scene in this hybrid space of the city. Here, however, "situation" is understood, not as context or background, but as "an agent and participant in the patterns of living."[61] This is not to posit direct links between urban form and social organization, but to insist that the flows and movements that define the bright lights scene are constrained and animated by material environments and are not willful acts of desiring subjects. To speak of agency in this way, in the context of gay life in a third-world city like Manila, is to simultaneously recall and depart from efforts to picture global sexualities as formations that challenge accounts that posit the existence of an increasingly uniform "global gay" culture.[62] In these efforts, emphasis is placed on the way "different societies appropriate the materials of modernity" in order to create alternative queer modernities;[63] on the production of sexual subjectivities through "the selective reception of transnational queer knowledges";[64] on the "crafting" of "transcultural gay identities" in processes of "cultural contingency";[65] and on "labors of reinvention and renegotiation" that stem from "the frictional relation between geopolitics and embodied desires."[66] The few published works on contemporary gay life in Manila follow a similar strain. J. Neil C. Garcia, for instance, has argued for a view of the gay Filipino as the "exceptional hybrid," a figure that "talks back" to imperialist projects and that demonstrates the persistence of the "local" despite the prevalence of the "foreign."[67] Ronald Baytan has similarly pointed to the "implantation of Western homo/sexual discourse in the Philippines" as a case of the "appropriation and *localization* of gayness."[68] Dana Collins, writing on gay tourism in Manila, likewise suggests that "gay identity is made through transnational relations that are rooted in the hybridity, struggle, and mobility that make up urban place."[69] Built along the lines of the anticolonial project of decentering the West, interventions such as these deploy hybridity as the state of a "new form of cultural difference," a difference that is, by definition, not caught in the trajectories laid bare by master narratives of modernity.[70]

Under Bright Lights echoes this concern with the production of difference. I do not want to suggest, however, that the fact of difference is necessarily the desired effect of a purposive agency, of a will to appropriate and indigenize circulating forms or of a longing to carve out spaces outside both local heteronormative space and global homogenizing space.[71] In this book, I want to hold at bay the language of *struggle* that surrounds talk of global sexualities, to suspend the academic desire to spot difference and *resistance*, and to acknowledge that *local agency* also works in the service of modernist aspirations, that it can be mobilized to reproduce the center in the margins, is constrained by the force of material environments, and remains animated by narratives of progress and modernity.

Here, I want to draw attention to moments and spaces that trouble the image of gay life in the third-world city as a form of living that mounts, from a position of liminality, a challenge to hegemonic projects and forces. In the space of the bright lights scene, subjects are submerged in the fantasy-desires that animate the third-world city. Here, a popular DJ can look you in the eye and say, with no apologies, that "what makes clubbing in Manila so good" is the fact that "we are closer to our Western counterparts." A writer can claim that "our lifestyles these days . . . look like something fished out fresh from the streets of Castro in San Francisco or Oxford in Sydney."[72] Set against the squalor of the third-world city, statements such as these can be read ironically, as juxtapositions that evidence the persistence of local difference and the capacity of subjects to appropriate the signs and styles that travel into the city.[73] Such appropriations, however, also mark the reproduction of forms of capitalist inequalities. More than just representative examples of how the local and the global are melded together to create spaces for sexual dissidents, they point to the dramatic contrast between the spaces that rise like havens where the *we* of the bright lights scene takes form and the outside that is refused access: the chaotic streets, the dilapidated infrastructures, the scenes of abject poverty. The *outside* functions as a reminder that the city where the spaces of the bright lights scene emerge and from which they cannot be separated is less modern than paramodern, a landscape teeming with the failures, paradoxes, and catastrophes that come in the wake of modernization.

To underscore moments and spaces such as these is not to resurrect the long-abandoned image of subjects duped by hegemonic forces but to account for the continuing salience of the dreams that animate the third-world city in the production of forms of gay life. It is to acknowledge that while the experience of modernity, as a global phenomenon, is marked by multiplicity and diversity, the trope of modernity continues to play an effective role in creating the conditions it designates. As Neferti Tadiar has argued, "It is precisely the representation of modernity as having already been played out (and therefore foreshadowed) elsewhere that informs the modernist drive."[74] Its "representational effects"—including architectures, road networks, identities, social movements, as well as sites like gay clubs that have emerged as signs of "gay modernity"—create the effect of an original, material reality that becomes the object of reproduction.[75] These representational effects, which stir desires for development and progress, engender real effects, from the new exclusionary protocols that proliferate in the bright lights scene to the broader inequalities that characterize life in twenty-first-century Manila. Ultimately, then, I stress the situatedness of the bright lights scene in the third-world city in order to demonstrate how a space for privileged gay life is carved from within the circuits of postcolonial desire.[76] In this space, forms of agency emerge out of a picture of a "place that holds no promise" and are animated by forces of seduction and propulsion that are too powerful and mysterious to resist.[77] Here, locality, hybridity, and difference persist not as the effects of a willful exodus from the imperatives of modernity but as painful reminders of how the particular emerges within the universal-ized and as the necessary leavings of the never-to-be-completed task of becoming modern.

An Ethnography of the Scene

As I have suggested previously, the *ethnography of the scene* I imagine here does not endeavor to make known an object that comes ready with codes, norms, and practices that need only be explicated. Rather, this ethnography is concerned with the moves of an unfinished world, "a poesis . . . that literally can't be seen as a simple repository of systemic effects imposed on an innocent world but has to be traced through the generative modalities of impulses, daydreams, ways of relating, distractions, strategies, failures, encounters, and worldings of all kinds."[78] In attempting to write such an ethnography, I am influenced by other attempts to rework ethnographic methods to account for unruly objects of analysis. From the aforemen-tioned "ethnography of forms" proposed by Gaonkar and Povinelli, I take the assumption that social life is composed of interlocked cultures of cir-culation that act as demanding environments that intoxicate, seduce, and materialize rather than just mean. From Anna Tsing's "ethnography of global connection," I borrow the "patchwork" method of honing in on "zones of awkward engagement" and on the "cultural friction" produced by flows, particularities, and the "grip" of universal aspirations.[79] Like David Valentine's "ethnography of a category," I confront the problem of naming; I try to track the ways a formation becomes a thing, but I am forced, time and again, to refer to that thing as an extant social reality.[80] Most of all, I draw from Kathleen Stewart's lyrical ethnographies of "ani-mate circuits" and "spaces on the side of the road" the patience necessary to suspend the search for meanings in texts and the acknowledgment that there are things that cannot be straightforwardly represented and that must instead be followed across disparate domains and evoked by forms of writing patterned after the "strange dance of spaces in flux" and the "sheer surge of things in the making."[81]

To depict connections between the forms of mobility and circulation that I have drawn attention to here as neatly ordered links would be untrue to the way they come together to form a lived cultural real. The connections I trace in the succeeding chapters are often vague, though perhaps, at an intuitive level, unremarkable. Modern systems and infra-structures of travel such as automobility and airports cannot but affect the way gay life is imagined as modern in the third-world city. The circulation of signs and images cannot but transform readings of local gay spaces.

The way expressive forms travel cannot be divorced from the interpretive processes of class formation. And all these mobilities and circulations cannot be isolated from the contradictions that are produced by capitalist modernity and that constitute the third-world city. To try to relay these connections, I bring various narratives together thematically, around particular forms of movement, from the intraurban to the imaginative to the transnational. Often these will be detailed ethnographic accounts of places, sites of encounter where different mobile forms pass and play key roles in gay world-making. I try to present these places as I encountered them, to convey the structures of feeling they elicit, before bringing them into conversation with the stories of my informants or with publicly accessible texts such as magazine articles and literary works. At times, the connections between the narratives I recall are not readily apparent: patterns are laid out through recurring tropes or made explicit only at the end of a story, when a voice—either my own or someone else's—airs an observation that suddenly enunciates links and logics that were always there, lying in wait. I do this in a manner informed by the asseveration that the structure of an ethnographic text suggests the shape of its object, to mimic how the scene remains a half hidden effect that "jumps into form" in moments of poesis.[82] Other times I switch to a more exegetical voice, in recognition of the limits of evocation. Throughout this book, however, I try to embed theoretical discussions in narratives. I do this, in part, as a response to reservations about importing theoretical architectures that emerged out of different contexts; more important, however, I want to recognize narratives *as* theories or ways of voicing epistemological positions that distanced analysis fails to capture.[83]

Though the object of this book is not the bounded culture for which ethnography was initially designed, it is derived primarily from narratives acquired through conventional ethnographic methods. I draw primarily from eighteen months of fieldwork, conducted over six trips to Manila between 2006 and 2010. During those trips, I conducted extensive semi-structured interviews with thirty men, each of whom I met at the clubs through snowballing methods or through networks I had established prior to fieldwork. The interviews were held in cafés and restaurants and were guided by a set of general questions that focused initially on experiences at bars, clubs, and on the Internet; media consumption practices; and travel stories.[84] Often, however, the interviews would spiral off to personal stories and to general assessments of gay life in Manila. Comparisons were routinely made to gay men and gay spaces overseas, and sweeping conjectures about how things had changed for gay men in the city over the years were frequently raised. I made no effort to keep the conversations tied to the questions I had prepared and let them wander off and take unexpected turns, to much reward. I recorded as much of the interviews as I could, but there were—as in most, if not all, ethnographic endeavors—instances when this was impossible to do. During those instances, I reconstructed conversations from memory, filling them in with as much detail as I could. Early on, I had grown adept at this process of reconstruction, when it became apparent that though the interviews were invaluable, much was also revealed in the innumerable casual conversations held while smoking outside clubs, while driving around the city at night, and over break-fast after a big night out dancing. Those nights out sit at the heart of the observations I document here. I hung out with people primarily at gay dance clubs and also at the homes of gay men and at other commercial sites that were integrated into the patterns of gay life in the city. In many ways, spaces appear here as equally central objects of analysis as the sto-ries relayed in interviews and conversations. I treat spaces here as cultural texts that have grown layered over time and make an effort to *listen* to and relay the fragments of larger narratives about the city that are embed-ded in built environments and landscapes.[85]

Unlike most ethnographies, however, this book does not have an arrival story, no moment of first encounter marked by the shock of what appears as radical difference. What frames the narratives I have included here are stories of departure and return and my own memories of gay life under the bright lights of Manila. This book thus also takes form, in part, as an autoethnography or what can be thought of, broadly, as a form of writing that connects the autobiographical and personal to the cultural and social.[86] It shares with autoethnography the desire to go beyond the now routinized practice of self-disclosure, to use personal experiences as an inroad to the inner workings of social formation, and to produce an "orphan text" that turns the writing of the self into an allegory of the ethnographic project.[87] However, unlike autoethnographic writings that excavate the personal histories of their authors, the self-narratives that appear here are limited to prefieldwork experiences and anecdotes that speak directly to the process of scene-making. I write of nights spent at the clubs prior to my return to Manila as a researcher, of memories of how particular places appeared years before the fieldwork proper, of rec-ollections of classed, gendered, and racialized discourses that have come and gone or that persist as constitutive elements of the bright lights scene. The point in doing this is not only to thicken descriptions with details drawn from memory but to remind the reader that whatever is relayed in these pages is filtered through investments hardened over time. In some ways, it seems to me that I have little choice in this matter, for to veil the memories that came rushing to me during fieldwork or in the process of writing would be to feign innocence and ignorance, or worse, to mimic the objectivity of the disinterested observer in order to claim a measure of ethnographic authority.

The personal voice I use in narratives of prefieldwork experiences is a voice I extend to ethnographic encounters. In part, this is a stylistic move motivated by a desire to implicate myself in the processes I critique, to treat the theme of complicity as an ethical injunction. Indeed, one of the issues I encountered while writing this book is that unlike most ethnographic projects, the central concerns that emerge here (most notably, complicity in class hierarchies) demand a tone that is more critical than empathetic.[88] I want to acknowledge that the materials that serve as my objects of critique were made available to me because I was also read as a member of a particular class. For instance, classist statements were routinely made in my presence with the tacit understanding that I shared the sentiments being expressed. It is out of a sense of responsibility to those who shared their views with me that I make a concerted effort here not to extricate myself from the violences I make apparent.

More fundamentally, the persistent presence of the "I" throughout this book is part of an effort to reconstruct the processes that enable the production of the scene, to convey them as palpable realities, and to relay ineffable structures of feeling that elude rationalized accounts. The "I" here is thus not a trusted "insider" that has mastery over the spaces and processes under investigation but an opening into the production of an "inside" and "outside," a perspective through which a worm's-eye view can be approximated. At certain points, there is a slippage between this "I" and the "we" of the bright lights scene. This is by no means a suggestion that the former can substitute for the latter but a demonstration of the moves between the personal and the social that are part of the process of materializing worlds. In a similar vein, the narratives included here are often written in the past tense rather than in the "ethnographic present." By emplotting observations and stories, my aim is to highlight their mutability and to avoid presenting ethnographic objects as though they were not given to change.

The writing of this book must thus also be seen as a kind of performance. It enacts the twists and turns of the constituent parts of the bright lights scene by narrating movements and lingering on the sites where circulations pass. Its hybrid style, its shifts from the general to the personal and back, mirrors the loose connections that enable the emergence of the scene as an imagined space that is felt and made through individual encounters but that exceeds the realm of subjectivity and personal experience. It suggests the shape of the scene by honing in on moments when borders become apparent and by cobbling them together to highlight patterns and constitutive logics. It tries to mimic "felt impacts and half-known effects" and to relay the force of settings and places and of the bright lights scene itself as it takes on a life of its own through detailed descriptions saturated with memories.[89] I want to convey, through the narrative voice adopted through much of this book, some of the force, pathos, and power involved in fashioning this scene within and against the drama of life in the third-world city. To do so, I have tried to suspend the desire for quick explanations and neatly ordered frames and to substitute for what Stewart called the "'you are there' realism of ethnographic description" a more fractious set of stories that re-present the scene as a space of desire, intensity, complicity, distributed agency, and the unruly movement and circulation of forms.[90] The end effect of this writing, as I imagine it, is not a *good enough story* of gay life in Manila, but an *immersive fiction* of being in something that feels like something.[91]

CHAPTER ONE

Automobility and the Gay Cityscape

It is the goal of the voyage that destroys the road, it is the target of the projectile-projector (of the automobile) that seems to trigger the ruin of the interval, it is the fleeting desire to go right to the end as fast as possible that produces in the opening out of the traveling the tearing apart of the landscape.

—Paul Virilio, *Negative Horizon*

Metro Manila has no gay village, no neighborhood or individual street seen and identified as gay. There are those who would claim that the formerly bohemian district of Malate, in the old City of Manila, has become such a place, but such claims are contentious and belied by the emergence in recent years of what I have begun to describe as a bright lights scene that resists straightforward mapping.[1] This is a scene that appears only in the form of nodes scattered across the megacity, including transient nodes, as in the case of the circuit parties that occasionally inhabit Manila's World Trade Center. Indeed, when I recall Manila's gay sites, I think of movement rather than districts. My memories of gay Manila are of driving and being driven to and from houses, high-rise apartments, sleek clubs, bars, and restaurants. These were satellites built for the upper strata: trendy havens cordoned off from the disorder of older quarters and joined by inadequate, pothole-ridden roads that betrayed their immersion in Manila's urban squalor. My memories also include the faces and bodies of strangers, people I did not know but knew of and whom I recognized from those pockets of privilege where we sat drinking cocktails under clouds of cigarette smoke and watched each other pose against dim violet backlighting. On certain nights, those familiar strangers and

I appeared at the same places at the same time. We passed one another without a word or even a single raised eyebrow, though we were utterly aware, as Manileños always were, of each other's recurring presence. On those nights, more than on any other, I could see us driving around in our darkened cars, tracing the same routes past the same soot-stained infrastructure. I imagine that we were all similarly thankful that so much of our lives were conducted late at night, when Manila's normally dense arteries slackened and we were able to speed through blinking stoplights, unmindful of the unruly streets of the postcolonial metropolis.

Nowhere do the streets of Manila feature less than in my memories of driving to Manila's gay clubs, which, as a consequence of the common desire to arrive after everyone else, came to life even later than the rest of the city's nightspots. I have many memories of such journeys, densely clustered in little time frames from the years I spent as a casual inhabitant of the clubs to my various returns as a researcher investigating those very sites where I might have been considered an insider. Recalling those journeys now, I am struck by how little they resemble the more obvious images of Manila: the ones that might feature a car stuck in standstill traffic slowly forcing its way into a treacherous shortcut dominated by garbage piling on street corners, gnarled wires and cables, remnants of posters from elections past, iron shantytowns, and packs of dogs and groups of street children only to exit at another road where the traffic was worse and cars were as immobile as the dilapidated buildings that surrounded them. I know those images well. I used to tap my fingers incessantly on the steering wheel while my car crawled through Manila's thoroughfares, seemingly millimeter by millimeter. I would start off seething with anger, muttering obscenities at the damp air and blistering sun, which made my back sweat against the leather seat and kept me from opening my window and having a cigarette. Then the anger would abate and I would find myself staring at and imagining the lives of the commuters who piled into dangerous-looking public buses and rickety jeepneys, or else peeking into cavernous, market-like commercial complexes that I knew I would never enter. In Manila, daytime driving was the stuff not only of road rage but also of contemplation and daydreams, and I have long suspected that it was this combination that made traffic a standard target of middle- and upper-class complaints.

At night, however, there was little time or reason to consider the city. Its edifices flew past windows, were blurred and disappeared like the buses that retired soon after rush hour and the smog that became indiscernible in the absence of daylight.[2] To reach the clubs, I often passed Epifanio delos Santos Avenue (EDSA), Manila's main thoroughfare. During the day, EDSA was the site of epic gridlocks, an experience made worse in those instances when you were caught between buses or next to a wet market and had no choice but to hold your breath or inhale the smoke and the stench of raw meat, which seeped through the windows and mingled with the odor of air-conditioning. My memories of EDSA at night, however, are clear of such intrusions. I remember seeing only large billboards featuring Eurasian models in their underwear and a smattering of video advertisements. In a city as poorly lit as Manila, these billboards and screens served as central guideposts and, on nights when I drove alone, the figures they contained were my only companions. Indeed, at night, the cityscape seemed to evaporate under the cover of darkness and the aesthetic of speed.[3] The frustration and introspection of daytime traffic were replaced by the thrill of the freedom to accelerate and the anticipation of the destination. I was a member of my class and took pleasure in all these disappearances.

Driving alone at night: there is perhaps no more mundane experience of pure singularity. One hand on the wheel, another on the gearshift, a foot on the accelerator, your whole body conforming to familiar dents on the car seat—the wonders of ergonomics from which the car-driver emerges, the automobile as exoskeleton.[4] There were other car-drivers on the road, but the curious quality of the automobile is the absence of eye contact, that most perfect reciprocity.[5] (On the road, fellow travelers are even less than the familiar strangers one runs into at night; they are more like the inhabitants of Sirius: "They do not exist for us at all; they are beyond far and near."[6]) Yet, among these other alien–machinic assemblages, I imagined a common love, of onward movement and of the exhilaration of unobstructed circulation. I remember driving in Manila at night as the closest approximation to objectlessness, as a substitute for freeways and as the temporary fulfillment of a secret desire to see the city abandoned and desertified. This was, however, a conditional desire. It waned as I approached the clubs and felt the pang of another longing: to see a caravan of cars parked along the surrounding streets, other bodies extracting themselves from their vehicles and making their way to the entrance or already parked by the bare facade, catching their breaths, resting their ears, chatting and laughing, and spiting the city with their flippancies.

Once I came to the clubs before midnight to do an interview with one of the owners. I remember how eerie the empty club seemed without bodies and without the smell of sweat and the thumping of dance music. There was one padded bench on the ground level, a three-seater bench I did not recognize without the quiet boys that were usually stationed there. I saw for the first time the geometry of the sunken dance floor, its angular edges, the raised platforms where the serious dancers displayed themselves and the depth of the back section where tireless boys spun around shirtless, toting the water bottles that were the emblems of narcotic-laced life on the circuit. I climbed the narrow staircase to the second floor and crossed the velvet rope to the makeshift VIP room, where once I caught drag queens brought in from seedier clubs sitting quietly before a performance, looking bored and uncomfortable in their military-themed costumes. At the end of this section was a door, painted black to blend in with the walls, which led to the club's central office—a tiny rectangular room shockingly awash in fluorescent lighting and adorned only by two small desks, a few stacks of CDs and magazines, and old posters tacked onto the walls. I sat there with Henry, who wore his hair short and spiked and who was clad in jeans and a black shirt with three buttons undone, revealing a small gold chain with a tiny crucifix.

Henry had grown up in New York and Toronto, a city where I too had lived, and we spoke quickly and knowingly of the clubs there that we both had frequented. He reminisced about his return to Manila and recalled his disappointment at finding that the city had no clubs, just small bars tucked away in corners of the old city: "Before us, there was nothing," he said, leaning back. "No place where gay men could dance like in Australia, Hong Kong or Singapore." He remembered planning the opening of the club and investors asking if it was going to be explicitly gay, because back then "gay" and "homosexual" were words that belonged to Manila's underbelly, to the spaces where go-go boys stripped to love songs in front of older queens who only loved "real" men. He spoke of educating the market, of playing in the big league with the big players, and of emptying taboo words of their old meanings and injecting them with "pride" and "dignity" and a sound system that was the best in the city. He spoke of pride above all things, and he told me how so many boys have confessed to him that before the clubs opened they were embarrassed to be gay. Now, he said, everyone was so happy and "numb"; and once a year on his birthday, he would come in drag and stand on the stage and scream, "How are you homosexuals in the house?" and everyone would cheer. He called the boys who frequented the clubs his "children" and they called him *"Motherrr."* Before I left, he told me to check the website where they chronicled most of the club's events. I said I would, even though I had already seen it and remembered it saying that "a spectacular visual feast" would prepare me "for the journey I was about to undertake." I was thinking about those words as I walked out of the club and crossed all its still barren spaces. I suppose it was then that I began to realize that emptiness was the condition for the journey and, in the context of Manila's density, a spectacle in its own right.

Shortly after, I found myself back on the road, driving around the Makati CBD. I drove down Makati Avenue, past the red-light district of Burgos Street, with its tawdry neon signs advertising girly bars with names like "Wild West," "Dimples," "Hollywood," and "Manhattan," and toward the Paseo de Roxas intersection, where prostitutes could be seen in full view, standing outside a large white building, which for years wore bullet holes, scars from the coup attempts of the late 1980s. At the end of that same block stood two five-star hotels, across from which was Green-belt, the upmarket development where I planned to have a drink until it was late enough to return to the clubs. It was only half past midnight, early for Manila's standards, and the roads were still packed with people driving home from extended dinners or late movies. It took me twenty minutes to drive two-and-a-half blocks to Greenbelt. I walked around for a while, running into people I knew, exchanging exaggerated pleasantries and kisses that missed the cheek by a good two inches. I parked myself in the outdoor section of a popular bar and sat conspicuously alone next to a band of underdressed Brazilian models (*fly-ins*, as the local fashion industry calls them). By the time I left again for the clubs, the traffic had begun to subside and I had smoked less than one cigarette before I found myself parking in almost the same spot I had vacated earlier that night.

Inside, the club had changed dramatically from when I left. The music and lights were on, and the crowds had come out in full force. It was a different, more welcoming traffic—squeezing through, bum to crotch, searching for familiar faces among bodies sharing empty space; it was, like driving at night, the experience of singularity bound by a common love. At the club, however, eye contact was a possibility, though it was carefully and sparingly used, because there, more than anywhere perhaps, it meant perfect reciprocity.[7] I ran into Henry on the second floor working the crowd and with his drink in one hand and a slim camera in the other: "You're back," he said, smiling. I smiled back and posed with him for a photo. Then I headed off to make rounds up and down the stairs, in and out of the club, and back and forth through the crowd. At the top of the stairs was a small smoking area, an aquarium bordered by sliding doors that smelled worse than smoking rooms in airports or EDSA at noon and caused my eyes to turn blood red. It was there that I returned intermittently, laughing and gossiping, thriving in the rare frivolity of willful circulation.

Intersections, Flyovers

Cars coasting through roads at night, dancers moving rhythmically in empty space: car-bodies and bodies tearing down spatial barriers, mirroring what Marx described as the work of capital.[8] Indeed, the capacity of both celerity and barrenness to enchant lies in the veiling, glossing over, and titivation of the contradictions carved on the streets of the metropolis. These contradictions, however, are more than just the effects of capital; they are the legacy of a larger cast of dreams: of the modernist goal of ineffable space to which club architecture seems at least minimally indebted, of the trajectories laid bare by the birth of the global city, of the American Dream that saturates the air in the ex-colony, and of the choking, painful pang of wanderlust that sits at the heart of a thousand gay stories.[9] These dreams cannot be disentangled; they are too tightly coiled together and make their way through the city and into our imaginations like knotted filaments coming from all directions. On the road, they find common enemies: slowness, stasis, torpor—those states that force us to come face-to-face with the beggars who knock on our tinted windows; the underpaid traffic enforcers who swagger to our cars, palms itching for bribes; the young boys who bathe in rain and swim in the flood waters that follow the steady drum of moderate downpours. Even late at night, we are reminded of our emplacement, even if only while parking on a side street near a club, where we are obliged to pay forty pesos (one U.S. dollar) to have an enterprising vagrant protect our cars from the threat he himself subtly poses. In Manila, driving can never serve fully as a form of amnesia (as Baudrillard once claimed); there is always some reminder on the ground that our imagination outstrips the city we call home.[10]

So frustrated are we by the rift between the world we know and the ground we have inherited that the roads themselves have become the targets of our aspirations. In the 1990s, our hammers and drills tore the roads apart, forcing whole sections of them to rise anew as flyovers—overpasses that leapt over the city's most congested intersections. It was Neferti Tadiar who first saw that these new structures were more than a way of managing traffic, that in promising height in a city so traditionally flat (no real skyscrapers, no subways, not even a deep underground sewage system), they also offered to suspend us from the urban turbulence on the ground.[11] Indeed, they offered the possibility of being hoisted from the sites of contradiction, of flowing through the city unencumbered, of materializing the networks of the rich by building concrete bridges between private islands of privilege. Tadiar pointed out that flyovers were more than a traffic solution, even more than a representation. She saw that they were, in fact, a mode of symbolic production: "A medium of desire which helps produce the effect of (transnational) subjectivity."[12] Much of the promise of flyovers, however, has remained unfulfilled. During those earlier years, many no doubt dreamt that one day all the elevated pathways could be linked and we would be able to keep most of our travels above ground, away from the buses, the commuters, and the garbage. Today, that fantasy seems foolish and distant. Flyovers have granted little more than brief respites from the horrors of traffic, lifting us up momentarily and giving us the quick pleasure of an aerial view of the city, but just as quickly slipping us back down or, worse, forcing us to contend, resentfully, with the standstills along the narrowed passages beneath them.

Once, I was headed to an interview at a bar at the Rockwell Center in Makati City and found myself trapped underneath the two flyovers that hovered over the intersection of EDSA and Ortigas Avenue. The columns and on-ramps of those flyovers had taken up so much space on that short stretch of EDSA that there were only two southbound lanes left on the base level. That night unmoving public buses commandeered them both. I was caught behind them, watching the minutes pass on the digital clock on the dashboard and sending frantic, apologetic messages to Carlos, the older gay man whom I had hounded for an interview. I could imagine him sitting on a barstool, playing with the olive in his cocktail, appalled at having been made to wait. I was reading the antigovernment graffiti on one of the columns when the driver of the bus next to my car jumped out of his seat and onto the road. He knew it would take longer to get past that intersection. He stood facing the side of the bus, thrust his crotch against the gap between the front tire and the bus's arched metal rim, undid his worn-out jeans, and started urinating. It was a common enough sight in Manila, so common in fact that walls along major thoroughfares were painted with signs that read, "*Bawal umihi dito* [No urinating here]." Still, I grimaced and thought about the gallons of piss that have been spilled on Manila's roads. I watched the bus driver wipe his hands on the sides of his jeans and clamber back onto the driver's seat, his passengers unmindful of his brief disappearance. Seeing him relieve himself, I remembered reading an account of Los Angeles and how there, once you got out of your car you immediately became a delinquent, like a dog wandering the roads.[13] In Manila, I thought, that observation was almost too precise to be a metaphor.

Half an hour later I found myself nearing the turn to Estrella Street, which bordered Rockwell's Power Plant Mall and where cars coming down from another flyover were met by a large billboard advertising new condominium units. The billboard featured a glittering skyline, a young couple, and bold lettering that read, "The Home of Fashionable Manila." I drove alongside the green metal fence that separated the upmarket mall and the surrounding residential and commercial buildings from the nearby string of low-income apartments and the notoriously polluted Pasig River. I parked next to a manicured green island—itself a sign of luxury in a city where so much greenery had been wiped out in the name of road expansion—and walked briskly past the shops and restaurants and the café where the students from the law school around the corner hung out, all dressed in mandatory business attire. I found Carlos sitting at an outdoor table typing on his laptop, unbothered by my lateness. We began talking about art and design, which were his fields, and about travel, his preferred pastime. He was, for the most part, retired from the scene and I knew almost immediately that I would be unable to use much of our conversation. He did, however, speak at length about cruising online. I asked him how he filtered messages and personal ads and how he selected men to meet in person. He paused for a moment and then confessed, with a guilty smile, that he usually tried to find out if the people who sent him messages drove their own cars. I laughed conspiratorially and did not ask him to elaborate on this criterion; it seemed, to me at least, novel yet self-explanatory.

I remember heading to another interview, this time at a serviced apartment building along Legaspi Street, right across from the glass and concrete structure of the Ayala Museum. To get there, I had to pass the intersection of EDSA and Shaw Boulevard, where a flyover competed for airspace with one of the busiest stations of the Manila Metro Rail Transit, an aboveground line that traverses EDSA at a pace slower than most cars. Underneath the shadows of both structures, I watched the swarm of pedestrians. Most of them were walking down the concrete steps that led to the train station or flowing out of Starmall, a run-down shopping center where, over a decade ago, Claire Danes played pool in between shoots for a film about Western tourists accused of drug smuggling in Bangkok. (After her visit, she told *Vogue* and *Premiere* that Manila was a "ghastly and weird city" and that it "smelled of cockroaches, with rats all over . . . that there is no sewage system and the people do not have anything—no arms, no legs, no eyes."[14] We railed against her and banned her movies, but I suspect we merely envied the accuracy and eloquence of her insult.) That night, the crowd at the EDSA–Shaw intersection seemed to move faster, more frantic than usual. Middle-aged women and working-class men kept walking in front of cars and even between them, a blur of silhouettes with shopping bags and backpacks that could not be deterred by the crossing signs. I missed two green lights and was forced to endure the quarrel of indecipherable chatter and blaring horns, the chugging sound of trains and the hum of impatient engines on the ground. I knew better than to wonder if anything extraordinary had happened that night, if there had been an accident on the road, a coup attempt, or some protest. In Manila, nights full of panicked energy just happened. I sat patiently and wished that the other cars would stop honking their horns. Then I turned up the volume of my car stereo, checked if my doors were locked, and let my mind wander.

(I remembered the old woman who used to beg on that intersection. I was driving with a friend the first time I saw her. We must have been chatting or laughing when she appeared suddenly outside my window, a shock of white hair on her head, her eyes bulging, her skin transparent. My friend and I jumped in our seats. She tapped on my window with a frail hand. I looked straight ahead and tapped back, the city's agreed upon gesture of refusal. She refused to leave and I imagined her face coming closer and closer, pressing against my window. My friend and I both turned silent and fidgeted in our seats, itching for the light to turn green. When it did, we breathed audible sighs of relief, sped off, and made jokes about the incident. We saw her a number of times after that, but my friend gave her a name, Rose, and we were no longer afraid of her. Months, maybe a year after we first saw her on the road, I recognized her on one of the local news programs. She had apparently moved to Manila from the provinces with her daughter and her daughter's family, but somehow they had lost her in the city and she ended up living under the cover of the Shaw flyover. The reporters called on the family to contact the network. They must have known, however, that the chances of that were slim and that there was a real possibility that she had been lost deliberately.)

By the time I reached my destination, I was cranky and dazed and half an hour late. Tristan, a popular figure among Manila's fashionable set, was even later. I had to sit by the curb in front of his building, smoking cigarettes and wondering why I was always anxious about time when I was on my way to interviews, knowing full well that in Manila tardiness was always expected and thus forgiven. When Tristan arrived, he was with Nathan, his eighteen-year-old boyfriend whom he hid possessively from other gay men, and Carl, a forty-something entrepreneur who barely looked thirty. The interview turned out to be a long, enjoyable conversation, punctuated mostly by Tristan's multipronged theories about various changes in the gay scene ("There are four reasons," he would say, "number one . . . number two . . . number three . . . number four.") and by Carl's sporadic objections. I suspected that much of Tristan's bold, authoritative tone was for the benefit of Nathan, but I did not mind. I thought it would make him easier to quote. In the end, however, what I remember most from that interview are its final, unrecorded minutes. Tristan had moved to sit on the floor, across from the chairs where Carl and I were perched. His legs were stretched out and he was chewing on ice chips. Nathan looked even younger leaning against his left arm. Tristan looked up at Carl and me and asked, "Have you ever slept with a *jologs?*" The term was an untranslatable pejorative, used primarily to refer to young, lower-class Filipinos. It appeared routinely in many of the conversations I had with gay men but was conspicuously absent from recorded interviews. "But what do you consider as *jologs?*" I asked, eager to hear him define an unwieldy though ubiquitous insult. Carl began listing his own criteria: bad grammar, a certain accent, cheap jeans, colored hair. It was a while before Tristan finally responded. "You know what it is?" he whispered. "It's the smell of cheap cologne mixed with the odor of public transportation."

On Nearness

Nothing seems to take longer than trips where you have to keep guessing where to turn or are perpetually staring at the sights outside your window, getting to know your location out of fear, excitement, or both. Proximity is a sensation; it is born of intimacy, not the absolute measure of kilometers.[15] Think of being lost in unfamiliar streets, only to realize upon several fortuitous turns that you were only a minute away from a familiar landmark, a hotel you are staying at, or your house even. Indeed, it is the repetition of routes that makes distance disappear. It is also what takes us in certain directions, orienting us toward some places more than others, the way a footpath carved into a forest might lead to a secret clearing.[16] Edmund Husserl termed this familiar realm the "near-sphere," a circle of nearness.[17] It is a slightly misleading term, if only because Husserl knew that the only reference of nearness was the body, and if the body is mobile or, better still, auto-mobile, then the shape of nearness is less spherical than constellational, amoebic—a tangled network of paths beaten by tires.[18] In Manila, this relationship between proximity and repetition bears extra significance, for the already puzzling twists of the road network are complicated by perpetual reconstruction, the dearth of signs, the changing of street names in accordance with political tides. Moreover, maps of the city are rare. They are absent from glove compartments and even from many hubs of public transit. In Manila, we navigate the city without mental aerial maps and instead get around with "images of seriality" or routes that can be traced "by imagining the flow of adjoining objects on particular pathways."[19] Tadiar called this an aboveground, "imaginary urban tunneling"; and if one considers the relative blindness involved in such an act alongside the unreliability of roads, names, and signs, then one might get a sense of how significant memory and familiarity are in our intraurban travels.[20]

During the mid-2000s, I lived in a high-rise apartment in San Juan, roughly midpoint between what were the twin centers of the gay club scene: Government (Henry's club), located at the fringes of the Makati CBD, and a club called Bed, located in the district of Malate. The fact that I was a short drive away from Malate was a late discovery. Whenever I went there I took a circuitous route: exiting at EDSA and then driving down Buendia Avenue all the way to the coastal road of Roxas Boulevard, which brought me to the intersection of Nakpil and Orosa, touted as the "X" that marks the spot of gayness by travel guides that insist on locating a single center. This was a reasonable route from the gated village where I grew up, but from my apartment in San Juan, it was almost comical; and yet, no one I drove with knew better, or perhaps they all took comfort in the unadventurous straight lines of the path I was used to taking. One night I found myself with someone who knew another path and I let him steer me westward, through roads I had never seen, dirtier roads crammed with more jeepneys and people. It was a more treacherous drive, but in a matter of minutes we were crossing the rusted old rail tracks that I regarded as an informal entrance to the old City of Manila. After that crossing, the roads became visibly narrower, the buildings older, more colonial, and the street lamps more garish, wrapped in the strange technicolor neon cages that were part of the city government's oft-mocked beautification program. Then the traffic became heavier, restaurants began appearing on the sides of the road, and then there it was: Malate—a dense cluster of small bars converted from two-story apartments, a smattering of street vendors, and young people walking in packs. During the late nineties, I could walk the streets of Malate the same way I did the sleeker pavement of Greenbelt. Everything was familiar, the places were known to me by name, the faces on the street recognizable. Then the winds changed and one by one the places I knew died under the weight of whispers that Malate was passé and were replaced by new venues that catered to what many saw as an underclass. The exodus that followed was quick. Many fled to Makati, gentry under siege, and I was wholly unsurprised when I heard someone say, condescendingly, that Malate had become a democracy.

In some ways, Bed survived this small revolution, and it was there where we were headed that night that I discovered the shorter route to Malate. Bed was larger than Government, but the two were cut from the same cloth. They shared a modern aesthetic, common prices, and indistinct lights and music. Even the bodies that inhabited them were similar: mostly hardened by hours in the gym and sporting the same uniform of tight T-shirts and jeans. During the years I was in Manila for fieldwork, however, Government acquired a reputation as more exclusive, more *sosyal*.[21] Many of the men I knew, including almost all my informants, preferred Government. Bed was sleazier, they said. It was dirtier. One informant said that the boys there looked like they stank. Still, such distinctions struck me as somewhat exaggerated. The crowds at both clubs were more mixed in terms of class than people implied, and it was only by calling on a lifetime of privilege that my eyes were able to see through the strobe lights and split the hairs of class distinction, spot the stylistic differences, and catch the threads that connected persons to the right networks. There were, however, more bodies at Bed that bravely bore the markers that signaled class difference: perhaps a little tail of hair at the back of their necks or the dead giveaway of poor English. *Jologs,* Tristan and Carl would call them, and their presence, even if it was not overwhelming, was enough to drive many away. We knew, after all, what their presence meant; we saw them (or figures callously likened to them) arriving in the days, weeks, and months before the deaths of other establishments in Malate and of hundreds of other bars, clubs, restaurants, even entire malls scattered across the city. In Bed, they appeared like signs that the streets were about to pour in. Thus the prudent ones became nothing more than occasional visitors and found safety in Makati, rallying around a center far away from the rest of what passes for a circle.

Government's very distance from the cluster of gay spaces in Malate was thus, ironically, the source of its cachet. There was nothing around Government; it stood alone on the northern end of Makati Avenue, flanked only by a bank and a midpriced hotel. A couple of blocks away, there was a branch of the fast food chain Wendy's, then a 7–Eleven, then a twenty-four-hour Chinese restaurant. There were no people on the streets other than those coming to and from the club. There were only cars speeding down Makati Avenue. (Makati Avenue, a major thoroughfare: this was the site of Government, not a village or a neighborhood, but a pathway, a non-place; "the landscape is a passage."[22]) Still, no one ever spoke of that part of the city as dead. In fact, Government became the site of the after-parties for the large circuit events, the fêtes thrown by glossy magazines, and the destination of DJs from overseas. For many, Malate became a distant, other world, home to a different set of gay men and to those who clung to the dream of gentrification.[23] No such pretense hung over Government. It stood alone, proud of its isolation, comfortable sitting alongside an ATM machine, a temporary abode, a fast food chain—the symbols of quick, ephemeral commerce. I, too, was comfortable in those surroundings and knew all the routes to get there, even the obscure one that cut through the Mandaluyong rotunda and jumped over the murky waters of the Pasig River. Once, during an interview with a group of men who were regulars at Bed, I was asked why I was at Government more often. It was a minefield of a question and all I could do was shrug sheepishly and say that it was "nearer."

Other(ed) Places

Still, it would be too simple to assert that the scene was moved only by the logic of distance, for even in the midst of struggles to rise above, elude, and speed through the contradictions that surrounded us, there existed a secret, perverse desire to see the very things we avoided, to come close to them, touch them, smell them. I am thinking now not even of Malate, which in its erstwhile separation still remained recognizable and unexotic, but of the darker, older, poorer recesses of gay life in Manila: the world of strip clubs and *callboys*—not tourist sites like in other Asian cities but somber places frequented mostly by older queers.[24] There were nights when we were seized by a sudden urge to visit these other(ed) places. We journeyed to them like schoolchildren on fieldtrips, eager to break the rhythm of our overprivileged boredom.

I once went with a small band of young gay men to one of the largest strip clubs in Quezon City. I remember that none of us knew its exact location and that we had to drive slowly, staring out of the car windows in order to read the neon signs that dotted the wide, sparse stretch of Timog Avenue. We found the club at the tail end of the road, marked by a modest pink sign and a lit canopy. We parked half a block away and rushed to the entrance, keeping our heads bowed between the collars of our jackets and chuckling about the embarrassing possibility of being seen in that part of town. Inside, the club was large and pitch-dark. The only lights shone on a wide catwalk in the center, where strippers came out one by one in identical denim cutoffs and motorcycle boots, dancing in slow motion to ballads that radio stations had retired long ago. It was a peculiar sight and not at all what we expected. We laughed under our breaths and earned irked looks from the lonely figures that occupied the surrounding tables. The strippers themselves, however, were uninterested in the behavior of the crowd. They danced with their heads bolted straight, staring out at an invisible dot on the wall opposite the catwalk.[25]

I was still on my first drink when the manager came up to us, beaming. He seemed to recognize us for what we were—tourists in our city, "false natives."[26] He asked if it was our first time there, if we were having a good time, and if we were interested in using the VIP room. I said something noncommittal and told him that we would call for him if we needed anything. We watched the show for a while longer, though its monotony became unbearable, and I caught myself staring at the wall behind the catwalk where the paper-thin plaster had peeled off to reveal concrete hollow blocks. We asked for the manager and he led us through the tables and into a narrow hallway at the back of the stage. On the way there, I could feel the weight of the other patrons' stares at the back of my head and could hear someone from the waitstaff yelling ahead of us, "*May* VIP! *May* VIP! [There are VIPs! There are VIPs!]" The dancers began rushing into a small room at the end of the hallway. We stopped outside it, in front of a long, narrow slit window from where we could spy maybe fifteen or twenty of the dancers. Some of them were laughing and chatting with one another, some were quiet and indifferent, and a few were jockeying for position, smiling and posing and looking directly at us, even though we were told that the slit was a one-way window. Outside the room, there was a portly Chinese man in his thirties gossiping with the staff, a counterfeit Louis Vuitton bag dangling from his shoulder. He introduced himself to us and began inquiring excitedly if we had tried this before, what we were interested in, and if he could offer some recommendations. "Who's the biggest?" someone asked, laughing. "Who's the most game?" said another. The man began describing each of the dancers in detail. I wondered if they could hear him and if they cared. It took a long time for us to decide, and in the end we ignored the man's advice and chose a tough-looking dancer in a skullcap who sat in a corner chewing the insides of his cheeks.

The VIP room turned out to be a small room with two couches and another slit window, this time looking out into the main hall, granting a view of the ongoing show and the backs and heads of the other patrons. The dancer, Paolo, was surprisingly shy and soft-spoken. None of us knew how to interact with him, so we looked at one another awkwardly, waiting for someone to take the lead. Finally we started asking him questions about his work, the industry, and his past experiences. Despite our stuttering efforts, Paolo relaxed. After a while, he asked if he should start dancing and if it was OK if he dimmed the lights.

The slit windows! Someone told me later that they were installed for economic reasons (to save on glass), but the effect they produced was more profound. To get a full sense of the figures they masked—the bodies of the dancers, the catwalk from inside the VIP room—we had to bob our heads up and down, shift our eyes from side to side, or let our imaginations do the work and extrapolate whole images from the bits that were uncovered (perceptual faith).[27] Paul Virilio once commented on what experts call anorthoscopic vision, the restriction of vision to a slit: "The frame, the limit of visibility, is clearly what makes conscious objectification possible," he wrote. "We combine our search to maximize perception at all costs with *the quest for minimal perception* by means of a *slit*, a slit that limits without ever ruling out our perceiving the whole of the object or image masked."[28] Indeed, the visual limit imposed by the slit was not a nuisance but a thrill and a promise. It preserved the enigma of the fractioned image and gave us nothing more and nothing less than what we had come for: "*perceptionless* perception," a glimpse.[29]

There were times when our desire to wade in darker waters took us farther than we intended. During those instances, even the car offered little security: I was in a suite in a four-star hotel in Ortigas, sitting in front of large windows that overlooked the city. It was September, a Sunday afternoon, and though in theory it was the time for rains and storms, the sun was streaming hard into the hotel room. It shone on the wreckage of a party—sheets were scattered about; empty glasses and bottles cluttered the coffee table, the nightstands, the desk; and ashtrays overflowed with cigarette butts and matchsticks. Across from me sat Bernard, dressed only in a thick white bathrobe, his legs crossed. A cigarette, his breakfast, was dangling from his right hand. Bernard was only twenty, but he looked older as he recounted the events of the previous two nights under the harsh glare of sunlight.

He and a few friends had gotten bored at the clubs and decided that they wanted to see a live sex show, but they only knew of one place that offered them and another friend had denounced it as unremarkable, full of ugly boys that could only get half hard. So they decided to create their own show and hire callboys from a prostitution block called Gold Loop, located a few minutes from the hotel we were at and also, ironically, from a university run by the Opus Dei. They drove in separate cars from the clubs and split up in Ortigas, with some going ahead to the hotel to book a suite while Bernard and a few others drove around Gold Loop in search of callboys to pick up. The Loop itself was a small square block in a neighborhood dominated by moderately expensive condominium buildings. It was an unlikely site for prostitution and only gay men seemed to know that late at night, johns and callboys moved in like ghosts.

Bernard was driving and driving slowly. None of them had picked up callboys before, and they were all nervous, unsure of the protocol and wary of the authorities. They drove several times around the block, spotting a few stray figures standing in corners or walking under the shadows of trees, away from the few, scattered street lamps. There was a patrol car on one of the streets, but it looked abandoned and uninterested. Bernard and the others ignored it and kept driving around in circles. It might have been over half an hour before they slowed down in the darkest part of the block and turned off their headlights. One of the other boys quickly opened his door and got out, rushing off to talk to a dark figure in a tank top standing next to a telephone pole. Bernard wanted to tell him to get back in the car, but he had gotten out in a flash, emboldened and deafened by alcohol, and was making the transaction that Bernard and the others were too sober to attempt. Inside, Bernard was getting more anxious. He turned to look behind the car and saw that suddenly there were callboys coming out of all directions, walking slowly toward them. They were hovering around his car. It was, he told me, just like *Night of the Living Dead*. Finally, the one who stepped out returned and squeezed into the backseat with the callboy he was talking to. By then, they were all too worked up to find another callboy to hire and decided to speed back to the hotel.

The following night, they decided to return to the Loop. They were experts this time, they thought, and would be able to carry through with their plans. They were more relaxed when they drove again around the block, buoyed not only by the previous night's experience but also by the absence of the patrol car. At one point, two of them even got out and pretended to be callboys, trying to see who could fetch a higher price. But when they got to the business of finding men to bring back, they found that few were willing to do a live show. None of them, it seemed, wanted to be watched. It took almost an hour for them to find someone, but as soon as he joined them in the car, a police motorcycle appeared out of nowhere, overtaking them and blocking their path. Bernard and the others started panicking and screaming obscenities. Bernard tried to back up and drive past the motorcycle, but the police officer had jumped out of it and was now blocking the rest of the road. He was yelling into his radio. Bernard opened the window and screamed at the officer. "*Bos, pag-usapan natin 'to!* [Boss, let's talk about this!]" It was the standard euphemism for a bribe offer. "*Wala tayong pag-uusapan!* [We have nothing to talk about!]," the officer screamed back. "*Dun na lang kayo mag-usap sa presinto!* [Do your talking in the precinct!]"[30]

Inside, the others were still cursing, while the callboy sat frozen in the corner. Bernard kept yelling out to the officer, gesturing at him to come closer to the window. But he kept ignoring Bernard and speaking into his radio. At one point, Bernard changed tactics and spoke in straight English, a means of intimidation that sometimes worked with traffic enforcers. "*Huwag mo na 'kong Ingles-in* [Don't bother speaking English to me]," replied the officer. "*Walang mapapala 'yan!* [That won't get you anything!]"

Three more motorcycles appeared at the scene, surrounding Bernard's car. Bernard was dreading the thought of having to call his mother from the precinct when a more senior-looking officer approached the car and leaned into his window. He asked a series of questions: what they were doing there, their names, where they lived, and if they were picking up men or women. He told Bernard to get out of the car. Bernard ignored the order and all the questions asking for personal details. Instead he ran through a litany of unrelated, contradictory excuses. He said they were just passing through, that they were picking up a friend, and that they were on their way home. The officer bought none of it.

"*Huwag mo na 'kong lokohin* [Don't lie to me]," he said. "*Kanina pa namin pinapanood kayong paikot-ikot dito* [We've been watching you go around and around the block since earlier]."

Bernard switched tactics again and apologized, saying that it was their first time to do anything of that sort. In the background, the callboy they picked up started protesting. "*Hindi po 'ko callboy! Hindi po 'ko callboy!* [I'm not a callboy! I'm not a callboy!]"

Bernard and the officer both ignored him. Bernard continued, "*Pasensya na Bos. Hindi na namin uulitin. Bababa na lang namin siya tapos kayo na lang mag-usap?* [Boss, we're really sorry about this. We won't do it again. We'll just drop the callboy off and you can just deal with him.]"

"*Huwag niyo nang ibaba. Ayusin na lang natin 'to* [Don't drop him off anymore. Let's just fix this]," replied the officer, his voice softening. "*Basta sa susunod kung gusto ninyong pumick-up, sa ibang lugar na lang. Nagrereklamo kasi yung mga nakatira dito.* [But next time, if you want to pick up, do it someplace else. The residents here are complaining.]"

With that, Bernard reached for his wallet and pulled out a one thousand-peso bill (twenty-five U.S. dollars). He folded it quickly and slipped it to the officer, who gestured for the other cops to back off and let Bernard and his car through.

It was around five in the morning when they started driving back. The sky was quickly turning gray and already a few joggers had appeared on the streets. They were laughing now, thrilled by their narrow escape. Bernard asked the callboy where they could drop him off, assuming that the night was over. The callboy said anywhere was fine. Bernard was getting ready to stop at the nearest intersection when someone else turned to the callboy and said, in a sweet voice, "You can still come with us if you want." Bernard wasn't expecting a positive response, especially after he had tried to give the callboy up to the cops, but the callboy only hesitated for a second before smiling and saying, "OK."

When Bernard finished telling me this story, he stood from his chair and faced the floor-length windows. I stood next to him as he pointed out where Gold Loop was. I nodded, though all I could really see were rooftops.

Beached

Whenever I remember Bernard telling me that story in his white robe, standing against the large windows of that hotel suite, I think of Michel de Certeau's modern spectator, the anonymous body "lifted out of the city's grasp," at the summit of a high-rise building: "His elevation transfigures him into a voyeur . . . puts him at a distance," lets him look down with a "solar Eye . . . like a god."[31] I think also of Le Corbusier, flying above South America, thrilled by the bird's-eye view and at the same time appalled at the present disorder and enthused by the prospect of reshaping the ground, of modern engineering guided by an aerial, cartographic eye. De Certeau, however, wrote of a caricature, a foil for his pedestrian; and, in some ways, Le Corbusier himself was almost fictional in his disdain for the streets (he was the aviator, the man of the city of tomorrow, Ayn Rand's Howard Roark made flesh).[32] Bernard, no less a modern spectator, was bored by height. As were we when we drove through the less-familiar streets of Manila in search of cheap thrills in strip clubs that were, invariably, less sordid than we had hoped or imagined. On those nights, we relished the descent; it was a dip, a glance, a fall couched by romance and by the wealth that bought private rooms and safe passage back to loftier sites. This was modern spectatorship as lived in the third-world city by those who benefited from the privilege of class—an economy of heights and distances traversed and ruled by the multiply mobile.

There were, however, places where the distance between the sky and the earth did not need to be bridged, where they blended together and became indistinguishable naturally like the horizon viewed from a beach. There was an island off the coast of Luzon where every summer gay men from Manila flocked to escape the tremendous heat in the city. In the dark caves a short trek from the shore, there was always sex, performed unself-consciously, under the yellow lights of mobile phones. Those caves were like the backrooms of clubs, or the fantasy of backrooms, since no such thing existed in a gay Manila obsessed with washing away the classed stigma of sleaze and filth. At the beach, the urban fantasy of an unbridled gay sexuality could be realized with no constraints. We fled there—to the middle of nowhere—only to urbanize it, to turn its crevices into a back alley, to hear the drum of dance music in the sound of waves breaking against rocks. We could not escape the city, or the concept of the city.

We tried to escape once on a hot night in June, the end of summer in Manila. I remember sitting on the hood of my car, drinking beers with two gay men I had known for several years. We thought of hitting the bars and clubs, but the stickiness of the air seemed to strip the city of its capacity to enchant. "Let's go to the beach," someone suggested, "someplace empty." We drove for hours, past the hazards of EDSA and then through the long stretch of the South Luzon Expressway. We sped through Makati City, Pasay City, and Parañaque City, until we crossed the waterparks and amusement parks and the only thing in sight were rice paddies. Our destination was not the port where boats left for that famous island frequented by gay men but the quieter beaches behind the mountains of Batangas. It was morning by the time we arrived, and we spent that first day on the rocky beaches where divers and fishermen parked their boats, content to be bathing in the breeze blowing with no discernible direction. The next morning, however, that beach was no longer enough, and we longed for someplace with purer sands and fewer people. We hired a fisherman to take us to a nearby island. There, we baked in the sun and were completely alone. Even the fisherman left us and came back only after having caught a small octopus. I swam out and left the other two on the shore. I was a good swimmer and felt comfortable heading out into the open water. I kept swimming until the men I was with had become nothing more than two dots on the shore. I saw that there were no fish in the sea, no coral, not even (as you were likely to see in many of the country's beaches) a stray piece of plastic. It was as barren as a desert. It probably should have felt empty, but instead I thought the space fully consumed by the water. It felt saturated and dense and claustrophobic. I choked and might have drowned had I not managed to calm myself down and swim back to the safety of the shore.[33]

We left later that same day. The trip went by fast (home was always near), and we found ourselves back in the thick of the city right in the middle of rush hour. By then I was too tired to be bothered by the traffic and found myself half asleep in the passenger seat watching the orange skeins streaked across the sky disappear from behind the quasi-opaque windows of the car. The heat was no longer coming from the city but bouncing off the sunburned skin on my knees and shoulders. It was a quiet drive until we got caught at a standstill along Ortigas Avenue. There, a boy about ten years old started knocking on the driver's side window begging for change. We ignored him, and after a few seconds he backed off and walked in front of the car. Midway, he turned to look at us. There was sudden recognition in his eyes. He smiled, a nasty smile, and yelled, "*Bakla!* [Fags!]"

He ran off, leaving us sitting there with our mouths open, paralyzed as much by the traffic as by the shock of being called *bakla*, a word that bound us to the older queers lurking in the shadows of the strip bars, the cross-dressers who ran the low-end beauty salons scattered all over the city, the classed figures for whom the term *bakla* was often reserved and whose lives took place (in our minds, at least) outside the world of bars and clubs and privilege that we called our own. At that moment, the traffic-clogged roads and the street child who took advantage of them seemed to hold us in a state of arrest. Named, recognized, and held in *place,* our ties to the city seemed suddenly visible, as though the walls we built through speed and wealth had, in an instant, become transparent.[34] For a moment, I was stunned. I did not know whether to scream or yell something back, how to react to this grave insult from a child. Then the moment of shock passed, and the three of us in the car looked at each other and burst out laughing: "Fucking kid," said my friend who was driving. "If the traffic wasn't so bad, I'd run him over."

Detours

In writing movement, there is always the risk of getting lost.

I wanted to write about gay men in Manila, to zoom in on a scene, only to find that I had to keep stepping out into the city. Stepping out—not stepping back or zooming out—for Manila makes no sense when viewed as a panorama, even less when viewed from above. It is only on the streets that one can get a feel for the stark contradictions of the third-world city, the relentless crumpling together of privilege and marginality. In some ways, the bright lights scene is the perfect site of contradiction, for there the sexually abject are also aligned with the interests and hierarchies of capital. It is in light of such an alignment that I have begun to weave together memories and anecdotes, stories that foreground complicity rather than resistance. These stories have invariably been about driving through and inhabiting space. I chose them in part because I can only remember Manila as a combination of nodes and travels but also because that combination is precisely what allows for the mastery of the contradictions etched onto the city streets. It is what allows us to see and hear some things more than others, to erect imagined borders and perceptual limits, to be sunk but flying, beasts and angels. Flyovers, hotel suites, VIP rooms, clubs, intersections, caves, standstills, and traffic jams: these are not only mundane sites but also the means for a play of heights, of density and emptiness, of speed and slowness, the very shifts that disturb and sustain the dreams of mobility that underpin life under the bright lights.

CHAPTER TWO

Elsewhere, between Palawan and the Global City

The future has ceased to exist; the idle circle of traveling closes in the land that lies before us, beyond the horizon. Elsewhere begins here, we become what is unknown to us.

—Paul Virilio, *Negative Horizon*

There is no more exile; the elsewhere is our abode . . . Another day is breaking in a world that is being born.

—Marcel Hénaff, "Of Stones, Angels, and Humans"

I have begun to track the way gay life in Manila takes form as an intra-urban network, a series of sites brought together, if loosely, through ways of navigating and inhabiting the city streets. In the previous chapter, the automobile, what might be regarded as both a metaphor for and an avatar of modernity, appears as the iron manifestation of ideals of progress, mobility, speed, and freedom.[1] It takes form as a "machine dream" that enables acceleration, elevation, swerves, fleeting contacts, and other spatial practices that subject the contradictions on the streets to the possibility of elision.[2] These spatial practices are the gestures that give the bright lights scene its metropolitan form; they are the moves that produce a world within the city and that assemble fragments of gay life into a local constellation.

The destinations that make up this constellation are, however, more than just islets in a sea of turbulence and decay. They are also nodes in worldwide networks of signs and messages, spaces filled with messengers or what Michel Serres called "angels": ancient and modern figures of a plural Hermes, of relations that outline a virtual space that serves as the locus of experience.[3] Indeed, ordinary spaces such as bars, clubs, commercial developments, and the streets themselves are teeming with things that come from afar—objects and images, names and styles, bodies and architectural patterns—apparitions that evoke lives lived in distant sites and that bring into view horizons that are both fantastic and remembered. As Hénaff once noted, urban spaces can no longer be imagined without their "elsewheres," their *limes,* their furthest borders. "To think the city, one must leave it and see it as part of the world, *extra-muros.*"[4]

The "elsewhere," as I employ it here, is a designation for a place of "forms that remain inaccessible."[5] In Derrida's terms, it is "the always further"[6] or that which always lies "beyond a certain limit."[7] Taken in the plural, elsewheres name a panoply of worlds that are not only cast as geographically distant but also imagined as bearing states that are still "to come," states such as modernness and globalness that stand as the telos of metropolitan change. This is not to say that elsewheres cannot be glimpsed or that they have no real presence in the city. Rather, it is to suggest that in Manila (like all cities, a city of angels), elsewheres arrive in the form of signs. They hover in the background. They are read in the things that circulate in the city and come from afar. They are plied from their referent sites and (like all signs) acquire force through "fleeting, half-visible associations that dwell in the corners of the mind."[8]

In this chapter, I am interested in how signs that evoke elsewheres are woven into the built environment of the city: how their appearance shapes and is shaped by the material landscape or the "stone" of urban life.[9] Here, local space emerges as what Wlad Godzich referred to as "the space of the inscription of the sign to come."[10] The urban fractures and differences that I have begun to describe appear as the limit conditions against which imagoes of distant sites rub up. How, I ask, do the meanings nesting in different material sites and the meanings ascribed to elsewheres collude and collide? What desires, dreams, divides, and aspirations are revealed and magnified by the relations that exist between spaces and signs or stones and angels? How do these relations inflect gay life under the bright lights of Manila and inform the manner in which local sites are seen, experienced, and integrated into the bright lights scene as destinations, as nodes in a network that not only is profoundly urban but also opens up to real and imagined places that lie beyond the limits of the city?

To answer these questions, I offer a picture here of three sites where elsewheres are materialized: Global City, a commercial development where clusters of sleek nightspots are set apart from the disorder of Manila; a party patterned after the U.S. version of the television program *Queer as*

Folk hosted by Club Government in Makati City; and a gay club named "Palawan," after a paradisiacal island off the coast of Luzon, in a run-down district called Cubao. These sites reveal how, in Manila, dreams of being elsewhere come to life in myriad ways and are set against the intense differences that mark and cut the urban landscape. I write them together here, in series, in hopes of beginning to shed light on how the scene takes form not only through moves that link cityspaces but that bridge or attempt to bridge the gap between near and far, here and there, the world outside and local space.

The Desert in the City, or Names Lodged as Signs

The Global City is a twenty-five-square-kilometer commercial and residential development that lies northeast of the Makati CBD, just a short drive across Epifanio delos Santos Avenue (EDSA) and down McKinley Avenue, a narrow tree-lined road that cuts through the mansions of the gated subdivisions known as Forbes Park and Dasmariñas Village. Many residents of Metro Manila still refer to the Global City as "the Fort" or "Fort Bonifacio," a name that recalls its prior incarnation as part of the headquarters of the Philippine Army. Despite the persistence of the name, however, the Fort has retained few, if any, signs of military life outside the small bases and the Cemetery of Heroes, which stand forgotten, or at best ignored, near the southern edge of the development. What one finds at the Global City in lieu of historical markers are upmarket condominiums occupied by wealthy locals and expatriates, office towers, a few clusters of shops, bars, restaurants, embassies, international schools, and the headquarters of multinational corporations such as HSBC, Deutsche Bank, Fujitsu, Sony-Ericsson, and Hewlett-Packard. On paper, these human and non-human inhabitants lend credence to the renaming of the Fort as a global city within the third-world city. On the ground, however, the new name rings hollow, belied as it is by the barrenness and quietness of the Fort, the large gaps between its high-rise buildings and commercial pockets, the absence of pedestrians on its major sidewalks. In a city notorious for its density and unforgiving traffic, the Fort stands out for its excess space, its often vacant, gridded roads and the sight they afford from moving cars of large swaths of land and dust rising from sites of protracted construction.

In the midst of the Fort's emptiness, it is difficult to imagine the thick flows of information, money, and people that have become, for better or worse, the yardsticks for a city's globalness and that pervade popular images of places grown dense, complex, and dirty under the weight and violence of both material and immaterial transactions.[11] During the day, the rush that percolates through the metropolis seems to die at the Fort. Viewed from above, it appears like a wound between two highways, a bubble kept apart from the swerving buses and jeepneys that compete with private vehicles on Manila's major thoroughfares, the vendors and beggars who work the roads, the shantytowns that surround even wealthy subdivisions: in other words, all those contradictions that seem to mark the rest of Metro Manila. Indeed, little of the city's disorder seems to flow through the Fort. Its spaces are all exposed, bereft of "possibilities for hidden life"—of secret passages and crevices where the city might seep through and linger.[12] On sunny days, the Fort seems hotter than any other part of the city, for there everything is laid bare and no respite is offered from the desert-like heat beyond the steel-gray lobbies of office towers and the narrow canopies of disjointed structures like the strip of restaurants and apartments called Serendra or the hulking form of the MC Home Depot that dominates its busiest street.

There is, in fact, something in the Fort that bears the qualities of a desert. It is all ordered plains and straight, concrete roads that evoke, if partially, that "pure geometry" to which Baudrillard once credited the disappearance of cities.[13] On weekday afternoons, you can drive around the streets of the Fort for hours and not see a single soul on foot, except maybe a stray security guard standing bored in front of an office build-ing or next to a parked motorbike; or you can walk around in circles, searching for a cab, only to realize that there are hardly any means of commuting at the Fort, just parking lot after parking lot; or you can stand at the edge of a large, untouched block and be struck by the fact that the Fort is one of the only places in Manila where you can see across wide distances, where few objects obstruct vision beyond the outlines of scat-tered buildings, the dry land and patchy grass of parking lots, the craters and lonely tractors that serve as early signs of construction projects. At the Fort, there exists that striking juxtaposition of barren expanse and the synthetic ambitions of human construction. There, pockets of develop-ment spring up in the midst of nothingness, like pale, third-world versions of the fantastic structures that rise from the sands in Dubai or the urban vistas that emerge out of the hills and plains of California.[14]

If another part of Manila were to be renamed "Global City," it would invite skepticism, if not outright ridicule. The emptiness of the Fort, how-ever, seems to make its ambitions plausible and hence palatable, if only because it offers bare space through which the world might enter the city and gain tentative hold. Still, the Fort is not exempt from the limits of Manila. The dearth of capital that marks the city keeps the dreams of the Fort—its wistful promise of reinvention—in check and manifests itself in the languid pace of construction and in the modesty of its engineers. There, all the structures are uniformly modern and a few have made the pages of local architectural digests, but among these structures that have been erected at the Fort, there are no skyscrapers that demand recognition, no landmarks other than a nondescript steel and glass sculpture by a famous local architect that stands alone at the corner of an empty block. There are only names that evoke lives lived in distant cities: A major artery is named "Fifth Avenue," though few seem to know exactly where First, Second, and Third Avenues are located. A two-story building is emblazoned with a large metal sign that reads "32nd and Fifth," though no one in Manila identifies addresses using street intersections. A popular restaurant and retail space is called "Bonifacio High Street," despite the absence of the British metonym "High Street" from the local vocabulary, and high-rise apartments rise in quick succession with names like "Palm Spring" (*sic*), "Hamptons Place," and "SoMa" (not an acronym for "South of Market Street," as in the San Francisco district, but for "South of 'Market, Market,'" the name of the mall that borders the C-5 highway).[15]

All throughout the Fort, familiar yet foreign names such as these dot the landscape. They emerge unremarked, as quotidian illustrations of how the dream of globalness might be approached through the weaving and writing of "elsewheres that resonate" into the spaces at hand.[16] What the appearance of these elsewheres brings to mind, however, is not the irony of pastiche or caricature that marks the emergence of *copies* in other desert and desert-like spaces like Dubai's World Islands or pyramids in Vegas or English towns at the outskirts of Seoul, but the uncertain life of "names lodged as signs," the gap between signs and their meanings that enables the blurring of "original" contexts while retaining the mysterious allure of the foreign.[17] At the Fort, names reveal how bare space and the magic of global circulation work in tandem; how distant places are attenuated, given new lives, and rematerialized in unexpected ways (districts and beach towns become condominiums, landmark avenues become sparsely populated roads, etc.) that nonetheless reveal the power of words to "make image"—that is, to set imaginations into flight, even when the destinations they evoke are only faintly penciled onto the sights/sites on the ground.[18]

The Fort, you could say, is a place where imagined elsewheres arrive. There, the "evocative force of names" becomes apparent, not as a derivative of similitude or resemblance, but as the effect of half-hidden associations and of the images of progress, wealth, and modernity ascribed to distant sites and that appear in the city as absent presences.[19] These names "open the question of signification to include not only the symbolic aspect of the sign with its reference to (first-order) meanings but also the indexical and iconic aspects of the sign that . . . give signs the power to point to an association regardless of their message or meaning in the cultural order of things."[20] The barren landscape of the Fort—a space that stands in a relation of negation to the disorder of the city—is where the global can be localized as a *sign*, a surface inscription overlaid onto the sites at hand, a vector that draws in all those who might take comfort in the tough alliance of emptiness, reinvention, and dreams of globalness. The name "Global City" and the names of the other elsewheres scattered throughout the development, in other words, do not speak of promises fulfilled or of transformations completed; rather, like desert oases or signs planted in the "space of a gap," they register aspirations and trajectories and index desires and dreams.[21]

There are, strictly speaking, no "gay-identified" establishments at the Fort, but among those who are drawn to the Fort's promise of being elsewhere are gay men, who arrive in packs and in enough numbers to merit the listing of the Fort as a key destination in online guides to gay life in the city.[22] During fieldwork, I found myself driving to the Fort routinely on weekend nights, when its commercial pockets burst into life and lit up with signs. Waiting for the right time to head to the clubs, I would walk with groups of gay men down High Street, and we would get lost among the couples walking purebred dogs, groups of young people smoking outside cafés, the yuppies heading to the wine bar hidden behind an untrafficked corner, and the artists and musicians making their way to an art gallery where rock bands sometimes played long sets and a famous movie director hosted a monthly party where people danced with flashlights. Often, we would begin walking from the westernmost end of High Street, where a specialty shop sold brands familiar only to the fashionable elites, alongside merchandise that spoke directly to a gay clientele, like old copies of *BUTT* magazine or coffee table books on Tom of Finland. From there, we would walk past all the other shops and up to Serendra, where we would stop at a bakery that sold cupcakes that looked and tasted exactly like the ones from Magnolia Bakery in New York or sit in the outdoor section of a restaurant named "Chelsea," after the Manhattan district, from where we would watch the young professionals who dominated the scene, the expats and college kids, the occasional model or celebrity. Among them, we would often spot other gay men we knew or knew of. The different men I found myself sitting or walking with would spot acquaintances whom they would greet across distances and kiss on the cheek. They would point discreetly at men on dates, the ex of an ex who was now seeing someone who looked like his twin, a man they recognized only because he was constantly online looking for sex, and a host of familiar faces from the gay clubs. Once, one of the men I interviewed asked me why I thought so many gay men brought dates to Serendra. I shrugged and threw the question back at him, since I knew he himself had gone on dates there. "I don't know," he said. "Maybe it's because it feels less public than other parts of the city."

There were nights when hours spent at High Street or Serendra did not precede trips to the gay clubs but led instead to other parts of the Fort that suggested states of being someplace else. On Fifth Avenue stood what was, at the time, the city's largest and most expensive club, Embassy, a large white box that used to be the headquarters of MTV Philippines and that was named, fittingly, after a structure defined by its displacement, an outpost located in a city and yet tied, belonging, and loyal to a distant land. Outside Embassy, you could catch celebrities and socialites flitting about and, as in the real embassies of foreign governments in Manila, lines of people waiting to get in. There were nights when I found myself just standing outside Embassy with other gay men. We would do nothing but smoke cigarettes and survey the crowd and walk in and out of the bar next door. And there were other nights when I got whisked through the crowd by people who could take me straight into the club, past the club's head bouncer, a towering American woman whose foreign presence at the door seemed to signify Embassy's separation from the city.

On those nights, I would catch sight of men I knew from the gay clubs dancing, more dressed up than usual, forming little circles in the middle of the crowd. Seeing them there, however, was never a surprise, for in Manila, even the men whose nighttime existence seemed firmly rooted between the narrow walls of the gay clubs lived in the continuous flow of the movements of the bright lights scene. At Embassy, gay men were not an excluded minority. I would spot them standing at the VIP section, raised just a meter off the ground like a stage right next to the main dance floor, or snaking confidently through the mass of bodies below. During my earlier visits to Embassy, I thought that their presence there was simply a sign of how sexuality was subordinated to class belonging in places like the Fort. Later, I came to realize that there was something kindred between my other memories of gay Manila—speeding through the city at night, nights spent at a club located on a major thoroughfare—and the promise offered by Embassy's bare white facade, its adoption of a name that recalls a structure *in* a place but not *of* a place, its self-promotion as a place "where the real thing happens." That line, coupled with the name

"Embassy," made it clear to me that the strange gathering of signs and spaces at the Fort and the dreams of speed and disappearance that marked my other memories of gay Manila worked in tandem; together, they illustrated how the real can and does happen in places at once in the city and someplace else.

There were nights when this connection between gay-identified spaces and the Fort was traced in almost literal fashion, when gay men moved from Embassy to the gay clubs at around 2 or 3 a.m. More than anything, those nights seemed to reflect a desire for continuity, a collective will to extend the experience of "displacement in place" until daylight, when the Fort once again emptied out, the rest of the city filled in, and the fabulation of a fast life was threatened by the sudden visibility of the detritus of the city.[23] There were nights, for instance, spent at Embassy or at the neighboring NBC Tent dancing to music played by famous DJs visiting from Europe or North America.[24] Once those events began winding down and the other patrons started stumbling back to their cars, many gay men would drive out of the Fort Strip, down Fifth Avenue, past High Street, and over to the gay clubs, where material from that same DJ might still be playing or where another event might still be going strong, perhaps a marathon of hits from Madonna or Kylie Minogue or from another pop star whose album was just launched overseas. Those nights, more than any other, exemplified the logic that underpinned the experience of the scene as a continuous movement, one that cast the gay clubs as an endpoint, a viable destination once the roads that led to them had cleared. Within such a movement, gay clubs appeared not as sequestered havens for those who were excluded but as extensions of other pockets of privilege, final holdouts where those who refused to go to sleep could sustain the dream of being elsewhere exemplified by the Fort.

The continuity of the scene, however, was contingent on the ability of different sites to similarly realize displacement and to effectively harmonize the images recalled by signs and the material landscape. In a city like Manila, this was no easy feat and there were times, for instance, when the gay clubs failed to match the credible promise of being someplace else offered by the Fort. One night, I found myself moving from the Fort to a gay club, only to find myself doubling back. It was the holidays, and a group of gay men had taken me along to various Christmas parties across the city. We were moving from Embassy to Club Government, which was hosting a party called "Evolution." We were told that it was going to be a winter party, that the club had hired out snow machines and ice sculptures and that there would be living art in the form of drag queens dressed as ice princesses. I remember that in the weeks leading up to the party, the club had sent out digital flyers touting it as "the ultimate dance party" and announcing that entrance for the special event was set at a higher-than-usual rate of five hundred pesos (twelve U.S. dollars). I also remember, however, that several gay men I knew greeted the event with a certain sense of comic apprehension. They chuckled at the thought of snow machines and compared the concept of the party to the low-end amusement parks set up near Manila Bay, where children were known to play in dirty crushed ice, in giant freezers dolled up as snow castles. Still, on the night of the party, we made our way out of the Fort Strip, through 26th Street and up the large, unlit, swerving flyover that linked the Fort to the Makati CBD. Approaching the club, we saw two men exiting wearing sweaters and snow vests, prompting one of the men I was with, an informant who had spent some years living in Europe, to start laughing. "How absurd," he exclaimed. "Do these people know where they are?" He suggested that we skip the party altogether and return to the Fort. We took his suggestion and headed back to a bar on Fifth Avenue. There, the question of "knowing where you are" was never raised, for the state and practice of being elsewhere did not produce contradictions and was accomplished more deftly and subtly through the collaborative work of a desert space—a blank slate—and desires indexed in signs.

Pirated Elsewheres

In the order of signs, reality is always mediated by the socially contingent.[25] Location, or knowledge of one's location, is hinged on the integration of or the friction between images and ideas spied and felt from across distances and the immediate world of surrounding, concrete space.[26] The elsewheres inscribed onto the landscape of the Fort and the elsewhere of the winter party held at Government begin to reveal how the material life and meaning of signs get affected by the spaces onto which they are transplanted, the performances of being elsewhere those spaces inspire, and the memories they invite or expel, like the traces of national military life and urban disorder that have been disappeared from the Global City or the classed image of a run-down amusement park recalled by a winter party. More fundamentally, they point to a desire to materialize the "far" in the "near," to arrive without having to leave, or to "fix" what Virilio described as the "disorder of common perception"—that is, the splitting of vision between "presence here and now" and "telepresence at a distance."[27]

Indeed, it is Virilio, more than anyone, who has plumbed the question of how urban life has been transformed by increasing knowledge of places that lie beyond the city limits. Today, he says, urban gates and ports have been replaced with windows and teleports, with screens and "time-slots" through which city-dwellers see the world and the world enters the city.[28] His is an account of urbanity that echoes images of the world wrapped in information,[29] of architecture as increasingly immaterial,[30] and of being as being "*hors-là*": "an out-there; a with-out; a here-there; an outside in; a there-beyond."[31] It is an account that recalls now-familiar pronouncements of the "annihilation of space by time"[32] but dwells less on the nature of flows than on their phenomenological effects, on the myriad ways they distort perceptions of distance, proximity, and imme-diate space.[33] Out of Virilio's writing emerges a montage or collage of optical effects that point to the "confusion of near and far" and the "rapid evaporation" of the "optical density of the landscape."[34] Objects come flying past the windshields of cars and the windows of trains; cinema and air travel combine to enable "retinal take-off"; and "audiovisual vehi-cles" outstrip the "perspective of real space," producing a world where "the far prevails over the near and figures without density prevail over things within reach."[35] "How," he asks, "can we really live if there is no more *here* and everything is *now*? How can we survive the instanta-neous telescoping of a reality that has become ubiquitous . . . ? How can we rationally manage the split, not only between the virtual and actual realities but, more to the point, between the *apparent* horizon and the *transapparent* horizon . . . ?"[36]

Virilio poses these questions with eyes vigilantly cast on the world of instantaneous tele-technologies, optoelectronics, real-time telecommuni-cations, virtual reality, and so on. Caught up in an urgent effort to critique forms of life hurtling forward, he was not thinking of the perceptual splits that mark a third-world city like Manila, with all its fits and starts, its nervous tempi, its gaps and "time-lag."[37] And yet his questions haunt my own images and memories of Manila, for there, perhaps more than anywhere, the tensions he describes and portends between the near and far appear more real, visceral, anxious, and nervous. Urban decay rubs up against the signs and styles, images and ideas, ideologies and practices that have become the ubiquitous objects of global circulation. Abject pov-erty sits side by side with privileged ways of life. Sights of contradiction erupt everywhere but have become unremarkable, veiled, and integrated into an order of business as usual through strategies hinged on visual effects: nighttime driving reduces the city streets to a blur; beggars are spied through tinted windows; flyovers rise above traffic and disorder; and, at the Fort, a "culture of desertification" goes to work.[38]

What can be said, however, of the names plucked from elsewheres that appear in the Fort? What of the bars and clubs that link together to form a scene, those places suffused with dreams of a fast life and an otherworldly air and that we might be tempted to dismiss as the epiphe-nomena of global capital or celebrate as the effects of an autonomous will to appropriate things that circulate? What of DJs who roam the Inter-net for hours to make sure their playlists are in step with the rest of the world, of party promoters and club owners who journey to Paris and New York to "find out how things are really done," of clubs decked out with chairs plucked from *Wallpaper* magazine that cost twice the monthly sal-ary of their employees and that send out flyers for parties named after events overseas? We might say, in contrast to Virilio, that in Manila the "grand optics" that see past the "apparent horizon" of real space do not necessarily result in the waning relevance of immediate space.[39] Rather, they function as a generative force. They give rise to a place like the Fort, determined to reconstitute itself as a "global city" within the third-world city, sequestered from the city but open to the world: a "ruptured enclo-sure" that lets "everything—absolutely everything—back to that place which has no place."[40] It animates the transformation of local spaces not into sites where "the gap between near and far ceases to exist" but into spaces marked by a yearning to reconcile the contradictions between the immediate and the distant.[41] It fuels longings for outward movements and purposive returns, inscribed, for instance, in those sleepless nights DJs spend scouring over playlists online or in the appraisal of the gay scene offered by one of my informants: "We have a long way to go," he said, "but we're getting there . . . We want to *see* what's out there . . . And we bring it back. We bring everything back."

Indeed, Virilio's pronouncement that "elsewhere begins here" reverber-ates throughout the city, not as a claim about the present order of things but as a never-to-be-completed task, a project to be realized in geographi-cal space. As a project, it is prone to both success and failure, like the gay clubs that could, on most nights, serve as viable extensions of the dream of being elsewhere and then become objects of ridicule on a night like that of the winter party. Still, it would be too simple to cast the emergence of else-wheres within Manila as a strategy to effectively reconcile the world we spy across distances and the territory we inhabit, for the desire to materi-alize the far in the near is charged with other desires, with the intertwined dreams of progress, escape, mobility, and wealth laid bare by the adoption of names like "Fifth Avenue," "High Street," "Hamptons," "Chelsea," "SoMa," and the like. These names arrive in Manila but lose their weight and bulk in transit. They appear not as alternates for the actual places they refer to in the cultural order of things but as signs that point to "a gap in which strange associations remain possible."[42] Their power comes

from their ability to articulate dreams and to project them onto a generalized other place, perhaps that imagined space we have learned to refer to
as "the West" or the "global" recalled by the name "Global City" or the
unspecified homeland of "Embassy." As José Rabasa once pointed out,
"The space of *elsewheres* remains neutral"; it is, by definition, never fully
inhabitable or expropriable.[43] The emergence of elsewheres in Manila, in
other words, can be taken as an attempt to materialize the far in the near,
but only if the "far" is understood not as a set of discrete places that exist
but as a composite of images and fictions produced through global circulation and filled with the force of local desire.

   There was a night in 2007, for instance, when Club Government's
weekly event, Pink Saturday, was transformed into a party inspired by
the U.S. version of the television series *Queer as Folk*. Originally a British
series set in Manchester's gay village, the American adaptation of *Queer
as Folk* revolved around the lives of five gay men in the middle-class gay
district of Pittsburgh, Pennsylvania.[44] While the program touched on various aspects of the characters' lives, a substantial part of the program
focused on their experiences at gay bars and clubs, most notably at the
fictional megaclub Babylon. It was this, the image of a gay club culture,
a culture absent from Manila until 2003, which seemed to spark interest
and imagination in Manila. Several weeks prior to the event, an invitation was circulated by e-mail featuring a picture of the two *Queer as
Folk* lead characters kissing and superimposed on a disco ball. On the
invitation, the name "Government" was reduced to a small "G" on the
bottom-right corner, its usual spot taken over by bold lettering that read
"Club Babylon." "Ever wonder what Babylon is like?" asked the invitation. "Well honey, we will take you there!" The e-mail promised that it
would be "the gayest Pink Saturday ever" and asked everyone to come
as *Queer as Folk* characters. On the night of the party, Government was
full, but its promise to transport clubgoers to Babylon was not mirrored
in mimetic spatial transformations.[45] Everything looked the same as on
any other Saturday night, though music from the series soundtrack was
blaring from the speakers and footage from the show was projected onto
the walls. Held nearly two years after the program aired its final episode,
the promise of the *Queer as Folk* party to take people to Babylon seemed
to hinge less on the imitative capacity of Government than on the force
and power of desire and nostalgia. During countless casual conversations
that took place while I was on fieldwork, talk of the party and of *Queer
as Folk* in general elicited recollections of the days when the program first
began circulating around Manila. People would remember those years just
prior to the emergence of piracy hubs throughout the city and the advent

of easy downloading over the Internet, when episodes were burned onto generic discs and passed around in private circles. The quality of the videos was poor, they would say, but it did not matter. They would watch them on their friends' couches or alone, with the sound turned down, in the bedrooms they had in their parents' houses.

A few years ago, one of my informants, James, wrote of his anticipation for the fourth season of the program. He said that the show always generated strong feelings for him, not because of the story itself, but because it brings up memories of the time when he first started watching the series, when he was nineteen and beginning to come out.[46] He would sneak out of the house and take a taxi to the apartment of the man he was seeing at the time, an hour away, and they would sit together and watch the program, copied onto blank CDs: "What I loved was the fact that there was a show about how gay people lived," he wrote. "I was so happy during those times . . . being able to pretend, if even for a moment, that my life was just like theirs."[47]

Later on, I found myself with James at a commercial complex called Metrowalk, a large block of land located at the heart of Ortigas Center and occupied primarily by gravel and a few rows of midpriced restaurants. We were on the second floor of a nondescript two-story building tucked away at the back of the complex, browsing through rows and rows of pirated DVDs. We stopped at a stall where the attendants knew James by name and stocked many gay-themed films: from mainstream Hollywood fare to independent productions stretching back to the seventies. Like most of the other pirate stalls at Metrowalk, that stall also carried box sets of *Queer as Folk* sold for as little as three hundred pesos (seven U.S. dollars) and thrown in with other American dramas. Spotting the copies of the series, James recalled that when the pirates first started selling copies of *Queer as Folk,* they hid them in secret boxes along with pornographic films. Now, he said, they were on display everywhere, and if you could not see them out in the open, it only meant that they were out of stock. Over coffee, he told me that *Queer as Folk* was inseparable from his experience of the clubs. He pointed out that the year he started watching the program was followed by the opening of the city's first major gay club, Bed, located in Malate in the old City of Manila. He said that going there for the first time was like "meeting the image" he first encountered during those months he was illicitly watching *Queer as Folk.* He said that Bed was, in fact, very much driven by that image: when it was new, they also screened episodes silently on the screens while everyone danced; its expansion in 2005 made it look a lot more like Babylon, and Government could also elicit that same feeling whenever you found yourself leaning on the railing on the second floor and watching the people below.

I remember James's account and I am struck by how, under James's desiring gaze, the clubs become extensions of pirated images, space acquires mnemonic force, and images travel and grow ubiquitous, not through the windows of instantaneous technology of which Virilio writes but through the secret passages of the third-world city. In James's account, the picture of "how gay men live" comes in through the back doors of the city. It arrives in secret boxes and gets passed around on generic discs. It enters discreetly but then circulates wildly, so much so that a few years after its initial circulation, the owners of Government could assume that practically everyone had seen the program and that many had wondered "what Babylon was like." In this account, the gay clubs serve as sites into which the image of an elsewhere leaks out even while outside the city loomed as an ineluctable and inconsonant setting.

In this way, the gay clubs appear continuous with both the city and the images of *Queer as Folk*. Like the pirated DVDs stacked in Metrowalk, their arrival marks the city's insistence on being in step with the world. Their power comes from the ability to evoke an *original*, which most may never see but is assumed to exist, somewhere, lost in the processes of transfer and transit. This is a power that stems less from similitude than from the force of desire itself. Indeed, on the night of the *Queer as Folk* party, Government did not need to make any spatial changes. James, armed with his memories, could read the very architecture of the clubs as signs. For him, the clubs had already materialized the dream of how gay men lived; they were, in a way, always already Babylon.

Dreams of Elsewhere

If desired elsewheres come across as fictions, as signs that emerge in circulation more than sites that have an a priori existence, then indeed they can be imagined not as places spied from across distances but as images that resemble dreams. They are like dreams not only because they are wishes but also because they are constrained by "imaginary structures," by what Sigmund Freud called the "unconscious," or by what Neferti Tadiar referred to, more accurately, as "the logics of organization of our material realities."[48] Dreams, says Tadiar, "cannot be understood apart from the global material imaginary . . . [from] the dominant field of reality on which they play out."[49] They do not open up into spaces that are entirely new, but they are always already occupied by the objects of modern life.[50] James dreams of how gay men live and finds a picture of men dancing under the laser lights of Babylon. The Fort indexes dreams of being global and takes on familiar names that evoke a life of privilege. Dreams, in both cases, become intelligible only through available scripts: they take the form of images or, better still, of cultural raw materials stocked in a repository built on the logics of capital and modernity. With Tadiar, we could call these scripts and stock images "fantasies"—that is, forms of expression that have become hegemonic or "abstract forms into which the concrete work of imagination (dreams) get subsumed."[51] Slavoj Žižek, similarly, termed them "fantasy-constructions" that "support our 'reality' itself."[52] Whatever name they are given, *fantasies* or *fantasy-constructions* order apprehension and constrain the shape of dreams. The task of materializing the far in the near—animated and impelled by the force of fantasies— might thus be taken as a form of dreamwork, as the labor of reproducing fantasies or of re-membering "dream elements in waking."[53]

Not all dreams, however, are created equal, and not all dreamwork is considered effective. In Manila, there are dreams of elsewheres shot through with ideals of progress and that are made real in spaces of luxury. But there are also *other* dreams that sag under the weight of the city and that seem unable to shake the exigencies of place.

In 2007, word spread that a new gay club had opened in Quezon City, in a lower-class district called Cubao. Unlike talk of new bars, clubs, and restaurants opening in Makati City or the Fort, however, knowledge of that club was passed around, always, in the form of a joke:

> "Have you heard? They've opened a gay club in Cubao."
> "Really?"
> "Do you know what it's called?"
> "What?"
> "*Palawan!*"
> [Laughter]

The name "Palawan" functions as a punch line in exchanges such as this because it, too, signifies an elsewhere. Unlike the names that appear at the Fort, however, the elsewhere it refers to is not a place that belongs to the realm of global cities but an island off the coast of Luzon—the so-called arm of the Philippine archipelago, the long sliver of land renowned for its white sand beaches, coral reefs, rainforests, foothills, caves, and valleys. Like Babylon, Palawan evokes a paradisiacal image, but not one that has been tied to notions of spectacular growth, empire, and, through *Queer as Folk,* modern gay life. In the national imagination, Palawan remains the sign of a time prior to urbanization and development. It is, precisely, the name of an unassimilated place beyond the *limes* of progress, a node outside the network, or a spot beyond the expanding reach of global space.

When I first heard of the club Palawan, I too laughed at its name. It brought to mind strange juxtapositions: tropical paradise and urban decay, virginity and hedonism, and the rejection of modernity and the very modernness of gay clubs. Beyond these images that immediately came to mind, I did not give much thought to the reasons why Palawan elicited laughter; why I, too, could barely suppress a smile whenever its name was raised in conversations. As with the punch lines of all inside jokes, it required no explanation and presumed meanings that were, at once, known, obscure, and shared. One night, however, a man I met at a bar in Makati City ran the joke by me again. I laughed politely, but by then I had begun to wonder about the transplanted names scattered throughout the city and, thus, found myself asking him why he thought the name "Palawan" was so funny. He looked at me, a bit incredulously, and said, "Well, hello! It sounds so cheap!" After a pause, he added, "Only a club in Cubao would call itself Palawan." That exchange made clear what perhaps should have been obvious to me from the beginning: the joke did not stem simply from the contrast between the name "Palawan" and urban gay life but from its location in an othered place (another elsewhere), the district called Cubao, which was already thought to abide by its own curious logic ("only in Cubao") and where, apparently, the dream of materializing the far in the near extended only to the edges of the archipelago, to the paradise untouched by the wonders of distant sites.

If Cubao could be regarded as "someplace else," someplace other, it was not because Cubao was seen as a place where gay men were unwelcome but because it was tied, intimately, to an image of gay life that preceded the rise of the sleek bars and clubs that now dominated the scene. In the topological imagination of privileged gay life in the city during the mid-2000s, Cubao was seen as a place "respectable" people did not go to at night, if at all.[54] It was a district better known for the rundown go-go bars with broken neon signs, for the brothels masquerading as massage parlors, and for giving rise to the term "*bakal* (metal) boys," a reference to the hustlers who used to stand by the steel railings around Araneta Coliseum and who were immortalized in Tony Perez's novella *Cubao 1980,* about a hustler named Tom, from whose vantage a picture of the district emerges.

> They say Cubao looks ordinary—like a local street cat . . . You can
> feed it garbage. It sleeps on the side of the road, rarely getting sick.

Kick it, throw it to the gutter, it won't surrender, it stays alive. Sometimes, it will run—sometimes, it will fight back. Under the sun, it
casts nine shadows. That's what Cubao is like.

That's what Cubao is like, in the daytime.

At night—ask Butch, he'll say that at night, that cat Cubao is full
of lust. Its eyes glow in the dark, lots of lights, everything moves. Go
to Ali, Superstore, Fiesta Carnival, Farmers'. A cat in heat, gibbering
in the music, rolling on the cement, twisting, searching, filled with
amusement.[55]

Tom presents a picture of Cubao as a district at home in its metropolitan
disorder, which is able not only to survive in the filth of urban refuse but
also to thrive in the lust that reverberates in its various corners. Through
the eyes of Tom and his friend Butch, who introduces him to hustling, the
streets of Cubao and its commercial centers emerge as spaces of desire:
parlors become the sites of backrooms where beauticians take their tricks;
public toilets become the haunts of cross-dressers who sneak peeks at
boys standing at the urinals; the malls and the carnival become cruising
grounds; married men hang around bookshops in search of hustlers; and
rape takes place in parking lots. Cubao appears as the polar opposite of
a place like the Fort. It is all grit, shadows and dark corners, garbage and
debris: the underside of the dream of globalness that finds its erstwhile fulfillment in the Global City. Here, gay life does not take place in the open;
it is hidden or hidden in plain sight and is apparent only to those who, like
stray cats, are able to navigate the crevices of the district.

Gay men appear in *Cubao 1980* as tragic and predatory figures. Hunted
and hunting (or *hanting,* as Tom says), their movements are marked not
by the leisurely flânerie that takes place in sites like the Fort but by the
sense of secret danger that constitutes Cubao. Indeed, the recurring metaphor of the "hunt" portrays gay men as part of the environment, of the
urban jungle: "the metropolitan apparatus of capture" into which Tom
and Butch sink deeper and deeper and that they ultimately try to rise
above.[56] After a series of more and more intense encounters, Tom and
Butch find themselves atop the Araneta Coliseum, the highest point in
Cubao. There, beyond the grasp of the streets, they vow to forsake the life
of hustlers. "*Ayaw na namin. Ayaw na.* [We don't want to anymore. No
more.]" Butch takes out his book of contacts and sets it on fire. He hurls
it down to the city below, a dramatic act that makes it clear that Cubao's
gay men—present atop the coliseum only as scribbled names—belong in
the throes and pandemonium on the ground. It is cold and windy atop
the coliseum, but Tom and Butch do not want to come down. They do

so only late into the night, when there are only a few people and cars left on the streets. Even then, however, they find no reprieve from the gay life that marks the district. On their way home, they see a group of gay men laughing inside a convertible sports car. In a final statement of disavowal, Butch screams at them, "*Puking ina n'yo—mga bakla kayo!* [Fuck you—you faggots!]"

Afterward, Tom and Butch's lives appear to revert to a picture of innocence. They attend a party at their high school, where Tom, sporting a new T-shirt and a new pair of pants bought for him by his older brother, flirts with a girl who had been ignoring him. He tells her he has changed ("*nagbago na 'ko*"). She smiles at him. Butch gives him a wink. The love of a girl, Butch tells him, is different from the love of a fag.

The grasp of the street, the turbulence and violence of Cubao, are, however, not that easy to rise above. One day, a storm strikes. Tom and Butch find themselves walking on an overpass, among hordes of pedestrians battling the rain and the winds. Suddenly, they spot a familiar figure on the street, looking up at them. It is Butch's spurned ex-lover, Hermie, a man who had showered Butch with presents and whom he had avoided since that night atop the Araneta Coliseum. Tom had forgotten about Hermie, but his sudden appearance on the street sends a jolt through Tom, who remembers Hermie as a figure from the past (*nakaraan*), a ghost in a dream (*multo sa panaginip*). Tom and Butch descend the steps of the overpass. Hermie approaches them. "Butch," he says, shaking. "*Hindi ko kayang tanggapin* [I cannot accept it]." He pulls a gun from his jacket and fires a shot at Butch. Screams erupt from the crowd. Hermie disappears and Tom finds himself on the ground, crouching over Butch's bloodied body until people pry him away. "*Ang lakas, ang lakas nung ulan* [The rain was so strong]," he recalls. "*Bagsak nang bagsak sa pusang nasagasaan, pinaliliguan, hinuhugasan iyong Cubao* [It kept pouring and pouring over the cat run over on the road, bathing, washing Cubao]."

If Perez paints a picture of gay life in Cubao as miserable and predatory, it is because he himself dreamt of an *other* gay life, of liberation from homosexual abjection, understood in terms of the acquisition of modern rights and a movement out of the strictures of local gay subjectivity. In his more overtly political writings, Perez speaks from a self-consciously gay liberationist perspective and reveals dreams of eradicating the gay life that he describes in *Cubao 1980*—that is, of effacing the dominant image of the Filipino homosexual as a tragic queen; of the need to abandon the desire for "real" men like Tom and Butch; of acquiring "equal employment opportunities"; and of recognizing gay men as honorable laborers, soldiers, priests, professors, businessmen, and athletes.[57] *Cubao 1980* is, in fact, but the title piece in a collection subtitled "*Unang Sigaw ng Gay Liberation Movement* [First Cry of the Gay Liberation Movement]," a cry that takes place, he clarifies, "only in one's dreams [*sigaw sa pangarap lamang*]."

The movement toward liberation only happens in a dream because the urban condition—*place*—is its limit condition. Perez's depiction of gay life as part of the landscape of Cubao hints at a connection between the gay liberationist dream of being something else and the dream of being some*place* else that marks metropolitan aspirations, the same dream that is being realized at the Fort and that finds its undoing on the streets of Cubao. Indeed, Perez's imaging of Cubao as a sexual underworld is necessarily incomplete. It presumes an audience that knows that the sexual underworld he describes thrives beneath attempts to establish Cubao as a prime commercial district. From the 1960s up until the late 1980s, before the rise of the megamalls in Ortigas Center and the upmarket shopping centers in Makati City, Cubao was seen as a viable destination for the privileged classes. The Araneta Center, the commercial heart of Cubao, was purchased in 1952 from Radio Communication of America (RCA) as part of a broader process of urban renewal. Like the Fort, that area offered bare space onto which desires for commercial development and dreams of globalness could be projected. When it was built, for instance, the Araneta Coliseum was the largest covered coliseum in the world. Ali-Mall, where Tom and Butch often *hanted* for clients, was the first multilevel commercial mall in the city and was named after Muhammad Ali, following his victory over Joe Frazier in the global event, "Thrilla in Manila." Fiesta Carnival, a central cruising site in *Cubao 1980,* was the country's first all-year indoor amusement center. The very names of the streets of Cubao reveal the age and provenance of the dreams of elsewheres that now mark the Global City. The prime commercial area begins on a street named "Fifth Avenue," and the road that fronts Ali-Mall was once known as "Times Square."

These names, like those that are present in the Fort, also go unnoticed, albeit for altogether different reasons. At the Fort, elsewheres lodged as signs go unremarked because there, the dreams and desires they index remain credible. Overlaid onto modern structures rising out of a pristine landscape, they offer up the possibility of transforming the city and city life. In Cubao, names of distant sites index failed ambitions, plans so deeply buried in memory that most taxi drivers would not know where to take you if you told them you were going to Times Square. If there is any reminder of the old dream of turning Cubao into a global city like New York, it is only the existence of a street named "New York Avenue," which, like "Palawan," is often raised in the context of a joke:

> I'm going to New York.
> Really?
> New York, Cubao.
> [Laughter]

No such laughter follows the suggestion of going to Fifth Avenue in the Fort or of bringing Babylon to Club Government, for in those cases, there is no readily apparent contradiction between the fantastic, distant sites recalled by foreign names and the local spaces onto which they are transplanted. Not only is the Fort an empty space, but it is also, as a former military base, a space that most of Manila's residents had not seen before, a space that holds no memories that would contradict the meanings inscribed in names like "Fifth Avenue." Club Government, as my informant James indicated, was always already read as akin to "Babylon"; its attempt to transport clubgoers to the fictional megaclub was, in a way, only a literalization of fantasies that were established long ago. The idea of "New York" in Cubao, however, much like the idea of a "winter party" in Manila, involves the juxtaposition of signs and sights filled with classed meanings and memories that are difficult to reconcile and that make the collapse of the distance between "near" and "far" appear ironic and absurd and, thus, open to ridicule and humor.

In Perez's Cubao, such juxtapositions are also largely absent. There are no middle-class families shopping in Ali-Mall, and Araneta Coliseum is but the site of an evangelical gathering rather than of the concerts of foreign artists that draw crowds from all walks of life. The wealthy appear only as clients—that is, as figures lured by the secret pleasures offered by Cubao rather than by its shops or restaurants. The contradictions between the dreams of Cubao and its occupation by hustlers and johns are barely articulated by Perez. The district as a whole emerges in the novella as a seedy underworld, its ambitions rendered invisible by Perez's adoption of a hustler's penetrating if selective gaze. In that way, the picture offered by *Cubao 1980* resembles more the state of the district in the year of the novella's publication than of the late 1970s and early 1980s. By 1992, the ambitions of the district had begun to fade. The middle-class patrons that once peopled Cubao had started to move to new developments in other parts of the city and the image of Cubao as a place that belonged exclusively to the underclass had begun to set. In certain respects, this image was tied directly to whispers about the illicit and dangerous gay world that subsisted in Cubao. In the late 1980s, for instance, middle-class families began avoiding the cinemas that lined the streets of the district when rumors spread of gay men hiding in the shadows and stabbing strangers with syringes full of HIV-infected blood.[58]

By the time I began fieldwork in the mid-2000s, the privileged classes had long dismissed Cubao as a run-down district. Those years, however, were also marked by the emergence of new plans to rehabilitate Cubao, spurred in large part by the construction of new train systems that connected the Araneta Center to other parts of the city. Those plans gave rise to a new shopping center, Gateway, which heralded the return of upmarket shops and restaurants to Cubao. The construction of Gateway, however, represented an altogether different dream for Cubao. No longer was there an aim to create streets where middle-class patrons could roam freely and leisurely. Rather, developers seemed resigned to building a haven in the midst of the run-down surroundings, a place (a gateway) where outsiders might pass through—by train or by car—and conduct their business without spending much time in or even seeing the surrounding area. Even then, the idea that Cubao hosted a sexual underworld could not be erased by attempts at commercial rehabilitation. Often I would hear talk among gay men about the rampant cruising that went on at Gateway or "Gay-tway," as many of my informants joked. The people there stare at you with no discretion, I was told. They hang out by the railings or hover around the cinemas. The implicit comparison was with the other malls that were occupied primarily by the middle and upper classes, spaces where you could also find many gay men but that were not marked by the uninhibited desire that belonged, properly, to a district like Cubao.

Though the construction of Gateway made Cubao an acceptable destination in the daytime, the district remained, at the time, firmly outside the circuit of nightspots frequented by privileged gay men and by wealthier Manileños in general. Talk of gay spaces there revolved exclusively around the strip bars near Aurora Boulevard and the scattered massage parlors that offered "extra" services. The way the news of Palawan's opening was greeted revealed how dominant this image of Cubao had become. Often, word of the gay club opening in Cubao was followed by qualifications: "It's not a strip club. It's a *real* club." It was a real club in the sense that it no longer featured straight men dancing for or being solicited by gay men. It was a place where gay men met, drank, and danced with one another, a version perhaps of what Perez had once envisioned, albeit written under the fantasy of a commercial gay life that Perez's overtly political dreams may have eschewed or, at the least, failed to anticipate. Though Palawan was talked about as a "real" gay club, it was nonetheless seen as something else: an *other* place that resembled, only partially, clubs like Bed, Government, and Embassy. This was how Roland, the informant who first told me about Palawan, described it: "It's an actual club, but it's really lower class. You can go there in *pambahay* [house clothes]. You should go there in really comfortable clothes, 'cause it's really hot. I think the air conditioner was broken when we went. But it's really fun. Just don't drink the vodka. When we went, there was one bottle of Absolut (Vodka) and it looked like it hadn't been touched in decades. Everyone just drinks Colt 45. And park near the entrance. It's not exactly the safest area."[59]

Another informant, Christian, told me that many people had begun talking to him about Palawan: "I keep asking, 'So what's there?' And everybody says, 'Beer is cheap.' I'm like, 'But I don't drink beer.'" Bernard, who had a fondness for what some of his friends called "slumming it," told me that whenever he went there, he walked around thinking, "Excuse me, everyone! Princess coming through!"[60] Patrick, with whom I first made plans to go to Palawan, said that it was described to him as "the Government or Bed for blue-collar workers." "That's the upside, but also the downside," he said. "One thing I hear is that they take off their shirts a lot more so there are more shirtless people in Palawan. They're blue-collar workers who are totally straight outside but totally gay inside." This was a picture of a place that simultaneously drew on and yet departed from older images of gay life in Cubao. It took on the derided but fetishized air of a sexual underclass—of men free of middle-class inhibitions—while moving away from the world of effeminate queens chasing after straight men that Perez had disavowed. In this way, Palawan also represented a desired elsewhere. It was imagined as a site where the gloss of privileged gay life in the city could be let go in favor of an unbridled sexuality, which was coded as lower class and which, in a roundabout way, coincided with the image recalled by the name "Palawan" of a space outside the folds of modern city life.[61]

I first went to Palawan in September of 2007. Patrick had ended up going there a few weeks earlier than me but had agreed to meet me there anyway. "It was worth a second visit," he said. I drove there with two of our common acquaintances and I remember that it was raining hard and that we had trouble finding the club. We were driving along Aurora Boulevard, a major thoroughfare that cut through Cubao and that served as the site of the new aboveground train that led straight to Gateway. The only landmark Patrick gave me was a drugstore on the opposite side of the road. At close to midnight, however, with most establishments closed and with the rain pounding hard against the car windows, we could hardly see anything but the neon lights of a few scattered strip bars. We made several turns around Aurora Boulevard before we found Palawan on a narrow side street occupied by nothing more than jeepneys parked for the night and a small motel that charged by the hour. "Where are we?" one of the men I was with asked. "Is there even going to be anyone here? It's raining really hard!"

We ran from the car to the entrance of Palawan. The front area was a small passage lit by fluorescent bulbs, which shone on old yellowish walls with posters of local celebrities and a ticketing counter where a bored, quiet woman handed out stubs for two hundred pesos (five U.S. dollars), less than what we were accustomed to but more than what we were expecting. The modesty of the entrance made the size of Palawan's interior almost shocking. Inside, it might have been the size of Bed and Government combined. But apart from the dim lights and the sound of dance music pumping from the speakers, Palawan was quite unlike the other clubs in Manila. There was a large rectangular stage in front, surrounded by cramped tables where men sat around drinking beer. Someone whispered that it looked like an indoor beer garden, but what it reminded me of were the strip bars of Quezon City. Instead of strippers, however, what was featured on Palawan's stage was a pair of singers, a boy in a sleeveless shirt and a girl in a cocktail dress, belting out pop songs in a manner reminiscent of the noontime variety shows that were staples of Filipino television. The club was near full despite the rains, but no one paid any attention to the singers. Everyone seemed content to sit quietly, chatting and drinking.

We found an empty table near the bar and from there watched the show and the crowd. The men I was with were amused by the show, the likes of which were never staged at the clubs we were familiar with in Makati or the Fort. I was, however, more interested in the crowd. Looking around, it seemed to me that the descriptions Patrick had heard of blue-collar workers dancing shirtless were rooted less in the composition of the clientele than on fantasies about Cubao and its underclass. The crowd at Palawan resembled crowds at Bed and Government more than anyone seemed willing to admit. The bodies at Palawan made up a familiar scene: there were the tight T-shirts and jeans, the gelled hair, and the muscled torsos. What Palawan offered was not a picture of the world of cross-dressing *bakla*, which Perez had railed against, nor of the closeted blue-collar workers that Patrick had imagined, but the recognizable dream of modern gay life in Manila, as materialized in a district we had learned to think of as part of an other Manila.

By the time Patrick arrived, the two singers had left the stage and were replaced by several drag queens. Patrick told me that the drag shows were the best feature of Palawan and that they were superior to the drag performances that were, on rare occasions, staged at Bed and Government. At Palawan, the drag show was not a brief number inserted in between DJ sets but an extended program. Drag queens did number after number, solos, duets, and trios, and unlike the more serious performances at Bed and Government, the drag show at Palawan was humorous and self-deprecating. There was an overweight drag queen with no teeth doing Beyoncé, an older one who did Tagalog songs from the sixties, mock fights, and wardrobe malfunctions. The closing segment was a beauty pageant where about eight drag queens just stood in a row waving to the crowd. At one end, the crowd favorite, a "little person" in a sequined dress, grinned from ear to ear, while on the other, a young drag queen slumped to the floor, looking bored and indifferent, chain-smoking cigarettes. We cheered and hooted for them both and lamented the lack of similar shows at Bed and Government.

I had wondered when we entered where people danced in Palawan, since the whole floor was full of chairs and tables. I got my answer when the program ended and the music turned into the familiar beats of house music. The people at the tables began standing and moving toward the stage. They climbed up and began dancing. It started with just a few men standing by the edges, nodding along to the beat, but quickly built up into a thick mass of bodies. We stayed in our seats and watched as the bodies began to spill out of the stage-turned-dance-floor into the area surrounding the tables. "This is what Palawan is about," Patrick shouted into my ear. "The people here don't care about what other people think. They have much more fun than people at Bed and Government." We decided to check out the scene from the second floor. We got out of our chairs, climbed up a narrow spiral staircase located at one corner of the club, and positioned ourselves among the row of bodies standing by the railings. "Some of these people are doable," someone was saying, surveying the crowd below. "If you're not being too picky."

We watched the crowd for a long time, moving up and down the stairs and positioning ourselves at different parts of the club. I do not know how long we spent walking around and watching, but throughout the night, the crowd seemed to just keep getting bigger and bigger, while outside the rain kept pouring. At one point, we found ourselves seated again at one of the tables surrounding the stage, still just chatting and surveying the crowd, maintaining our imaginary distance from the goings-on. Suddenly, one of the men I was with stood up and announced that he wanted to dance. The other man and I looked at him, eyes wide in surprise, but he just shrugged and said, "I don't know anyone here." He walked away and climbed up the stage. At first, he just stood and danced awkwardly near the edges. But after a few minutes, he began squeezing through the crowd until we lost all sight of him. When he returned, flushed and sweaty, I smiled at him and said, "We thought we lost you. You were there for quite a while." "Really?" he said, "I didn't notice. I was having too much fun. This place is really something else."

Reading Displaced Signs

The bars and clubs at the Fort, the *Queer as Folk* party at Government, and Palawan in Cubao are spaces caught in between in a city caught in between. Taken individually, they might be deployed to reveal how gay life in a city like Manila bridges the near and far; how gay space is carved out at the interstices of the city and the world, producing ironic juxtapositions that might be taken as manifestations of a capacity to play with notions of here and there. Taken together, however, they reveal how such juxtapositions are read differently on the ground; how emplaced subjects, individually and collectively, experience in starkly dissimilar ways the material facticity of location while maintaining spatial imaginations that look to places beyond the city limits; and how local fractures run deep and are shaped by variegated relationships and connections to circulating signs, spaces full of messages, and the local class order. They illustrate how being in between is never simply a case of being caught in the juncture of local life and global forces but always already laden with the drama, pathos, and cultural politics of built environments and dreamworlds inhabited.

It is this—the particularity of ways of reading and experiencing the juxtapositions of signs and spaces that appear all over the city—that is often lost in the celebration of cities such as Manila as spaces where notions of distance collapse, as sites of hybridity full of negotiated difference, gaps, fissures, and de- and reterritorializations.[62] Indeed, talk of liminality, of states of in-betweenness, contains the danger of obfuscating the persistent role of aspirations and dreams of elsewheres in the production of forms of urban life in third-world cities like Manila. In the drive to make visible complex differences, there lies the temptation to take the intermingling of the near and far as the effects of a will to challenge universalized accounts of modernity, as though the differences that emerge when spaces are reconfigured with reference to distant sites could be prized apart from the powerful dreams that "fuel and further the logics of the dominant global order."[63]

Take, for instance, Neferti Tadiar's critique of Arjun Appadurai's reading of Pico Iyer's account of the Filipino love for mimicking old American pop songs. Appadurai sees, in Iyer's account of a space suffused with sounds that come from afar, an example of how third-world subjects are able to "appropriate the materials of modernity differently"—that is, to establish their (or our) own "alternative" or "vernacular" modernity.[64] While indeed it would be foolish to suggest that modernity is experienced everywhere in the same way, Tadiar notes that it is nonetheless necessary to ask what the limits are of his ironic reading of the Philippines as "a nation of make-believe Americans" or of a parallel reading of Manila as a hybrid space "for possible expressions and/or interpretations of (post-colonial) difference as well as the resistance and opposition this difference betokens."[65] How, after all, would such readings account for the varied ways the materialization of the far in the near is read on the ground and for the (classed) meanings always already ascribed to the places where such materializations take place? How would they address debates within a city like Manila about who or what counts as modern and global? What is at stake in taking "the ironies of subordinate third world dreams" as evidence of "agency" and, thus, as counterpoints to the seductive force of centripetal dreams of global belonging?[66]

Tadiar points out that "irony as critique creates an interpretative boundary between dreamers and analysts, between those who dream and those who unpack the meanings and consequences of their dream-ings."[67] This boundary, she reminds us, finds its provenance in a longer history of apprehending images of places full of ironic juxtaposition from a place presumed to be free of unconscious irony, in the delight taken from images of natives holding cameras or hijab-wearing women hold-ing mobile phones. This delight "stems from the inner knowledge on the part of the viewer that the alien modernity in the hands of the ever non-modern is really theirs. Or at least it is one they are already fully familiar with."[68] More important, for the point I am raising here, Tadiar points to the fact that the appreciation of Manila's ironic juxtapositions is not limited to outside observers but is shared "by present and wait-listed post-colonials" plugged into systems of privilege.[69] "They too," she reminds us, "appreciate the irony of seeing street children in Manila wearing T-shirts with Ivy League university names or first-world logos whose references and connotations these urchins cannot possibly understand. They too can appreciate the irony of more Filipinos singing perfect renditions of American songs . . . [in spite of] the fact that the rest of their lives is not in complete synchrony with the referential world that first gave birth to these songs."[70] Put differently, "the dreams of Filipinos, rulers and ruled, cannot be understood apart from (their relationship to) the global mate-rial imaginary . . . To cast these dreams as expressions of autonomous, self-contained . . . subjects (whether they aspire to or resist world power) is to ignore the global order of dreamwork."[71]

Remember, for instance, the night I found myself driving to the winter party at Club Government. That night could be read as a quotidian challenge to the problem of location. The organizers' attempt to realize the dream of a white Christmas, of being someplace else, could be taken as an appropriation of the American Dream itself, as a way of utilizing that dream in order to carve out a space of revelry in the heart of the third-world city. In the sight of men dancing, wet from snow machines, next to Filipino drag queens dressed as ice princesses, there lies, undoubtedly, the seeds of ironic critique, cultural raw materials that might make up a kind of backtalk against the global order of things or an imaginative attempt to relocate the space of the club out of Manila and into the fantastic world of gay dance parties. And yet, remember that in the car, we too were able to spot the irony of winter being reproduced in a gay club in Manila. We did not, however, take the sight of men dressed in winter clothes as the effect of a deliberate act (being ironic) but as a sign of an unwitting state (an ironic condition) worthy of ridicule.[72] "Do these people know where they are?" was, indeed, a rhetorical question; it functioned only to iterate the distinction of those fully familiar with the elsewheres being evoked. Remember that we were also coming from the Fort, where the irony of names like "Fifth Avenue" and "High Street" transplanted into the third-world city was lost to us, overlaid as those names were onto barren lands kept apart from the startling juxtapositions that marked the rest of Manila. At the Fort, the dream of elsewheres, of becoming global, and of being in a "global city," appeared realizable and seamless; the challenge posed by strange juxtapositions seemed to dissipate in the wake of the promise of reinvention.

This challenge dissipated, too, in the *Queer as Folk* party hosted by Club Government. During that event, the elsewhere of Babylon was materialized only in the form of images projected onto walls and of a declaration that, for one night, Government would become a mode of transportation, a way of arriving without having to leave. Indeed, for my informant James, the *Queer as Folk* party at Government did not appear to involve the stretching of imagination. After all, even prior to the event, he had already read the very space of the club as a site full of echoes and traces of Babylon. In this way, the arrival of *Queer as Folk* at Government on the night of the party was a restatement of fantasy-constructions that were already in place. The party did not only point outward to a place where one could be taken but backward in James's memory to a time when a perceived lack appeared as a yawning gap waiting to be filled.

This space, the space of the gap, is the site where shifting commentaries take place. It is where difference emerges, but it is also the space where dominant fantasies are reproduced and sustained. Indeed, the dreams of modernness and globalness conflated and simultaneously indexed in the names that appear at the Fort and in images of fantastic sites that circulate in and around the city are older than those to whom such names and images speak might know or care to admit. In Cubao, a picture emerges of where these dreams might lead. There, a shadow configuration of the outward trajectories of desire that defines a place like the Fort becomes apparent. Street names that once indexed grand plans to become part of the world are forgotten, ignored, or turned into jokes. Structures that once stood as signs of progress become signs of danger and threat. Cubao as a whole can be taken as a reminder of how dreams are fated to fail, and it is perhaps for that very reason that the district now sits outside the circuits inhabited by the privileged, a site located in the city but not *of* the bright lights scene.

Thus the emergence in Cubao of a "real" gay club becomes a point of curiosity; its name, "Palawan," becomes the sign of an imagination that cannot extend to the fantastic world of global cities. It would not be enough, however, to cast Palawan only as a site excluded from the scene, for it was also treated as a destination, as a place that could be approached ironically, an elsewhere we could go to, but where we should not be. There, we could spot familiar signs and read them as things that were really ours or ours first. At Palawan, it was possible to get lost in a mass of bodies dancing, for one was always safe in the knowledge that one could get out, that whatever similarities existed between that place and places like the Fort or clubs like Government, which were integrated into the bright lights scene, would always be qualified by the fact that the former was built on a district (on stones) marked by signs of difference and otherness. It was, in turn, precisely the ability to read such signs that allowed us to play the part of visitors, figures from elsewhere who have the power to see, recognize, and determine what is or is not out of place.

CHAPTER THREE

The Specter of *Kabaklaan*

Effective exorcism pretends to declare the death only in order
to put to death . . . It is *effectively* a performative. But here
effectivity phantomalizes itself. It is in fact [*en effet*] a matter of a
performative that seeks to reassure itself but first of all to reassure
itself by assuring itself, for nothing is less sure, that what one
would like to see dead is indeed dead.

—Jacques Derrida, *Specters of Marx*

"Time is out of joint." This line from *Hamlet,* quoted repeatedly by Jacques
Derrida in *Specters of Marx,* reminds us of the instability of the present,
its openness to ghosts or those figures that can "disembark from the past
and appear in a time in which they clearly do not belong."[1] For Derrida,
the figure of the specter provides a means to speak of that elusive space
between presence and absence, life and death, "the non-contemporaneity
with itself of the living present."[2] It is that which disrupts the dream of
leaving the past behind—of time as linear, of planetary history as a project
of progress and enlightenment.

In the stories I have told thus far, there are figures that interrupt the
dream of being some*place* else that marks the bright lights scene. Beggars
appear outside car windows. Othered places hover at the edges of urban
imagination and become objects of desire and revulsion. The city itself
looms large in the background; its disorder and detritus stand as constant
reminders of the invincible facticity of location. In this chapter, I foreground the ways in which the scene is also imagined as some*time* else;
how its production is hinged on notions of "nowness" and "newness";
and how the imagined states of being present, simultaneity, and real time

that are often linked to global modernity and late capitalism are haunted by specters that are read as signs of the past.

In chapter 2, I began to show how the bright lights scene emerges through the deployment of a spatial imagination grown planetary—a psychogeography that stretches out beyond the city limits to distant sites that are both "real" and fantastic and that are transported to and materialized in the city through dreamwork, the transformation of the local landscape, and the evocative force of names lodged as signs. I continue in this vein here and look beyond the borders of Manila in order to shed light on the spatiotemporal practices that underpin privileged gay life in the city. I set the scene against the experiences of the Filipino gay diaspora, particularly as described in Martin Manalansan's ethnographic work on gay Filipinos in New York. I do this in part because, as I have begun to suggest, it is no longer possible to represent the scene as a geographically isolable space. Gay life under the bright lights of Manila involves knowledge of the world; its pathos lies in the sense that a (transapparent) horizon exists and in the desires, hopes, and dreams inspired by that horizon.[3] More important, I set gay life in Manila against the migrant experience in order to demonstrate the structuring force of distance and location, to show how emplaced class, gender, and racial hierarchies condition notions of global time and affect the way the charged borders between global and local forms of sexual identification are built and inhabited.

I am interested here, more specifically, in discursive attempts to reemplot Manila within a putatively foreign narrative of gay modernity and in how this emplotment reproduces and is produced through a fraught relationship with the figure of the *bakla*, a slippery term that is sometimes read as a synonym for gay but that is more accurately, though no less problematically, depicted as a sexual tradition that conflates homosexuality, lower-class status, and transvestism or effeminacy. The term *bakla* has already appeared in some of the stories I have narrated. It was thrown as an insult by the street child who accosted us that afternoon we found ourselves trapped on the traffic-clogged road of Ortigas Avenue on the way back from the beach (chapter 1) and was used by Butch in his angry disavowal of gay life in Tony Perez's *Cubao 1980* (chapter 2). In stories such as these, the bakla emerges as a fleeting point of disidentification, an accusation meant to wound and injure. In this chapter, I look more closely at the meanings nesting in the term bakla and at the violences that surround its embodiment in the caricatured figure of the *parlorista*, or the cross-dresser working in one of the many low-end beauty salons scattered throughout the city. Here, the unsettled arrival of the bright lights scene in the *present* of what I call *gay globality* is re-presented as an event predicated on the abjection of the bakla and on the wishful relocation of its image to a different space–time, to an elsewhere and an "elsewhen" that lies outside the ambit of the scene.

In saying that *kabaklaan* (bakla-ness) is being "relocated," I do not mean to claim that it is, in fact, disappearing; rather, I aim to highlight the ways it is being disappeared through strategies of invisibilization and discipline authorized by the local market, which participates in setting the contours of gay identity and its cultural visibility. These strategies of erasure are modes of reinvention that stand in sharp relief when set against the recuperative model adopted by Manalansan's diasporic informants, who, like other queer migrants, are largely unseen by the U.S. gay market and who recover kabaklaan in order to negotiate the violences that accompany their dislocation.[4] This contrast between life under Manila's bright lights and the migrant experience is, however, neither straightforward nor absolute. In the same way that the recuperations engaged in by Filipino gay men in the diaspora are always in progress, the strategies of erasure I speak of here are part of a never-to-be-completed task, for the dream of burying kabaklaan is belied by its ability to make its presence felt, either through the practices of others or through the anxieties of the scene's privileged inhabitants. Indeed, despite attempts to cast kabaklaan as anachronistic, it continues to permeate the city both materially and psychically; it is lodged in cultural memory and, as such, is inextricably tied to the production of "modern" gay subjectivity, not as a contemporary, but precisely as Derrida's *revenant*—that is, a ghost that keeps returning despite assiduous attempts to conjure it away by consigning it temporally and spatially to the past or home.[5]

This chapter is thus also an effort to rethink the relationship between the global and the local, the world and the third-world city, in terms of spectralization. For Derrida, spectralization is the incarnation of the autonomized spirit in an aphysical body. "There is no ghost," he says, "there is never any becoming-specter of the spirit without at least an appearance of flesh . . . For there to be ghost, there must be a return to the body, but to a body that is more abstract than ever."[6] I want to take this description somewhat literally here and treat the bakla as an abstraction in order to reflect the scene's physical and psychic distanciation from the *real* embodiments of kabaklaan. It must be noted, however, that the value of Derrida's spectrology lies in its refusal to distinguish clearly between abstraction and corporeality.[7] It is this indeterminacy—the oscillation between imagination and flesh—that allows us not only to imagine the figure of the ghost but also to figure it as both classed and gendered. More important for my purposes here, it allows for a rethinking of the bakla as a feared image, a site where the class and gender anxieties of the men who constitute the scene are condensed, projected, and expelled as incongruous to the blueprint set by an increasingly global imagination.

What this implies is that global–local relations, despite the binarized cartographic schema summoned by the term, cannot be mapped easily onto bodies and cities. Within spaces like Manila, axes like class enable dissimilar relationships to global circuits and myriad affective connections to "home" and to the images, bodies, and subjectivities with which it has been articulated. The spectrality of the bakla is thus particular to the bright lights scene and the neoliberal spaces that constitute it, from the bars and clubs that were featured in the stories I have told so far to the glossy publications and Internet portals that I write of here. The scene reemerges in this chapter as the site where gay globalization plays out as an internalized project that is at least minimally teleological—a space that necessitates a particular sense of history as well as an imaginative planetary geography built via the suturing together of other, distant cityspaces, from clubs in global cities to international party circuits to celebrity DJ networks.[8] This imaginative geography is what I refer to as *gay globality*: a network of urban sites and scenes, a metacity or city of cities, a "planet-spanning but spatially discontiguous urban sprawl" bound together under the universalized, mediatized, and commercialized sign of "gay."[9] Gay globality, understood this way, does not refer to actual "global gay" spaces or subjects but to a spatial imagination founded on claims and hegemonic representations driven by the market and sustained by the articulation of urban scenes that separately, though similarly, depend on the erasure of othered gay men, both in Manila and in those cities read as epicenters of the gay globe. In Manila, the dominant position of kabaklaan in discourses on homosexuality makes it the prime object for such an erasure. In this chapter, I examine how attempts to efface the bakla reify exclusionary class and gender protocols. I shift away, if momentarily, from the narrative-centric approach I have taken thus far and discuss, in more exegetical terms, the language adopted in publications, Internet portals, and other objects of public culture tied to the bright lights scene. In so doing, I hope to shed a different light on the scene's march toward gay globality's elusive modernity and to offer a critique of the self-representations and discursive claims that frame privileged gay life in the city and the struggles for global belonging they reveal and underpin.

Bakla/Gay: Impossibilities for Border Crossing

While there is some consensus about the articulation of lower-class status and effeminacy in the figure of the bakla within the popular Filipino imaginary, there remains no easy way to define exactly what the bakla is. It can be seen as a subculture, a subset of the Filipino homosexual population that has its own codes and activities and that exists in particular sites and industries (Tan), or as a form of "psychospiritual inversion," the performance of an "inner" gender grounded in "local" beliefs about selfhood (Garcia).[10] It can be understood as "the embodiment of an outside cultural other" (Johnson) or as "mimicry par excellence" (Cannell).[11] Subjected to new global flows of ideas, images, and bodies, kabaklaan can also be taken as an "alternative form of modernity," a complex amalgamation of cultural and historical elements, a form of subjectivity in constant mediation (Manalansan).[12] These varying ways of describing kabaklaan speak to its elusiveness, to the way its meaning shifts in accordance with contexts, with the perspective one takes and the vantage from which one writes.[13] While the competing conceptualizations of the bakla have their own relative merits, I am not interested here in adjudicating between them nor in presenting my own "more accurate" definition of kabaklaan. Rather, I hope only to present one way in which kabaklaan might be seen, how it appears from the view of a scene that has increasingly reached out to a global network both materially and imaginatively. I focus here on Manalansan's contribution, for it is his account of how kabaklaan is practiced by men who have been displaced that speaks most directly to the everyday politics of transnational mobility and its effects on the complex relationship that binds and separates kabaklaan and modern gay subjectivity.

In *Global Divas,* Manalansan tracks the moves between *bakla* and *gay* and argues for a view of kabaklaan as an enduring social category recuperated by the Filipino gay diaspora in order to carve out spaces in New York City and in the U.S. social imaginary. In the accounts that appear in *Global Divas,* the borders between bakla and gay appear porous. Filipino migrants draw on the former as a means of negotiating identity and difference through practices such as cross-dressing and *swardspeak,* a vernacular language that reconfigures elements from Filipino, English, and Spanish and is spoken with a hyperfeminized inflection.[14] For Manalansan, the deployment of swardspeak indicates resistance to assimilation and reflects Filipino gay men's struggles with notions of belonging in the context of their abject relationship to the (Philippine) nation and to the American (mostly white) gay community.[15] He argues that swardspeak has a blurry relationship with class, noting that while "some people contend that swardspeak is a communication style prevalent among lower-class queers who work mostly in beauty parlors . . . [his] informants, who are neither from the lower class nor work in beauty parlors, consider swardspeak to be a more democratic system of linguistic practice."[16]

During the years I was conducting fieldwork in Manila, however, swardspeak appeared to be a dying language. It persisted and continued to thrive only in certain pockets—in places like the beauty parlors, with which it remained most closely associated; in the drag shows held in clubs like Palawan, where it remained a source of comic relief; and in new sites such as call centers, where large groups of gay men learned to speak in code.[17] Swardspeak was spoken in spaces such as these, but in the sites most closely associated with the scene, it was nowhere near as ubiquitous as it was in the diasporic communities discussed by Manalansan. In the bars and clubs that emerged as central sites of privileged gay life, it was rarely used. Many younger gay men never learned it or knew only a handful of words, which they deployed sparingly or in the manner of parody, confident that they could speak the language without claiming it as their own. The practice of cross-dressing too had become increasingly rare, and the gay "uniform" of tight T-shirts and jeans greeted so warily by Manalansan's informants had become the norm.[18] Indeed, the years I document here were marked by a dramatic shift away from practices of kabaklaan, a change manifested not only as a generational difference but also as an individual choice. There were, for instance, groups of gay men who cross-dressed and spoke swardspeak as recently as the late 1990s who had dropped both practices by the mid-2000s. When I asked them what had spurred this shift, they simply shrugged and said that such things were no longer "*benta* [attractive]" and that they had become *unfashionable*.[19]

If, for Manalansan, the appropriative capacities of Filipino gay men were demonstrated by the recuperation of practices such as swardspeak and cross-dressing, then how can the intersections of global and local forms of sexual identification be conceptualized in Manila's upper market commercial spaces, where a seemingly overt desire to approximate hegemonic representations of global gayness overwrites putatively "local" practices? Any attempt to answer a question such as this must begin by acknowledging that the nuances of Manalansan's informants' diasporic experience are what make possible the underplaying of class consciousness, which in turn is what allows kabaklaan to serve as an acceptable source of adaptable practices. As Manalansan argues, "Class issues . . . are subordinated by the immigrant experience"; many middle- and upper-class migrants are forced by economic circumstances and exclusion from racialized gay spaces to abandon or at least temporarily forego investments in class identity.[20] The stories he tells are thus stories of compromise, of coping with unfamiliar states of displacement and eking out lives as outsiders within the interstices of a foreign city. His informants recall, for instance, how upon arriving in New York, they were forced to take menial jobs and interact with Filipinos who were not of the same class background. Others remembered how they established ties with the broader Filipino gay community as a response to the feeling of "not belonging" in the bars and clubs in the gentrified sections of Manhattan.[21]

The stories of Manalansan's informants demonstrate how the interdictory character of gay globality becomes clear for Filipinos in New York, how their proximity to one of its imagined centers allows them to recognize their difference, experience exclusion based on that difference, and discover that the global gayness ascribed to the city is a claim that excludes Filipinos, among many othered queer subjects. Moreover, the downward mobility experienced by migrant Filipinos enables the sublimation of class and foregrounds national identity and belonging. It is the combination of these factors that demands and conditions strategies of resistance; it is what offers the possibility of disparate individuals jointly reinscribing practices of kabaklaan as a means of negotiating sexual subjectivity in the age of diaspora. The queer migrant experience thus emerges in *Global Divas* as the process of becoming *local* by entering global space—a process made clear by one of Manalansan's informants when he confesses, in Tagalog, that he "used to think that (he) came to America to be gay, but then (he) realized that (he) came to America to be a real *bakla.*"[22]

This quote reveals how distance plays a crucial role in navigating the rocky terrain of gayness and kabaklaan, how becoming gay is tied to the dream of leaving home, and how this dream gets turned on its head when the contradictions between spatial imaginations and the "real" effects of cultural dislocation are exposed. Here "America" takes on a key role as the site onto which dreams of mobility are projected. As Mark Johnson notes, however, Filipino discourses on "America" cannot be taken as references to the literal space of America. America is a sign that evokes that which lies "outside"; it serves, primarily, as an idiom "through which the world is thought and imagined."[23] Similarly, Fenella Cannell, writing on the bakla in the Bicol region, notes that the outside world consumed via Manila-based films is "the world of the wealthy 'American' outside at one remove, mediated . . . through a portrayal of the life of the national élite who have access to it."[24] Johnson's and Cannell's observations point to the much-discussed close articulation of Filipino and American culture.[25] It must be noted, however, that while notions of gay globality in Manila continue to operate within a history of slippage through which America comes to stand in for the world, the scene has also begun to move beyond the binarized imaginative geography left behind by colonial history by adopting a gay cartography that is, more broadly, global and metrocentric. This is made evident by the now ubiquitous appearance of references such as the following: "Pretty soon partying in Manila will be at par with the parties of New York, Miami, Palm Springs, Montreal,"[26] or "Our life-styles these days . . . look like something fished out fresh from the streets of Castro in San Francisco or Oxford in Sydney."[27] More than examples of how the dream of America becomes undone, experiences of exclusion in places like New York can be read, in the context of such multisited claims, as instances that forcefully demonstrate disjunctures between the "real" of gay life in global cities and the simulacrum of gay globality.

Manila's movement into this simulacral circuit is itself an act of sub-scription, a "falling upwards" made possible by the fact that the scenes of gay globality are seen only from a safe distance, insulated from the exclu-sionary mechanisms faced by Filipino migrants in the imagined centers of the gay globe.[28] Thus, as counterintuitive as it may seem, it is Manila's very geographical separation from such sites that allows its residents to be more fully interpellated into the global gay identity than their diasporic counterparts, since the absence of shared experiences of displacement and exclusion is also the absence of any impetus to perform kabaklaan and to recover it from its subordinated position within local hierarchical systems grounded on the abjection of lower-class status and effeminacy. One could say in fact that Manila offers an inversion of the picture of global–local relations presented by Manalansan—for there, in the absence of the racial-economic politics of being diasporic, it is gayness that is recu-perated, mimicked without the threat of nonbelonging, and mobilized as *the* alternative modernity, contrasted as it is with the historically domi-nant, multiply marginalizing position of the bakla in Filipino discourses on homosexuality.

Indeed, the struggle of gay men in Manila against the heterosexism, if not the outright homophobia that continues to structure life in many parts of the city, has often been cast in terms of finding ways of perform-ing homosexuality without being coded as bakla. In 2004, for instance, Manila's first gay glossy magazine, *Icon,* was launched. In the editor's note of the second issue, Richie Villarin writes,

> "We cannot remain oblivious to your market."
> These were very powerful words, I thought, not because it came from one of our possible advertisers, but because it's about time some-one said so. This is an acknowledgment, a validation that the pink community is gaining recognition as an important part of society whose contributions cannot be ignored.
> And why shouldn't it be recognized? We are everywhere. We are no longer confined to the stereotypical image of the *parlorista.*[29]

Villarin's quote captures the thrust of the neoliberal reconfiguration of Manila's gay cityscape. His closing line, "We are no longer confined to the stereotypical image of the *parlorista*," echoes popular conceptions of the bakla as a restrictive image, a script all homosexual men *were once* obligated to follow or a screen through which all homosexual men *were once* viewed. The queer rallying cry "We are everywhere" here takes on a different meaning; it situates the bakla in a specific place (the parlor) and casts "validation" as the recognition of our newfound mobility, our presence in places other than kabaklaan.[30] These "new" places, however, include not only the heterosexual spaces of Manila but also the marketplace of gay globality. Indeed, the early 2000s were marked by an overwhelming sense that something new had arrived in the city, particularly with the opening of the clubs Bed (2003) and Government (2004), both of which were designed to cater to a market aware of global parallels, manifested not only in their spatial design, their lights, and their music but also in their mirroring of foreign gay events such as album and single release parties timed to coincide with similar celebrations abroad.[31]

Not only did the opening of both clubs provide a space for many younger gay men who saw preexisting queer spaces as "cheap" and "seedy," but it also allowed Manila to begin stepping into a global gay cartography. It paved the way for the arrival of foreign DJs and the entrance of an emerging CircuitAsia party scene, which, on holding its first event in Manila in 2005, was met by local gay organizers with a doubly triumphant language, one that heralded the arrival of the gay globe in Manila and Manila's arrival in the gay globe:

> Government: "It is truly an exciting time for Manila's gay
> community! . . . We are so excited with the 'sleepless' parties that
> are coming up; but more seriously, we are more thrilled with the
> positive economic impact their events will bring to our community."
>
> Bed: "It has been a time of growth and new experiences ever
> since the opening of Bed in 2003. With the advent of CircuitAsia
> we are delighted to see that the clubbing community has likewise
> grown. It is our intention to support CircuitAsia in an effort to
> promote Manila as a world-class party destination locally and
> internationally."
>
> *Icon*: "This is an event that is long overdue. Finally, CircuitAsia
> brings world-class entertainment that Filipinos truly deserve. We
> now have the chance to showcase to the world, the very best that the
> Philippines can offer—claiming our rightful place in the international
> circuit party arena."[32]

These quotes demonstrate the rhetorical force of globality, the world, and world-classness, all of which slip through despite the regional imaginary summoned by the name "CircuitAsia."[33] By making reference to the long wait endured by Manila and the newness of being global, they reimagine Manila's place in the world, embedding the city onto a map that is not only spatial but also temporal. The movement of Manila along the path of gay globality is here represented as a movement toward the present, toward contemporaneousness with other cityscapes coded as "gay." In this way, "gay" or "gay-as-modern" operates as "a historical signifier that reorganizes the temporality of homosexuality and society according to a sequence that places gay culture as a reference to the present, to the 'now'—a present defined in global terms."[34] It must be noted, however, that despite the references the testimonials make to Manila and the Philippines, the nowness or newness of gay globality is not acquired uniformly by the nation or the city or by gay men in general. Rather, it is reached via the vehicle of gay community, written under tropes of diversity but delimited by the ability to purchase instantaneity through participation in a local pink economy that accedes to the image of the global gay. This accession is exhibited forcefully by *Generation Pink,* a glossy gay magazine launched in 2005. The exclusionary power of newness embodied by its name was made even clearer by its introduction as "the newest quarterly publication especially developed for lifestyle-conscious, shop-savvy, socially-aware, party-loving and liberal individuals."[35] The specificity of this generational niche, however, is belied by the magazine's erasure of difference through representation. The disclaimer about its market comes in fine print and is buried under features that speak broadly about *who* the Filipino gay man is and describes events such as the White Party (borrowed from the U.S. party circuit) as "milestones" for "the LGBT community."[36] Through such descriptions, publications like *Generation Pink* are able to perform the unintended cultural task of converting market-specific texts into generalized ontological claims about those who belong to "*this* time . . . the time of the times, the time of this world . . . 'this world', this age and no other"; consequently, they are able to write kabaklaan as part of the past, not through direct admonition, but by rendering it absent from the sites that embody the *now* of Manila's gay history.[37]

Haunted by a Past That Is Always Present

In *The Location of Culture,* Homi Bhabha asks, "What is the now of modernity? Who defines this present from which we speak?"[38] In Manila, it is those whose imaginations and practices are tied to the city system of gay globality who can speak of the present, a present from which the scene can narrate local history and reinforce "the complementarity between the local and the global in a transparency that creates a new set of challenges and erasures."[39] Here, gay visibility is marked by a kind of tunnel vision, through which can be seen those elements that can exhibit global isomorphism; the rest are veiled, silenced by virtue of their links to the past. The erasure engendered by gay visibility is thus contingent on the splitting of temporalities. It works only under the premise that kabaklaan can be confined to the annals of a specifically local and implicitly outdated culture.

Such premises, however, are doomed by the instability of the plot of modernity and are perpetually plagued by the presence of the past in the present. Indeed, kabaklaan persists, both in cultural memory and in its continued practice by othered Filipino gay men. It makes real what Derrida called "the frightening hypothesis of a visitation" by continuing to appear on television and cinema screens, where the parlorista remains fixed as a source of comic relief.[40] It is resurrected in homophobic language and still performed on the streets of Manila, if not through the body of the parlorista then through the disarticulated appearances of femininity and lower-class status in figures that seek entrance into the spaces created by the scene's reorganization of gay culture. The speed of Manila's gay reconfiguration, in other words, does not presage the increasing obsolescence of kabaklaan; rather, it indexes a desire to imagine the bakla's obsolescence. This imagination, however, is subverted by the claims of diversity necessitated by the liberal politics attached to modern gayness and that opens the scene to traces of *kabaklaan,* which enter discreetly through passages laid bare by the putative openness of gay culture and its material and virtual sites.[41]

Such traces are cause for flight—sometimes literally, as when gay men abandon websites and clubs increasingly frequented by men who are seen as cheap or establish borders within those spaces to avoid engaging individuals who do not conform to privileged class and gender codes. Websites devoted to personal advertisements, for instance, are marked by a distinct emphasis on class markers. Guys4Men.com, a global site that served as the primary Internet hub for gay men in Manila during the years I was conducting fieldwork, stands as the most vivid example of how lower-class status and femininity seep into new gay spaces and are subsequently evaded or managed.[42]

Guys4Men first became popular in Manila during the early 2000s, a time when gay men in the city were only beginning to migrate from text-based chat rooms and long before the advent of gay networking applications for mobile phones. At that time, though the website had its share of men looking for one-night stands, Guys4Men seemed to function less as a space to arrange anonymous sexual encounters than a means for establishing social linkages among similarly situated men. The majority of early adopters appeared to come from middle- and upper-class backgrounds, which was evidenced most significantly by shared links to Manila's network of exclusive private schools and universities. During those earlier years, the website functioned mostly to reproduce that network within a gay subset, with many ties eventually carried over into nonvirtual spaces. The establishment of this community was aided in part by the relatively small number of users from Manila. With usually no more than a few dozen members online at any given time, the site appeared to be a tightly knit space and, though it was structured as a venue for personal advertisements, it functioned similarly to other social networking sites that were popular then.

By 2005, the number of users in Guys4Men had grown exponentially, reaching a total of 48,000 in 2006.[43] This growth was accompanied by the democratization of the site's membership, which was reflected most vividly in the dramatic shift in the overall class profile of its users. Though this shift cannot be evidenced by statistical data, middle- and upper-class users routinely remarked on the increasing presence of lower-class men, who were identified through the use of multiple codes, including those that were linguistic (English proficiency, certain linguistic styles), geographic (location in areas coded as ghetto), and visual (dress style, background imagery in shared photos).

Many users responded to the entrance of what was perceived to be the underclass through a policing of class difference, most notably by employing language as an index of desirability. "I'd love to have a decent conversation with someone who has sense," wrote one user, "someone who can stimulate my brains before my groin . . . someone who speaks fluent English without trying." Another noted that he was looking for someone with "a good general background . . . someone cultured . . . someone who can carry a good, sensible conversation (especially, but not exclusively, in English, because unfortunately for this country, having a good command, or at least an understanding of the language, is a very accurate gauge)." More insidiously, some members' profile pages mockingly quoted the messages they received, which were written in broken English in order to ward off users with similar language skills. Others directly made the link between language and sex by claiming, for instance, that "good English is a turn on" and that "it's a real turn-off to see or hear dudes who can't even put together a decent English sentence."[44]

Similar strategies were employed to patrol gender lines. When I first started visiting the website in 2004, there did not appear to be a popular way of coding masculinities. By the time I began fieldwork two years later, a large number of profiles had begun to include the caveat "no effem," a response to a parallel increase in the number of users who did not conform to the hypermasculinity increasingly prescribed by local representations of homosexuality.[45] The term *effem* served as a blanket reference to a wide spectrum of feminine gay men, including those who practiced cross-dressing (or were in fact female identified) as well as those who simply fell short of hypermasculine ideals. In some cases, the rejection of effems worked hand in hand with the abjection of lower-class status, particularly when directed against those who cross-dressed, given the centrality of that practice within kabaklaan. In light of the relatively small number of members who did cross-dress or were female identified in Guys4Men, however, the ubiquity of the disclaimer "no effem" appeared to serve more as a generalized rejection of all traces of femininity. Users guarded against such traces and those who tried to hide them. They warned against "fakers," or those who "pretend that they aren't 'effem,'" by including threats such as, "If we meet up and you don't match up to the hunky pic you sent, I swear I'll hurt you." Many distrusted photographs and sought the "inner truth of gender" by asking, "Are you effem?" or "Are you sure you're not effem?"[46] Correspondingly, some users began to "come out" as masculine, either through statements (e.g., "I'm not effem . . . I'm not into that") or through the staged performance of hypermasculinity. Shortly after joining the website, for instance, an informant who used to cross-dress began posting images of himself wearing baseball caps and holding soccer balls despite his complete lack of interest in sports.

While the denigration of femininity has long been a feature of gay male spaces in the West, so-called femme phobia was complicated in Manila by the historical dominance of kabaklaan in Filipino public culture and the associated, classed fear that one's homosexuality might be interpreted as female identification. Moreover, the hypermasculinity displayed in Filipinized virtual gay spaces presented a sharp contrast to the feminized image of Filipino gay men (and other Asian men) overseas.[47] The polemic that pervaded Guys4Men inverted this exoticized and eroticized image; it put forward a spectacle of remasculinized Filipino homosexuality more often associated with hegemonic representations of global gayness. This spectacle, however, seemed even more anxious than its foreign counterparts, determined as it was to smoke out the last vestiges of a suspected inherent femininity ("Are you *really* not effem?"). The exhibition of performed and confessed masculinity spawned by such suspicion, coupled with the abjection of lower-class status through language, served as a startling example not only of the disciplining power of Manila's gay reconfiguration but also of its instability, of the need to constantly secure and resecure gender and class privilege within the spaces of the scene.

In some ways, Guys4Men served as a site for the disarticulation of lower-class status from femininity, with many of those who might be read as part of the underclass being the most vocal about the undesirability of effems. Such disarticulation, however, only worked to fix the multiple marginality of the bakla, its imagined presence as the absolute condensation of both undesirable elements. Indeed, even when broken apart, these elements were separately policed through the disciplining strategies outlined previously and, when such strategies failed, could then be evaded. For instance, many of those early users whom I interacted with when I discovered Guys4Men began abandoning the website in the mid- to late 2000s. In fact, one of my informants sent me an e-mail in fall 2006 suggesting that I do the same; it was, he said, "time to delete your account."

During this period, the seeds of a similar movement could be detected in the gay clubs. Though the clubs continued to draw large crowds, there were those who saw themselves as more discriminating and who began abandoning the clubs in favor of house parties with what one host referred to as "the right crowd and the right address." There I found myself in the midst of a network of similarly situated men: men who spoke with the same style of English and *Taglish* (Tagalog-English), dressed similarly in designer jeans and T-shirts, and displayed the same gym-built masculinity. During my first visit to one such party, which was held at a gated subdivision in Makati City, one of the guests told me that they had similar gatherings every weekend and that I should come more often. "The clubs," he said, "were now only worth going to during special events." Later on, I would learn that there were other parallel parties being thrown around the city. They varied in terms of age and interests, but they were all similarly protected by the privacy of residences and by unspoken restrictions that had less to do with traditional class markers such as income levels than with language skills, shared cultural references, and dress style—those markers that signaled not wealth per se, but proximity to gay globality.[48]

These strategies of evasion were supplemented by attempts to incorporate kabaklaan into gay globality through a murky shift to a language of "drag" and "trans." Room was made for gender outlaws if they were able to work within the modern gay script. It was thus unsurprising that while the new gay clubs dissociated themselves from the famed bakla beauty pageants, they were nonetheless able to provide a stage for occasional drag shows. Similarly, cross-dressing or effeminacy seemed to fit in seamlessly if embodied by figures linked to high fashion.[49] These spaces, however, were not spaces for the bakla but for its metamorphosed form, its reincarnation under the likeness of bodies and subjectivities, which were made legible by their very foreignness.

Attempts to translate kabaklaan, however, were (and remain) fraught endeavors. Though its conceptual core of cross-dressing and effeminacy is shared by subjects in radically different contexts, the pool of meanings assembled over its long, painful history cannot be erased through the use of other categories.[50] Still, the translation of *bakla* into palatable modern counterparts was an enterprise that many parties had become involved in by the mid-2000s, including those who practiced kabaklaan, as seen, for instance, in online discussion forums where individuals struggled to determine which "trans" term best described them and in articles in the popular press, which spoke of a transgender community in lieu of a bakla one. In a forum on Guys4Men, for example, one member asked, "How far you know [sic] about transgenders, transsexuals, transvestites? Similarities? Differences? Feelings towards these type[s] of gay people?" The responses to this question were varied and confusing. There were those who simply declared their identification ("I'm a transvestite") and many more who attempted to pin down definitions for the terms, often through inferences taken from everyday interactions.

> Ok [i]n my own definitions of such terms base[d] on my experiences, people around me, psychologists and cosmetics surgeons I had conversation with and lawyers: crossdressers are people who dresess [sic] oppositely base[d] on their gender due to some reasons like job and such. These people are mostly drag queens and impersonators, but during their normal hours they dress as what is proper in regards of their gender. Transvestites are gays who dresses [sic] like girls wherever they are even if they sleep. Some of these are pre-op. [T]ransexuals are gays who have already undergone sex change. They are the post-op people. Transgendered are post-op people who filed a petition in the court for a change of gender (most cases are from male-to-female) and the court granted their request. [51]

This quote illustrates how fraught the translation to a language of trans is and also how the task of translation was read as both humbling and increasingly pertinent. A number of responses to this post, for instance, began with disclaimers such as "*Inaamin ko, marami pa akong dapat malaman tungkol sa sekswalidad na ito* [I admit, I have much to learn about this sexuality]" or "This is based on what I know, *ha* [OK]? I don't know if *tama* [it's right]." Others pointed to the urgency of the task of translation, with some participants in the discussion urging others to keep posting in order to bump the thread up the list of topics in the forums. "Remember . . . keep the thread going . . . promise sistah?" This task of comprehending one's gendered or sexual self using the language of trans subjectivity was mirrored in part by shifts within activist communities. In 2006, for example, the *Manila Times* published an article on the "Filipino transgender experience." In it, Francis Gomez, a gay-identified writer, recalls meeting members of the Society of Transsexual Women of the Philippines (STRAP), a support network established four years prior. He writes, "I excused myself before they went on to business and kissed all 15 of my sisters on the cheek. I casually said: '*O mga bakla,* enjoy *kayo ha!* [Have fun, *baklas!*]', to which someone politely but firmly replied, '*Hindi kami mga bakla, babae kami* [We are not *bakla,* we are women].'"[52] In the article, Gomez presumes that the refusal to be called bakla stems from an understanding of bakla as gay and hence distinct from transsexuality.[53] Though possible, the refusal remains ironic, given gay culture's othering of kabaklaan precisely due to its historical links to female identification.[54] In this light, STRAP's disidentification with the bakla might be taken as the apex of kabaklaan's abjection, a final translation whereby its very conceptual core of gender variance is transferred to a new body, a *trans* body.[55]

The translation into a vocabulary of "trans" and "drag" may be understood as an attempt to preserve kabaklaan's conceptual core while emptying it of its injured past. In that sense, one might read it as a form of resistance, an unwillingness to bear the burden of historical abjection. The abject position of kabaklaan, however, cannot be reduced to a nominal inscription; it is a response to the performance of femininity and lower-class status that shapes what Derrida might have called the *spirit* of kabaklaan. It is this spirit that persists and constitutes the local, abject realm. The translation of this spirit is an attempt to relocate it outside that realm and hence dilute the challenge that realm poses to our being global by rewriting its (gendered) elements as something more relevant to the present from which we speak. Such a strategy, however, does little to curtail the exclusionary violence practiced online and offline, predicated as such violence is on the memory of the identity of the bakla (the ghost is "a who," says Derrida), which pervades the scene's narration of the present and which is reflected directly by Villarin's declaration that "we are no longer confined to the image of the *parlorista.*"[56] This memory—at work even here in my ability to write about the bakla as a point of disidentification— enables us to see (and hence police) kabaklaan's traces in the bodies and

practices of others. In effect, Manila's gay spaces are treated to the sporadic yet routine reappearance of kabaklaan in figures that are not quite
bakla. But kabaklaan is there, recognized; it is seen via "the *frequency* of
a certain visibility" or "the visibility of the invisible."[57]

We might then say that the celebration of the newness of the bright
lights scene is predicated on the interplay of visibility and invisibility and
on the belief that the scene has left the bakla behind—a fragile belief
betrayed by our ability to see and hunt down its traces. Such sightings
speak directly to the spectralization of kabaklaan, how it is becoming
palimpsestic or, in ghostly terms, being "improperly buried."[58] Indeed,
like a palimpsest, Manila's gay scene bears the marks of its local history,
which cuts through, never fully erasable, always legible despite attempts
to overwrite it with something new. This struggle between history and erasure situates the bakla somewhere between there and not there, past and
present, appearance and disappearance, life and death. It is still visible but
increasingly excluded by or dubbed with a gay modernity made seductive
by the possibility of rescuing same-sex desire from the doubly damning
alignment of femininity and lower-class status. This possibility rests on
complicity with the current landscape of global neocolonial domination,
on the desire to occupy that aspirational space previously inhabited by
the colonial collaborator.[59] Like the collaborator, the scene is neither col-
onizer nor colonized but both at the same time; we—its purveyors—are
estranged from yet rooted in the homeland and only precariously belong
to the present of gay globality. It is this fragile belonging, threatened by
the bakla's rival claim to Filipino homosexuality, which reproduces the
bakla as a specter, as the other's intolerable other.

Phantom Global Gayness

I have thus far presented the bright lights scene as an imaginative, global-
izing, spatiotemporal project that anachronizes kabaklaan. The distorted
character of this present, however, is also effected by its relationship to a
phantasmic future, to the paradoxical vision of a present that is not yet.
For Derrida, specters are also promises of things to come, injunctions
that order us to summon the very thing that will never present itself.[60]
This, perhaps, is a way to speak of the dream of gay globality, marked as
it is by the impossibility of belonging, an impossibility made most visible
in the act of travel, when the third world, postcolonial subject attempts
to literally eliminate the distance between "here" and "there" only to
encounter his own otherness. I explore such attempts in greater detail in
the following two chapters, but here I would like to point out that even in

Manila, where Filipinos are not subjected to the same exclusionary protocols faced by the diaspora and where elite subjects can draw privilege from class and gender codes, gay globality remains nonactualizable. The aspirational transformations that underpin the semblance of gay globality do not constitute the imitation of a preexisting real but an inching toward a nonreplicable idealized model rooted in a history of colonial desire that involves intersections of class, gender, and race. As Bhabha writes, "The question of identification is never the affirmation of a pre-given identity, never a self-fulfilling prophecy—it is always the production of an image of identity and the transformation of the subject in assuming that image."[61] It is in this sense that we might say that the inhabitants of the bright lights scene, despite their or our introjection of global gayness, will always be chasing the phatic image. Manila itself seems bound to a perpetual state of movement, fated to never arrive in the present, hinged as that present is on a map of modernity, which periodizes the city as somewhere behind, almost but not quite global. Thus between the city and the gay globe and between the scene's inhabitants and the global gay sits a perpetual gap, a lag, a diastema, "failure, inadequation, disjunction, disadjustment, being 'out of joint.'"[62]

The aspiration that underpins this gap can, I suggest, be fruitfully rethought in terms of spectralization. Derrida speaks of the illusions produced through the "new speed of apparition . . . of the simulacrum, the synthetic or prosthetic image, and the virtual event."[63] We might start thinking again of how the high-speed global circulation of gayness, seen, for instance, in the widespread consumption of pirated gay programming in Manila, is implicated in the process of introjection, in our ability to imagine other, distant worlds, "to re-present to ourselves people and objects we cannot see . . . and to finally act accordingly."[64] Here, the market once again takes center stage as the "audiovisual vehicle" through which images and apparitions travel.[65] It must be stressed, however, that the market is more than a transmitter. It is also constituted by neoliberal mechanisms—including but not limited to the clubs, parties, magazines, and Internet portals I have named here—which facilitate the impossible yet seductive task of materializing the distant image. In this sense, we might say that our disappearing of kabaklaan works alongside a parallel invisibilization, the veiling of the impossibility of global gayness through the speed of global interpellation, which not only facilitates identification but also reconfigures distance. Gay globality becomes a space that is virtually accessible, seemingly within reach, bridgeable by a few more transformations (a few more erasures), so close that we have begun to announce its arrival.

Gay globality thus also stands on the line between presence and absence. It is a trajectory made seemingly plausible by the proximity effected by its mediatized apparitions. The subscription to this trajectory is what engenders the task of bordering off kabaklaan; it also creates a "specular circle" or a "paradoxical hunt" whereby the ostensibly "global" gay men of the bright lights scene require the presence of the bakla in order to assert their difference from locality and secure a sense of global belonging. Derrida mocks, "Come so that I may chase you! You hear! I chase you. I run after you to chase you away from here."[66] Therein lies the final snag: our inability to exorcise kabaklaan is the effect not only of its material persistence but of our perverse desire to see its presence, since the memory of being doubly damned and confined in the classed and feminized image of the bakla allows us to extract pleasure from being approximates of global gayness.

The ghost of the bakla is thus inextricably tied to us, "for better or worse—united."[67] Going back to Hamlet, Derrida reworks "to be or not to be" by claiming that the verb "to be" is always prefigured by the specter. "'I am' would mean 'I am haunted': I am haunted by myself who am (haunted by myself who am haunted by myself who am . . .)."[68] This perhaps becomes doubly resonant for the subjects who inhabit the bright lights scene, in as much as our search for a "new" subjectivity is compelled and propelled by specters from the past present and the future present. This dual haunting is a double-sided ethical demand. It requires us to take seriously Derrida's injunction to encounter what is strange and other about the specter of the bakla and at the same time to account for our complicity in the continued life of modernity's trajectories under the sign of gay globality. This second task requires us to put into words the phantom character of gay globality, its status as an impossible task grounded on modes of exclusion that take shifting configurations in different locations. By foregrounding this impossibility, the impossibility made clear to the excluded migrant but obscured by Manila's bright lights, we might finally begin stepping off the linear path and addressing the violent hierarchies we ourselves reproduce in the process of gay world-making.

CHAPTER FOUR

Transnational Transit and the Circuits of Privilege

Here we see the advent of airport politics . . . but this time, of airports that will no longer have the relaxed atmosphere of leisure that the traveling bourgeoisie conferred upon it . . . Air-terminals, terminuses, and ports of the anti-city that opens on the nothingness of a territory disappeared; a site of ejection that one occupies temporarily to buckle the empty buckle of an accelerated wandering; the air terminal, a spectroscope where popular shadows file past, migrants, phantoms in transit, postponing the last revolution, the revolution of the eternal return.

—Paul Virilio, *Negative Horizon*

Unlike most airports servicing major cities, Metro Manila's Ninoy Aquino International Airport (NAIA) is not located on the outskirts of town but inside the megacity, a few kilometers from the Makati Central Business District (CBD), near the invisible border that splits Parañaque City and Pasay City. Like most of my informants, I have lost countless hours on the road to NAIA, stuck in the standstill traffic at the southern end of Epifanio delos Santos Avenue (EDSA) or on the streets that branch to the east, the ones lined with sagging electrical wires, inexpensive streetside restaurants, gas stations, and old businesses housed in graying buildings. I remember the trips to NAIA and recall the frustration on the road, the absence of that rush that normally accompanies trips to other airports, of the sense of escape that comes with sharp breaks from urban centers, of long drives down sparse highways bordered only by bare industrial parks and the hulking buildings of outlet malls, and of the first up-close sightings of planes landing and taking off.

I used to imagine what it would be like if the city just flattened NAIA and the ground beneath it and built in its place an airport of glass and steel, a high-tech oasis like the airport-cities of other nations.[1] I used to wonder if I would feel more remorseful about leaving the city, over and over again, if leaving felt less like a battle waged against the city, if I could contemplate the act of flying on an open road instead of silently cursing the bumper-to-bumper traffic on NAIA's thatched perimeter roads, the black stench of smoke belched by aging buses and jeepneys, and the noise of horns. At times I still wonder what would happen if NAIA was razed to the ground, if the authorities would rebuild it elsewhere, maybe south of the city, where there is hardly anything but blue skies and open fields waiting to be colonized, or if, ten years from now, NAIA will be just as it is today: a concrete box baking in the heat; browning in the midst of the palpable smog bouncing from the asphalt; and suffering the encroachments of the squalor, the urban turbulence, the stale liquid mess that constitute Manila.[2]

I imagine NAIA as it once was: an architectural triumph among other architectural triumphs, one of the many imposing buildings that rose like concrete monoliths from the landscape of concatenated violence and beauty, luxury and abject poverty, demolition and construction, and death and progress that defined Manila from the late sixties to the early eighties.[3] I can see its arching structural curves, its marble floor, and its dim yellow lights, and I can tell (or intuit, at least) that it used to dominate not only that part of the city but also the story of the city: an imposing structure jutting out of barren environs in order to herald a coming modernity, to literally concretize the claim that Manila had become a destination and to evidence its supposed transformation into the "City of Man."[4] I imagine as well the wealthy travelers to whom NAIA must have belonged when it was completed in 1981—the privileged locals who were able to fly, the ones who thrived in the excesses of the dictatorship and who mingled with the foreign dignitaries and socialites who once welcomed stopovers in Manila. I can see them being driven up NAIA's unweathered ramps, standing on the freshly laid marble floor, marveling at the glamour of the cavernous high ceiling and at the modernness of NAIA. Imagining them there, I cannot help but wonder whether they were grateful that NAIA's predecessor on Nichols Field burned to the ground; whether they anticipated and dreamt of those fires, and if they did, whether those dreams were marked by the same destructive, wishful desire for a tabula rasa that grips me whenever I slip into my own classed, half-hidden daydreams of NAIA bursting into flames.[5]

I remember NAIA, but in my memories, the amber glow that must have once given the main concourse an air of luxury merely coats it in sepia tones, making it fittingly seem like an old snapshot. In my memories, the architectural details that once proclaimed the newness of NAIA function as remainders that tell the story of its age. The concrete slabs so loved by its modernist architect, the national artist Leandro Locsin, offer a heavy contrast to the metal and glass—the transparency—of airports overseas.[6] The marble floors have darkened veins. The green rubber floors leading to the gates seem like kitsch additions to a movie set in the sixties, as do the two flip boards hanging in the waiting lounge, which display the status of flights in the absence of digital screens. I do not know if I am alone in noticing these details, but growing up in the privileged corners of Manila, I have been party to countless conversations bemoaning the absences that speak the same tale of NAIA's immurement in time: the lack of duty-free shopping, Internet access, television screens, ATM machines, international fast food franchises, themed bars, and decent bookshops—all those "universal," transposable things that make airports recognizable as airports. NAIA is defined by these absences, these lacks that together constitute failure by recalling the patterns laid bare by the overwhelming uniformity of airports overseas. These absences keep me from remembering NAIA as a gateway to a space of flows, as a non-place linked to other non-places, as in the crisscrossing flight paths drawn on the foldout pages of in-flight magazines.[7] I can think of NAIA only as an avatar for the para-modern city that surrounds it—as a "place of memory," not because it is bereft of history, as Marc Augé once claimed of airports in general, but because it remembers the unrealized possibility of the city, littered as it is with the mnemonic traces of past decades and with absences functioning as gaps, ready to be filled with memories of what might have been.[8]

In this way, NAIA can be seen as a place that has grown textured in the vicissitudes of history, as a witness to the comings and goings, the ups and downs (but mostly to the downs), the mass departures, the hanging on that echoes what Kathleen Stewart once called "the desire of remembered loss."[9] Indeed, NAIA appears to be caught in a perpetual present, pointing at once to a coming global mobility and to the inertia that plagues Manila, to the promise of modernity and to the derailing of that same promise. It is a structure reaching outward but trapped in the place and time of the city, located in the third-world city and hence at the fringes of that archipelago of transit spaces that has become "the true city of the twenty-first century": "a centripetal city whose population forever circles its notional center, and will never gain access to its dark heart."[10] Thinking now of NAIA, it is easy to imagine that Manila has been forgotten by that population. There, the mythic figures of the "kinetic elite" are rarely glimpsed; they fly in and out but are mostly conspicuous in their absence, unwilling perhaps to brave this strange airport where there is nothing to buy and nothing to do but sit on one of the few metal chairs in the wait-ing lounge and bear the weight of nostalgia.[11] Marked by absences, NAIA has become an eerie portrait of aspiration and failure: an airport with no tourists, no businessmen shuffling along in dark suits with leather carry-alls and laptops. It stands now as a testament to the relegation of Manila to the outskirts of the world, a sad reminder of the rendering of the city as a place beyond the pale, well beyond the itinerary of the prototypical traveler, of the *supermodern* individual.[12]

And yet, for all the absences that mark NAIA, it is an airport equally defined by excess. In place of the gaps and lacks so visible in NAIA, there are the lines that stretch endlessly, the *balikbayan* boxes piled on top of one another on cumbrous trolleys, the din of too much chatter, the poor families waiting by the fences, the excess delays, the filth of the toilets, the smell of dust accumulated over decades.[13] Above all, NAIA is over-run with too many bodies—not with the individual circulating bodies of supermodern travelers, as in Augé's non-places, but a mass of bodies try-ing to exit: the Overseas Filipino Workers (OFWs) for whom Manila is so famous, the country's human excess, pushed out and funneled through the postcolonial metropolis.[14]

The few changes in the built form of NAIA's main terminal have, in fact, taken shape around the figure of the labor migrant. At the mouth of the terminal, OFWs pass through a special entrance, delimited by a brown and white sign and waist-high metal barricades and leading to a process-ing area where their paperwork is collected. Inside, there are two special lines, one that grants airport tax exemptions to OFWs and the other an "OFW express lane" at immigration that often moves, ironically, at a slower pace. I used to think of these alterations as nothing more than cosmetic extensions of the state's long-running attempts to facilitate the outflow of its excess inhabitants, as sites of final, official, farcical pats on the back before exportation. Thinking now of the inundation of NAIA, however, these clogged up passages seem more like last-ditch efforts to contain whatever excess possible by sequestering OFWs at the edges of the terminal, away from the privileged travelers who "choose" to move and hence have prior claims to NAIA's internal spaces.[15] Except, there are simply too many OFWs to be contained. There are no numbers that detail how much of NAIA is occupied by OFWs at any given moment, but my memories of NAIA are brimming with their presence, if only because those memories have been shaped by a gaze trained to spot class differ-ence, to see "otherness lurking in appearances."[16] Indeed, even before I took on the cataloging eye of the researcher, I could see that NAIA no longer belonged to the elites whose dreams I inherited but to their alter egos: to the seafarers clad in denim jackets with Philippine flags sewn onto the shoulder; the construction workers headed to the Middle East with *too much* gold peeking underneath their collars and shining on their fingers; and the groups of women with long straight hair cut bluntly at the edges and *too much* makeup off to serve the world as nannies, caregivers, cleaners, cooks, "entertainers."[17] These are the bodies that occupy NAIA, the ones that now stand in sharp relief against the traces of the airport's old glamour. Remembering them now, I cannot help but hear, guiltily, the same tale of loss whispered by the architectural details of the main terminal—that is, the story of botched modernity allegorized in the mutation of a structure meant to announce the arrival of the city in the world (and the world in the city) into a pathway for the underclass, a valve for a surfeit of "labor commodities."[18]

The Airport and Gay Globality

Picture NAIA and all its attendant lacks and excesses and cast it against the dream of gay globality.[19] Think of how NAIA reveals the abject place occupied by Manila in the archipelago of global and would-be global cities and the claims made about the arrival of Manila in the circuit of gay spaces; how those very claims have been enabled by a filling in of gaps in the city through the creation of spaces suffused with light and sound systems from France, manned by DJs who scour the world and the Internet for knowledge of what is "current," and crammed with bodies plugged into a global flow of images and producing their own images: the casual shots of partygoers in tight T-shirts that later make their way onto websites and the back pages of magazines, the advertisements with "gym-built" models in low-hanging jeans. Think of the upmarket bars and restaurants scattered across Makati City and the Global City, where on some nights you might catch threads of a conversation about a weekend of dancing in Bangkok or Hong Kong; a summer spent in Europe; or months or years spent in Los Angeles, San Francisco, or New York. Think of these places as dreamspaces protected from the excesses of the city but at the same time exceeding the city, housing an imagination that stretches outward and connects with faraway yet ideationally proximate places. Think of how some of these conversations might happen outside a club, interrupted or prefaced with comments about how the crowd that night is too cheap and *jologs* and how those comments might get passed on by text message, like warnings sent out to those yet to arrive. Imagine how later, living out the same stories of travel, those narrating them might find themselves caught in the pandemonium of NAIA, standing in line with the OFWs, with figures familiar only as laborers performing housework, chauffeurs, and construction workers passed on streets and spied from behind the tinted windows of private automobiles. Imagine how that same, rare intermingling of classes might have happened as a prelude to travel, at the long line that used to snake outside the gates of the U.S. embassy, where even the wealthy had to wait from before dawn until noon, when the sun shone so hard everyone hid under umbrellas, only to submit visa application forms and face the humiliating prospect of denial. Think of how, at NAIA, the spatial separation on which the bright lights scene is predicated becomes undone and how NAIA, perhaps more than any other site, ought to serve as the foundation of a classed global imagination.

Think of how the *nowness* and *newness* of gay globality rubs up against the time of the city. At NAIA, one confronts vestiges of the past, failed dreams of contemporaneity, and the sense of being left behind, of being at the outskirts. There, spatial imagination must contend with the materiality of location; the excess of urban squalor meets the excess of privilege; and faded traces of glamour reveal the heritage of gay globality, its roots in older dreams of a worldliness to come.

> *June 25, 2008.* I have just returned from a dinner hosted by Tony, an older gay socialite whom I met at the city's most exclusive bar and who, having heard of my research, had grown excited at the prospect of recounting the glory days of Manila and its subsequent decline into what he called an "unbearable cheapness." The dinner was held at a private room in Umu, a Japanese restaurant inside the five-star Dusit Thani Hotel Manila. I arrived twenty minutes late but was still only the second person to arrive. The first was an architect whose name I was familiar with from local magazines. Later we were joined by a fashion executive who kept disappearing to the toilets to snort cocaine and a wealthy Parisian in town after a weekend of debauchery in Thailand. Tony arrived last, his young lawyer boyfriend on his arm and followed by a waiter carrying a box of pink champagne. It took a long time for the party to settle down. Tony and the architect kept standing up to scold the waitstaff, first for bringing the food out too quickly in succession, then for taking too long to refill our glasses. Tony spoke with a confident drawl, for effect I thought; his voice drowned out all smaller, breakaway conversations. "Darling," he would say to me from across the table, "I can say nothing good about gay Manila today. Everyone is cheap, cheap, cheap. In the eighties, Manila was a happening place. Beautiful people came here from around the world to attend the parties of Mrs. M."[20] They too, he said, had traveled the world in search of the finest

clubs, the most lavish parties. He kept recalling earlier travels, the glamour of flying in the early eighties, perhaps even in the seventies or late sixties. I could not tell what decade he was referring to, since he made no effort to make distinctions between them, only to stress that they were in the past. "Back then," he would say, "there was no economy class. Economy class was by boat. The trolley dollies were all from good families, since they had to know their customers. And there were no direct flights. To get home from Europe, we had to fly from Paris to Athens to Abu Dhabi to New Delhi to Bangkok and, finally, to Manila. And before landing, there was always a rush to the restrooms, because even after twenty hours of flying, we had to look fabulous when we got off the plane." Today, he said, flying had become too cheap, the airport too democratic. He waxed nostalgic about discovering in his mother's dresser a Pan-Am ticket to New York, priced at a few thousand U.S. dollars, what must have been at that time a veritable fortune. I was surprised to learn that he had recently flown to Singapore on Tiger Airways, a budget airline that used not NAIA but Clark Airport, a former U.S. airbase located in the province of Pampanga and over an hour away from Metro Manila. He said that the flight itself was terrible but that he enjoyed disembarking because the plane and the terminal in Clark were so small that instead of going through a bridging tunnel, passengers had to go down a set of mobile stairs and walk onto the runway. Learning this, he and his friends put on their best coats and their sunglasses and stepped out into the empty airfield with their chins up and chests out, pretending all the while that it was the old days, when arriving in Manila was still an event.

Think of how, in remembering the past life of the traveling bourgeoisie and in condemning the "cheapness" of "gay Manila today," Tony was able to *ground* gay Manila in the undesirable present (the *nowness*) of the city. Think of how "gay Manila today" also attempts to displace cheapness by adopting a spatiotemporal imagination that relocates practices associated with the lower class, particularly those linked to the *bakla,* into a past that has been left behind. Think of how the fabulous past imagined by Tony gets reborn in talk of the present of gay Manila, which he reject but which shares, echoes, and rehearses his fierce rejection of the present of the city.

Think of how the "arrival" of Manila in the gay glob injunction to travel and hence casts trips to the a of vocation and necessity. There were the travel arti that extolled the wonders of cities like Amsterdam were the nights of listless boredom peppered with exclamations of need-ing to "get the fuck out of here." There was the boy who came back from years as an "angel," a dancer in an old New York club called Heaven, and who spoke incessantly about dancing on its ledges and his dreams of going back; the veteran of the scene who boasted about having been to every cir-cuit party held in Asia; the bits of conversation that veered to unexpected places like bathhouses in Cape Town, a gay club in Geneva, a cruisy street in Rio. During fieldwork, I asked many gay men to describe the inhabit-ants of the scene. "We travel more . . ." they would say, but their basis of comparison would often be left a mystery or else would shift nervously from older generations of gay men to straight Manileños, to those othered gay men we did not know and who existed only in the peripheries of the scene, to gay men from other cities across the region, and to gay men from all over the world. Left as an ellipsis or filled in with interchangeable straw men, the basis of comparison seemed, to me at least, to matter less than the claim that we were (or had become) a society of travelers.

Think then of this society as not a society at all but as a scattered set of individuals adrift in the world, at home in the circulation of bodies like the atomized figures thought to populate the centripetal city of the airport-network. Remember, however, that these individuals, among whose numbers I cannot but be counted, are also pushed by an exasperation with Manila and, in that way, are not unlike the abject figures that rush to exit the city via the gates of NAIA, whose looks bear the hallmarks of alter-ity but whose mobility mirrors the oft-dashed hope, carried by even the wealthiest of the city's inhabitants, that elsewhere things are better.

The Borders of Class Difference

Think of NAIA as a site where different temporalities and imaginative geog-raphies come to a head. Think of its location at the margins of the world and near the center of the megacity and remember that this is where the privileged and the marginal all pass through, that this shared space, the site where the borders of the nation are crossed, is also the site where the bor-ders of class difference erected all over the city begin to unravel.

In space-deprived Manila, poverty and privilege converge but are kept apart through the practices of bordering that mark the embodied expe-rience of moving in and inhabiting the third-world city. On the road, privileged motorists hide behind darkly tinted windows and stare blankly ɔrward while blind men and small children knock on the glass, begging change, and vagrant men and women, tanned deeply from years of ʌing the roads, peddle everything from cigarettes and gum to bottled water to peanuts, fish crackers, cowboy hats, visors, toys, mobile phone chargers, guitars, and technicolor rags. The large malls scattered across the city are tiered by class, and those that draw a wide array of shoppers find ways to keep the classes separate: like the Glorietta complex in Makati City, which is split into four quarters, each more expensive than the last, or the Trinoma Mall in Quezon City, which keeps all the upmarket shops at the top levels, lifting its privileged visitors out of the mess on the ground and allowing them to peer down at the masses that crowd the activity center at the basement.

Think of how Manila's nightspots follow a similar logic: how bars and clubs do not last long enough to establish enduring classed reputations, how they come and go in rapid succession, rising and dying following the movements of the fashionable elites, who move base once an establishment begins to attract figures who belong to the wrong networks. Think of the bar where I met Tony, which was guarded not only by the intimidating sight of drooping chandeliers and alcoves that could be closed off for additional privacy but also a list of admissible patrons held by a surly bouncer standing at the nondescript front door next to a metal sign that read, "Members Only." Think of how the gay clubs, though too few and too poor (or too enterprising) to turn away any paying customer, mirrored the spatialization of class difference that marked the rest of the city. There were the VIP lists that contained the names of preferred patrons who got in for free, the clustering of bodies that effected de facto class separation, the disparaging looks and whispers. There was one night when a group of men I was with had the entire second floor of a club sealed off, a request made for no reason other than a faint desire for exclusivity and granted eagerly by the management after they asked for bottles of champagne that the club did not even stock and that one of the bartenders had to frantically search for among the liquor stores several blocks down.

Think of how all these borders between classes cut through the dense thickets of the megacity, like improvised responses to the relentless crumpling together of privilege and marginality, subtle and not-so-subtle interdictions that maneuver and contain bodies along pathways and into spaces that effect the semblance of class order. Think of how these borders extended beyond the public space of roads, malls, nightspots, and into places of dwelling, like the gated villages where most of my informants and I grew up and, in several cases, still reside. Think of these villages as unlike the gated communities that litter the exurban landscapes of North America, Australia, and Latin America, which quell classist fears through the making of separate, idyllic worlds; how the villages in Manila appear instead like bunkers scattered throughout the metropolis, less self-contained communities than walled residential pockets, bubbles located next to major thoroughfares like EDSA or Katipunan Avenue or even shantytowns made of stacked homes of plywood and corrugated iron.[21] Think of how the borders between gated villages and shantytowns penetrate the interior world of privileged homes, which are inhabited not only by its owners but also staffs of domestic workers who live in small rooms hidden behind kitchens, rooms finished with cheaper materials like vinyl tiles that break from polished marble floors and fluorescent bulbs that reveal the secret life of discarded items: old mattresses, old televisions, old electric fans, old plastic saints and glow-in-the-dark crosses, old wardrobes, and old clothes passed on to maids in spates of "generosity." Think of these rooms as but the most literal of the strategies employed to keep the integrity of homes rent by class difference. There were also the separate bathrooms built for the exclusive use of maids; the timetables that had them eating after their employers, waking before them, and sleeping after them; the white, navy, or pastel uniforms that mark maids inside the house and enable the extension of domestic divisions to outside spaces such as churches, restaurants, shopping malls, the city writ large.[22]

Think of these borders—at home, among homes, on the road, and in commercial spaces—as drawn on top of one another like violent scrawls that split the city, spatially and temporally, in microscopic ways that elude the taxonomic and cartographic impulses of academics and urban planners. At times the edges of these borders were readily apparent, producing jarring visual contrasts like the sight of a well-tended garden and a shanty split by a wall topped with broken glass or of luxury cars stuck in traffic next to jeepneys with hand-painted portraits of Jesus or their owners' children. Other times they were barely perceptible, like the divisions that operated at the clubs, which were all but invisible to untrained eyes.

April 20, 2008. Outside the club, Karlo and Adrian were talking to Nick, an Australian who decided to visit Manila precisely because it was an uncommon destination. Karlo and Adrian were trying to explain to Nick the meaning of *jologs*. They were running through a litany of descriptors, pointing out particular articles of clothing like the oversized cardigans and desert scarves that were popular that year. "But just because you wear those things, it doesn't mean you're jologs," Adrian disclaimed. "And not all jologs wear them. Those are just for the *jumping jologs*."

"What are *jumping jologs?*" asked Nick.

"They're jologs who are proud of being jologs." It was Karlo who responded.

"No, that's not it," Adrian exclaimed. "Jumping jologs are jologs who think they're fashionable."

"Then how do you know if someone's jologs if they're not jumping jologs?"

"You can just tell," exclaimed Adrian, exasperated. "I can't explain it."

The rest of the night, Nick kept pointing at people and asking Adrian and Karlo if this or that person was jologs. At one point, they saw him being chatted up by someone they considered jologs. "He'll never get it," Adrian whispered to me while casting an exaggerated sidelong glance at Nick. "But of course," Karlo said, chiming in. "They never get it. Why do you think all those expats hang out with those skanks in Café Havana? It's not because they like cheap girls. It's because they can't tell the difference."

Think of how the failure here to articulate the borders of class difference reveals their very fabulation and exposes them as codes illegible to those unfamiliar with the local order of things; how the disagreement between Karlo and Adrian about what a *jumping jologs* is forestalls the assumption that the logic of the borders erected among Manila's inhabitants is simply hidden beneath local codes that can be systematized, translated, made legible through taxonomies, charts, and economic pyramids; and how their disagreement points instead to borders that are elusive yet palpable, emerging from a particular, nervous system that is nonetheless intelligible to those who *get it*.

Think of how the self-evidence of classed borders in Manila, among privileged Manileños, might be threatened at points of departure. At NAIA, the borders give way; the interdictory force of old glamour functions only as a relic, which is notable only to architectural historians and to those who share in the perverse nostalgia of the privileged. The outflow of laborers, their usurpation of the mantle of mobility, marks the poetic failure of the strategies of spatial containment that orders class difference in the city, for not only does NAIA emerge as a shared space where the underclass is unleashed, but it also evidences the fragility of class borders, exposed as such borders are to the danger of collapsing under the scrutiny of those who cannot get it. This is a danger that, in fact, emerges before even stepping through the doors of NAIA and that follows the privileged into the world at large. Think of the consulates and embassies where elites who have been made nervous by urban legends about middle- and upper-class Filipinos being denied tourist visas stake their difference from would-be labor migrants by making a show of their English language skills and by providing documents that detail their local assets. Think of the anxiety of arrival that reverberates through the lines at passport control, where once again class privilege must be performed under a foreign gaze. There, the privileged effect comfort with the vagaries and routines of travel, projecting the nonchalance of tourists, of those who have nothing to hide and nothing to be ashamed of.[23] Think of the anger that threads through stories of mistaken identity, the "anecdotes . . . retailed about the Europeans equating the word *Filipino* with domestic helpers, or Filipino tourists being asked by OCWs in Singapore shopping malls or Madrid parks if they, too, are on their day off."[24] Such is the danger posed by travel, the threat of the misrecognition (of class) from which emerges both fear and shame, the affective effects of the collapse of class borders, of the occupation of the word *Filipino* by the mobile underclass, prefigured by their occupation of the infrastructures of transnational mobility.

Think of how, at NAIA and at other airports, this fear and shame might turn to resentment, targeted against the underclass who can no longer be walled out and kept at arm's length and with whom the privileged must then share lines and seats, meals and toilets, just as surely as they share the desire to leave and Manila as their origin. In 2007, for instance, I received an e-mail from Alex, an informant who was, at that time, living in New York. The e-mail contained a warning ("Read this if you want to be pissed off by a social climber.") and an article scanned from *People Asia*, a travel piece on Greece, penned by one Malu Fernandez. She writes,

> To save on my ticket, I bravely took an economy class seat on Emirates as recommended by my travel agent. However I forgot that the hub was in Dubai and that majority of the OFWs were stationed there. The duty free shop was overrun with Filipino workers selling cell phones and perfume. Meanwhile, I wanted to slash my wrist at the thought of being trapped in a plane with all of them . . . While I was on the plane (where the seats were so small I had bruises on my legs), my only consolation was the entertainment on the small flat screen in front of me. But it was busted, so I heaved a sigh, popped my sleeping pills and dozed off to the sounds of gum chewing and endless yelling of "HOY! *Kumusta ka na? At taga saan ka?* Domestic helper *ka rin ba?*" Translation: "Hey there! Where are you from? Are you a domestic helper as well?" I thought I had died and God had sent me to my very own private hell.[25]

In recalling both the airport and the airplane as intolerable shared spaces "overrun with Filipino workers," Fernandez rewrites the mobility of the

OFW as "a threatening surround,"[26] a surround that had to be "washed off" upon her arrival at the Ledra Marriott Hotel and that she had to fend off again on the plane ride back to Manila, where she was "trapped like a sardine in a sardine can" with "OFWs smelling of AXE and Charlie cologne" and where her "Jo Malone evaporated into thin air."[27] In Fernandez's account, the airport and the airplane were the sites of a terrifying encounter that imperiled her distinction, contingent as it was on something fleeting: her scent, easily overwhelmed by the smell of otherness.[28]

Think of Fernandez's condescension as emanating from the darkest recess of a bourgeois imaginary besieged by class difference, a condescension and a repulsion rarely voiced in such public ways but which is echoed in the sneers and jokes whispered at NAIA and in the all too common insults launched at those who are "*mukhang* OFW" (those who look like OFWs). Consider, however, Alex's irate response to her account, a response belied by my memories of standing in NAIA with Alex himself and listening to him make snide remarks about another man's "OFW jacket." Consider how Alex's response would later find itself magnified in the onrush of angry middle-class voices that jumped from e-mail exchanges to online diaries to major newspapers and television programs, the outrage over Fernandez's "insensitivity" and "tactlessness" that made her comments seem shocking despite their familiarity.[29]

Think of how Fernandez was denied the very position of privilege she desires and identifies with by Alex's reference to her as "a social climber," by the questions raised online about her class status—"Who is *this* Malu Fernandez?"[30] "Where are all the 'friends' whose names she reverently drops between ill-conceived lines touting superficiality, vanity, and arrogance? Where are the members of the jet-set class who found her deplorable article so funny?"[31]—and by the statements that rendered her as the other of privilege: "Real rich people do not have to insult another social class";[32] "The real rich don't make such remarks—they have class"; "Malu obviously lacks breeding."[33] Think of how these dismissals and questions were voiced alongside epithets directed at the article's accompanying photographs (Fernandez dolled up in a white blouse and giant beads under the title "Fierce and Fabulous," in a black dress with a plunging neckline surrounded by the young men who staffed a beach resort, and in a wrap-around shawl and oversized sunglasses against the backdrop of the Aegean Sea); how people wrote of the thickness of her makeup, her "constipated smile," and most of all her weight, targeted relentlessly in references to her as "swine," "Miss Piggy," "the Abominable Snob-Woman"; and how the virtual lynching rendered her as a grotesque, monstrous exception.

Think of her eventual forced resignation from *People Asia* as the end result of her saying things "better left unsaid."[34] And, finally, think of how this result stemmed equally from her "elitism" as from her very position on the border of class difference, or more accurately still, from her failure to sustain those borders, dramatized by her experience of interclass communion thousands of feet above ground and condemned, flippantly and swiftly, through her relegation to the derided aspirational position of the "social climber." It is this, the precariousness of Fernandez's class position, that became the basis of her mockery. This was made apparent to me by Alex's e-mail and confirmed, a few weeks later, by another gay man, the celebrity blogger Bryanboy, who meted out perhaps the most damning response to Fernandez when he posted an entry that said little about the controversy but which had the seemingly innocuous title, "Malu Fernandez Rides Economy Class."[35]

Fellow Travelers

I saw Alex in New York in the spring of 2008. I was there for a conference and learned that he had decided to stay in the city after turning down an opportunity to study in London. We were catching up over Sunday brunch, trading stories with Jesse, a mutual friend from Manila who was also in town.

"I was at this club the other week," Alex recalled, "and this white guy asked me where I was from. I told him the Philippines. And then you know what he asked? He asked if I was a nurse! Can you believe it?"

"What did you say?" I asked.

"Nothing! I didn't know what to say. I was so mad I just walked out."

"Well," interrupted Jesse, "at least he didn't say 'domestic helper.'"

Here, the OFW takes form, first as the nurse and then as the domestic helper. One is a new addition to the master list of migrant figures that populates the modern global imaginary and the other an old familiar.[36] Each has its own history, its own politics, but here they are joined by a stroke of disavowal that invokes the abject place of the Filipino in the global circulation of bodies, or better, the story of the nation in an era of mobile labor, which haunts privileged Manileños whenever they leave the privileged pockets of the city. The nation or the "sensation of becoming Filipino" that looms large in the transnational travels of all Filipinos is here mediated by the image of fellow travelers, of the laborers who had come before and whose differences from one another cannot be fully apprehended through the gaze of those who are loathe to see the

underclass contained at home scattered in every corner of the wc
seared into the global imagination as *the* representatives of the natiᵤᵤ..

Still, the temptation to heap figure upon figure onto a pile of othered
fellow travelers does not make the emergence of the two figures in my conversation with Alex and Jesse incidental. The male nurse and the female
domestic helper are both born of the nation's role in performing the global
work of care and, in that way, are tied to the generalized state of gendered
subservience that threatens the dreams of global belonging, which persist
in the privileged quarters of the city.[37]

Alex's story about the club and about the speechlessness that overcame
him when his confession of national belonging was returned as an accusation, as an attempt to *place* him in the global division of labor, reminds
me of the travel stories of my other informants. These were proud stories
of lone travels to gay spaces around the world told at once as unremarkable parts of life under the bright lights and as intermittent yet wondrous
reprieves from life in the third-world city. Just as Alex's night at the club
was interrupted by the question of his origin and, hence, by the ubiquitous
specter of the labor migrant, however, the stories of my other informants
were interrupted by my questions about their encounters with migrant
Filipinos in bars, clubs, and bathhouses overseas. There were some, they
would say, but they did not speak to them. "I saw a few in Hong Kong,"
one told me. "I think they were nurses." Another told me that during a
year he spent in London, he met only one Filipino, a nurse he became
friends with online. Once, he said, the nurse introduced him to a local
white man at a club, whom he ended up sleeping with a few nights later.
When the nurse found out, he asked my informant to return the favor and
introduce him to some of the white men he had pictures with on a social
networking website. "But I couldn't do it," he told me. "He was, you
know, a nurse. He was too provincial."

During those conversations, I never had to ask why the nurse was an
acquaintance not to be made or one that needed to be hidden. In Manila,
nursing schools were emerging in large numbers, popping up along major
thoroughfares, often with large billboards advertising pathways to overseas work. So frenzied is the rush to fill the global demand for nurses
that a special report from the *Manila Times* describes a part of Manila
where a number of training centers are located as an "export processing
zones for nurses," a space where dreams of working abroad are mined
and courses like "Transcultural Nursing" make clear the outward trajectory of the industry.[38] Nursing education has become a way out and
all over the city there are stories of doctors, accountants, teachers, jour-
nalists, clerks, secretaries, and government employees rushing to enroll

as "second-coursers," willingly or even eagerly retraining, overwriting their careers at home in order to find work in foreign lands.[39] Inscribed within this broader story of mass migration are the anecdotes of gay men who, drawn to the prospects of life abroad, have begun to take on a central role in performing the global work of care, not only as licensed nurses but as paraprofessional careworkers, tending to the ill and elderly everywhere from private homes across America to institutions in Israel.[40] My informants' encounters with nurses might be read, in this context, as encounters with figures that embody the slippage between outward mobility and downward mobility. The national-cum-racial sameness that binds them to such figures is what erodes the borders painstakingly policed at home.

Gay spaces overseas thus become points of intersection. They serve as sites where those who dream of belonging in gay globality come face-to-face with the nightmare of their origin, their Filipinoness, embodied by the figures kept at bay by the class borders that order Manila. Still, the danger of mistaken identity has to do with more than just the collapse of class borders in the gaze of those who do not get it. It also combines the fear of downward mobility with the threat of feminization—a threat that is always already a part of the racial politics of gay spaces in the West (wherein all Asian men are feminized) but which is heightened here by the anxieties that surround the so-called feminization of migrant labor, a process recalled by Jesse when he raises the specter of the domestic helper as the worst of all possible comparisons, as the figure that genders the class politics of mobility.

Though the domestic helper is only one among many migrant Filipino figures, it is her profile that has become *the* profile of the Filipino labor migrant. Both at home and abroad, her travails have become a source of anxiety. The rehearsal of her suffering, or rather, the constant display of her suffering body in news reports and fictional and semifictional texts, have dramatized for a national audience the place of the nation in the world.[41] Her ubiquity marks her out as the dominant representative of the nation, allowing the people "to be manifest to themselves by staging the physics of their absence" and offering up a startling "convergence of violating images: the image of the destroyed, drained, destitute laboring body of the nation . . . the image of the violated, sullied domestic body, and the image of the shattered and scattered national body abroad."[42] Often, this convergence of images leads to a passionate identification, to an outpouring of grief and anger that swells and bursts in moments of collective mourning and protest like the tears and placards that greet returning corpses.[43] At the same time, however, the equivalence the domestic helper engenders "between Filipino as the name of a sovereign people and Filipino as the generic term for designating a subservient class" is also met with disidentification by those who are enfranchised, particularly when traveling, when the equivalence moves beyond the realm of metaphor and becomes "real." Jesse, for instance, responds to the offense caused by the stranger encountered by Alex by raising the image of the domestic helper, a specter seen as more abject than the nurse.[44] Malu Fernandez recoils, hides in pill-induced sleep from the echoes of the question, "Are you a domestic helper as well?" Another columnist, Emil Jurado, confesses that in Hong Kong, he is "embarrassed as a Filipino to see (domestic workers) spreading out mats at public places . . . and eating with their hands. Some of them . . . manicuring and pedicuring their compatriots." He points out that the domestic workers are now banned from congregating at the Landmark Mall because of complaints and claims, poignantly and sincerely, that his heart "bleeds" when he sees them "acting the way they do."[45]

The feelings of shame that bubble from the knowledge that Filipinoness and abject femininity are corporealized in the same figure are here linked directly to the spatial politics of class. The ownership taken by domestic helpers of public places overseas marks their entrance into global space, their hypervisibility making clear their occupation of the sign "Filipino" within the global imaginary. It is this, the ubiquity and mobility of the domestic helper, that sublimates the physical violence that they are all too often reported to endure. The force of shame subordinates the violence borne by domestic helpers to "the violence of the image they project of the nation abroad," a violence that is also figured as physical for the elite: it catches Alex's tongue, causes Fernandez to bruise her knees, and makes Jurado's heart bleed. Confronted by this violence, elite Filipino travelers have taken to manufacturing distance, to constructing physical, symbolic, and discursive separations from domestic helpers.[46] For decades, privileged Filipinos in the diaspora have attired themselves in ways that emphasize their higher-class status, spoken out against every reference in the mainstream media that defines Filipinos *as* maids, and learned to navigate cities in ways that elude the congregations of domestic helpers, avoiding the malls, parks, and churches frequented by the laboring women who have become "the new bio-geographical territories of the nation."[47]

Refuge from the unsolicited company of the domestic helper comes, in part, by way of the very gender and class positions they occupy. The former is evident in the more direct danger posed by the domestic helper to the class status of middle- and upper-class Filipino women, the latter in the distinction often made between "unskilled" or "semiskilled" workers and professionals.[48] The appearance of the nurse in gay spaces thus challenges the idea that national abjection can be contained in the bodies of laboring women and the spaces they occupy. The figure of the gay man who becomes a migrant careworker not only literalizes the ability of the mark of femininity to cut through the dichotomy of sex, but it also stands on the uncertain line between forms of migrant labor, for the nurse seen and avoided by my informants in gay spaces overseas cannot be disarticulated from the umbrella of carework that covers not only those who are licensed professionals working in hospitals but also the full range of laborers drawn in by the global care industry, including male domestic workers, personal caregivers for the elderly, and nursing home attendants. Indeed, the fact that my informants could identify the migrants they encountered as "nurses" without verification, without even an introduction, reveals the breadth of meanings covered by the term *nurse*, its emergence as a catchall name given to those conationals spotted in gay spaces who are seen not as fellow itinerants but as vessels that carry and embody the links between femininity, lower-class status, Filipinoness, and mobility into the sites of gay globality. The fact that nursing is viewed in Manila not simply as an occupation for the underclass but as an occupation taken up by familiar faces (old schoolmates, acquaintances, and friends of friends) who cross class borders in order to leave makes the nurse all the more threatening. The possibility of being mistaken for a nurse causes uneasiness not only because it foregrounds shared nationality and recalls the class and gender meanings always already embedded in it but because such misrecognition is not as implausible as Alex's outrage might imply. The figure of the nurse and the downward mobility often attributed to it speaks to the uncertainty of class position in Manila (and globally) and, consequently, to the vigilance with which the borders of class difference must be guarded. Put differently, the specter of the labor migrant in the form of the nurse poses a threat not simply because of what the nurse is but because it offers a portrait of what the privileged might become, a depiction of how class boundaries collapse in the act of travel.

> *September 30, 2007.* Three years ago, I had a conversation with Eric about a trip he took to London in November of 2003. He was telling me about how he had broken away from the group of friends he was traveling with in order to explore the gay bars and clubs in Soho. I remember that his story began with the same air of admiration I would later find in the stories of other gay men, with praise for the bigger clubs, the better music, and the more attractive men. But I also

remember asking him about the racial composition at the clubs and the fact that though it was *"diverse,"* the different men stuck mostly to their own. "It was," he said, "like the world map on the dance floor." He told me that he ended up meeting a group of Filipinos at one of the clubs and that he had gone home with one of them, a nurse. Back then nurse migration by gay men had not yet reached fever pitch. Schools and training centers had yet to emerge in large numbers across Manila and there were fewer stories about Filipino nurses being spotted in gay clubs the world over. I thought little of the fact that the man Eric went home with was a nurse. Eric himself seemed unbothered by it, though the fact that the man's occupation merited a mention reveals how, even then, the nurse was a curious figure seldom engaged at home.

Last night, he told me that he saw the nurse again, this time at a gay club in Manila. "I was at Bed," he said, "and he grabbed my wrist and asked if I remembered him."

"What did you say?" I asked.

"Nothing. I told him no and left."

"Why did you do that?"

After a long pause, he shrugged and said, "I don't know. It was instinct, I guess."

CHAPTER FIVE

White Noise and the Shock of Racial Shame

You are afraid of your anguish . . . you are afraid of noise, of this noise rising in the silence of our organs. It writhes, howls, breaks loose, insane. Keep the noise down.

—Michel Serres, *Genesis*

The last chapter ended with the story of Eric, who entered a gay club in London only to come face-to-face with the fact of his difference, his otherness, his unbelonging in gay globality. There, in a distant city, on "a world map on a dance floor," he saw men sticking to "their own" and found himself going home with a man who represented "home." Faced with the exclusionary logics that govern gay life overseas, Eric was able to open a gap in the borders of the bright lights scene, to occupy a space that cut across the boundaries of class difference. Eric must have known, however, that this gap could not hold for long and that it could only be opened away from the third-world city. Indeed, when Eric unexpectedly encountered the same Filipino man at home, in Manila, he found himself pulling away, feigning ignorance, and willfully forgetting their contact overseas. Under Manila's bright lights, Eric felt no desire or compulsion to wedge a gap in the solidity of the scene's borders; his *instincts* were attuned to the shifts in notions of sameness and difference, affinity and disaffinity, and belonging and unbelonging that accompany movements across local and global space and time.

Throughout the previous chapters, I have tried to shed light on the scene's shifting borders, to reveal, if partially, how these borders are shaped by the broader politics of class and gender, privilege and mobility, and aspiration and fantasy that operate in Manila. In many ways,

Eric's story offers but another example of how the boundaries of the scene emerge through what I referred to, at the beginning of this book, as micropolitical interpretive moves: *instinctive* responses to the imperatives of emplaced hierarchies, practices that appear less calculated than felt. Eric's story about London, however, also hints at how the dream of movement that underpins the scene is brought to a halt—how, when the locally privileged gay subject attempts to literally bridge the gap between *here* and *there*, he himself comes across unfamiliar borders that cannot be crossed. Like the borders of Manila's bright lights scene that Eric participates in establishing, the boundaries that greet him "outside" are not readily intelligible. Indeed, while they might appear, at first glance, as the effects of the *racialized* politics of gay life in global cities like London, they also take form, in Eric's imagination, as the reproduction of *national* lines on the dance floor, what he describes as "a world map." In this final chapter, I want to address the fraught relationship between race and nation evoked by Eric's metaphor. More specifically, I explore, in somewhat speculative terms, how the national–colonial past inflects affective responses to racial protocols that disrupt visions of gay globality.

In some ways, the question of race has been present throughout the preceding chapters. It has been hovering over stories of images and signs that are brought into the city from afar. It lies latent in the master narratives of modernity that inform ways of navigating and transforming the gay cityscape. In chapter 3, I drew distinctions between the experiences of the Filipino gay diaspora and of those who stay "at home" and suggested that what enables the sublimation of class investments, the foregrounding of national belonging, and the concomitant recuperation of "local" practices in the migrant experience is the encounter with race-based exclusion in gay spaces overseas. I want to return to and further complicate this point here. If, after all, one takes into account the stories of transnational travel I narrated in the previous chapter, then it becomes impossible to cast the men who inhabit Manila's bright lights scene simply as figures who stay at home. Eric's story makes it clear that even those whose movements out of Manila are fleeting and temporary come into contact with the fact of their otherness. They, too, in Frantz Fanon's terms, come "into the world" with their spirits "filled with the desire to attain to the source of the world" only to find themselves turned into objects "in the midst of other objects."[1] Indeed, all those who dare cross the borders of home and enter global space must face first encounters with racialization. These encounters, I suggest, can be imagined as moments of standstill, as abrupt pauses in the outward and forward movement toward the global/modern, or as times of "tense stasis" wherein the traveler finds his journey halted, his participation barred, and his mind reeling in an attempt to make sense of the grounds of his exclusion.[2]

During such moments, Manila's colonial past catches up with the would-be global subject. Indeed, if encounters with racialization in global cities can be considered moments of shock, it is not simply because such encounters are forceful and unexpected but because different racial orders operate in different sites and emerge out of histories that resist generalization. For those who come from Manila (or the Philippines, more generally), race is a minimally intelligible category, a sign loaded with uncertainties that can be traced to the early years of the anticolonial, nationalist project. It is in recognition of the enduring impact of colonial rule and of its lasting effects on understandings of race that I turn briefly here to an older, parallel story of travel—namely, to the movements of the colonial elite (the early nationalists), who journeyed to the colonial metropole also to find themselves recognized as others and cast out of the world they hoped to enter. The pained journeys of these men—the spiritual forefathers of the urban elites I write of here—are not only echoed in present-day travels. They were also the moves that led to the emergence of the name "Filipino" as an uneasy means of designating both race and nation and, ultimately, to the erasure of race from Philippine public discourse. These ambiguities and silences are the conditions that set the stage for the shock experienced by Eric, among others; they explain, in some measure, why experiences of racialization in gay spaces overseas are interpreted through geopolitical lenses that recall the place of the nation in the world. Put differently, I want to suggest here that it is not enough to acknowledge the fact that gay spaces in the imagined centers of the gay globe are raced. In order to shed light on how exclusionary protocols are experienced by gay men who travel from Manila, and other places like it, it is necessary to reimagine race itself as a sign that travels, a historical–political construction filtered through incommensurate interpretive frames, and a contested way of organizing difference in the wake of mobility, postcoloniality, and globalization.

Though the ambiguity of the sign "Filipino" affects all those who identify with it, it is clear that the way its meaning transforms in the face of the racial politics of a space such as a gay club in London is not uniform. For those in the diaspora, we might say that the experience of racialization serves as a starting point for the painful process of being *fixed* into a racial category, of being *sealed* into what Fanon called "objecthood," and also, as in Martin Manalansan's account, the precipitous point that jumpstarts the painful struggles of diasporic subjects to "stake out their own spaces" within "the topography of race and desire [of] the global city."[3]

For the inhabitants of the bright lights scene whose travels are brief and fleeting, the experience of racialization does not congeal into a point of identification. Rather, it is preserved as "crystallized shock": a never fully comprehensible instance that engenders a range of impromptu strategies, including Eric's momentary passage across borders of class difference, as well as the disavowal of national-cum-racial sameness with (and class distinction from) figures such as nurses and domestic workers that was apparent in the stories of my other informants.[4]

There are other examples, other means of coping with the shock-effect of racialization. I recall some of these later in this chapter. I am less interested here, however, in detailing these myriad examples than in shedding light on how the experience of racialization is brought back home; how it leaves a mark, akin to a wound, that is hidden in shame and shrouded in silence. Thus, like Eric, I come back full circle to the city. Eric's second encounter with the Filipino man he met and slept with in London, I suggest, is indicative of how shock is absorbed: how the moment in which the dream of global belonging is interrupted, unremembered, and masked by silence, a shrug, a pulling away. Indeed, whenever I spoke to my informants in Manila about their travels to gay spaces overseas, accounts of race-based exclusion and of the strategies employed in the face of such exclusion were never volunteered and were often hidden beneath conventional accounts of the wonders of travel. Encounters with racialization were recalled and narrated only when I asked directly about them or when conversations stumbled upon them by chance, and even then, retellings were marked by gaps and hesitations. I remember downcast eyes, pregnant pauses, stuttering—the telltale markers of shame or the feeling of being undone and of the "somersaulting movement of remembrance and amnesia" that accompanies shock.[5]

Shock turned to shame turned to silence. This is the series of affective responses that follows in the wake of encounters with one's difference through racialization and that becomes apparent when one follows the movements of those who inhabit the bright lights scene out of the city and back. The fact that such encounters cannot be articulated or are difficult to articulate, in other words, cannot be attributed to a single cause. Rather, it is the effect of the joint operation of the muting force of shame, the absence of a universal discourse on race, and the "stasis of anticipation and reflection" produced by shock.[6] Here, however, silence appears not only as the response of those who return to Manila with a sense of their otherness and of the marginal position they are fated to occupy in the imagined centers of gay globality, but it is also what sustains the dreams of globalness and modernness that animate the bright lights scene. What

silence accomplishes is the masking of the exclusionary racial log
which such dreams are predicated. Silence veils the impossibility of entering gay globality; it makes it appear within reach, accessible to all those
who are able to move past the borders of the third-world city. Ultimately,
then, silence emerges here as a manifestation of how complicity operates
among those who are (globally) marginal and (locally) privileged. It is, at
once, a feeling-full response to the memory of becoming other and a constitutive act that sustains and invigorates the never-to-be-fulfilled promise
of global belonging.[7]

Imagined as a promise, being global might be thought of, in Serresian
terms, as a message, one that is continuously being channeled by the other
mechanisms I have written of in the previous chapters: the circulating
signs that enter the city, the spaces where those signs are materialized and
that stand as pockets of the "first world in the third world," the magazines
and websites where claims are made about the "arrival" of Manila in the
now of gay globality. Correspondingly, race might be thought of as a form
of noise. It is an interruption in the transmission of the message; it is a dis-
ruption of the dream; it is what is not communicated; it is just there, the
part of difference that remains excluded.[8] As Jacques Attali once noted,
"Noise is violence: it disturbs. To make noise is to interrupt transmission,
to disconnect, to kill."[9]

The bright lights scene can, concomitantly, be reimagined here as a
form extracted from noise. Indeed, we have already seen how the scene
emerges in Manila through the exclusion of noise in its various forms.
There is the speeding through the city, the relocation of the din of the
streets to the "outside" of protective vehicles such as automobiles. There
is the flight to sequestered spaces, to the quiet of desert-like spaces such as
the Global City. There is the deafness to the *bakla* language of *swardspeak*
and the effort to shut out the chatter of OFWs on airplanes. I have shown
how such manifestations of noise disrupt the movements of the scene and
also how the scene manages these disruptions by exteriorizing them—
that is, by erecting and reerecting borders that establish an "inside," a
space where the dream of being global might endure. The noise of race, I
suggest, poses the stiffest challenge to the imagineering of a bright lights
scene, for the otherness to which it points cannot simply be exteriorized.
It is not akin to the noise of raucous run-down districts that can be cast
as "someplace else" or of figures such as the bakla or the OFW who can
be read as other through the lens of orders of class and gender difference.
Rather, it marks the difference of those who inhabit the bright lights scene.
It points to an otherness that resides inside or to what Michel Serres might
describe, aptly, as the "noise within."[10]

Race in Motion: A Detour

Rising under the ostensibly unifying banner of same-sex desire, gay spaces in the West (and elsewhere) are nonetheless riven by racial fractures that run deep. This observation is not new. Stories of race-based exclusion are well documented and have been inserted as correctives into the recent and not-so-recent histories of sites such as clubs and bars, as well as political spaces such as activist organizations and the virtual corners of the Internet where gay men (and other queers) meet.[11] Such accounts have put under question the implicit whiteness of signs and categories such as "gay." They have made visible the experiences of those who are marked as racialized others and thus have no access to the symbolic and material forms of capital that are privileged in gay spaces.[12] Still, the critical project of revealing the operation of racial politics in spaces such as dance clubs carries within it the risk of taking "black," "Asian," and other categories that are habitually used to name race in Anglophone worlds as unproblematic means of organizing difference worldwide. At the least, there lies, in attempts to account for race-based exclusion, the danger of glossing over the fact that the very grounds of exclusion are not always readily intelligible to those who are excluded or of assuming that all those who find themselves in a particular time and place operate with a shared script from which common knowledge of race emerges.

Race, Minkah Makalani reminds us, does not "translate easily across historical and national contexts."[13] Racialization is a divergent process. Race "inhabits" place; it coheres as part of structured hierarchies, but always necessarily in relation to methods of domination that vary across time and space.[14] For Arun Saldanha, the locality of race means that it is best understood as a "chain of contingency, in which the connections between its constitutive components are not given, but are made viscous through local attractions."[15] It is a tenuous unity, a substance that is neither liquid nor solid or an "immanent heterogeneity" that emerges out of "the movements between human bodies, things, and their changing environments."[16] Thought as such, whiteness, for instance, appears as the effect of "sticky connections between property, privilege, and paler skin."[17] It possesses no essence, but there is "a relative fixity that inheres in all the 'local pulls' of its many elements in flux."[18] Race, in this way, can be seen as something "creative"; it is "constantly morphing, now disguised as sexual desire, now as *la mission civilatrice*, all the while weaving new elements in its wake."[19] Correspondingly, the spatiality of race is not about the separations between races but about how subjects emerge out of or enter into racial formations that are themselves the products of chains of connections forged between bodies, spaces, and discourses. This is not to say that subjects are bound to racial formations that are unchanging and discrete but to say that when subjects travel they nonetheless remain tethered to the long-standing racial formations that operate in their places of origin. Transnational movement can, in other words, be seen not simply as the experience of becoming an "object in the midst of other objects" but also as the experience of inhabiting multiple racial formations at the same time.[20]

In Manila, race rarely enters public discourse. There are no official forms with tick boxes next to a list of racial or ethnic categories. There are no campaigns waged on the seemingly steady and familiar grounds of racial identity politics.[21] Even the conflicts that were once fought under rubrics of racial difference—from the ongoing war with Moro separatists in the south to the intermittent battles between landowners and peasant farmers—have been recast as quarrels based on faith and class.[22] Here, perhaps more than anywhere, race operates without congealing into easily delineable categories or being straightforwardly named, claimed, and mapped onto bodies.

Here, the somatic and cultural differences oft linked and tied to notions of race remain unsystematized. Differences persist but are inscribed within or are in excess of the unstable signifier "Filipino," a name that conflates race and nation and that possesses meanings that shift from one moment to the next.[23] Ask people here about their race and the answers you will get are diverse and contradictory. In the absence of any official or popular conception of race, people draw on overlapping and often incommensurate ideas about descent and parentage, culture, geography, and history in order to account for who or what they are. Some people simply say they are Filipino, while others claim that Filipino is a construct that has nothing to do with race. Some say that all Filipinos are mixed, in recognition of bodies that are difficult to classify and of presumed and undocumented histories of (colonial) relationships often described as miscegenation.[24] Those attuned to the racial categories adopted in the West say that Filipinos are Asians, summoning a regional imagination that sits uneasily with the long history of Filipino disidentification (and exclusion) from and indifference to cultural notions of Asianness.[25] Others say that Filipinos are Malay, a claim drawn from primary school textbooks that have long been challenged by historians and that is routinely unsettled now by the separation of "Filipino" and "Malay" under the classificatory orders of places like Malaysia and Singapore where many Filipinos live and travel.[26] Whatever response or explanation people might proffer when faced with the question of race, it is bound with few exceptions, to be prefaced with pauses and looks of surprise and qualified with confessions of uncertainty. People say that they haven't thought about it, that it's complicated and difficult to explain.

You might describe Manila, then, as a space where notions of race remain inchoate. You can imagine it as a space where race appears only as part of pained efforts to make one's self known using grammars of difference borrowed from someplace else. This is not to say that Manila has no racial politics of its own or that it can somehow be likened to a utopian pre- or postracial space. Race operates here, but in ways that are difficult to articulate. The children of working-class emigrants return, courted with promises of stardom and celebrity, and desire and power become palpable in their performance of whiteness as style.[27] Mundane scenes of violence erupt in schoolyards, where children with darker skin are likely to face insults. Skin-lightening products fly off shelves, as in other parts of Asia, but here they evoke notions of wealth attached to the figure of the mestizo/a.[28] If, in these instances, racial politics appears as a half-glimpsed logic that remains unnamed, it is not simply because notions of race have not mattered enough in Manila and the Philippines to engender hardwired systems of racial difference but because the racial politics of Filipinoness is marked by gaps, ambiguities, silences, and excesses.

Indeed, the relationship of race and Filipinoness is a historical problem that remains unresolved, one that has appeared, alternately throughout the last three centuries, as an ignorable puzzle buried in the background of national(ist) thought and an urgent identity crisis that demands immediate attention. There is no room here for a full account of the long and still underexamined history of racial politics in Manila and the Philippines, but consider, for instance, how the elite, Europeanized mestizo youth known as the *ilustrados* (literally, the "enlightened") transformed the term *Filipino* from a name given to Spaniards born in the Philippine islands to a point of identification for those who possessed a "fatal attachment to the *patria*" at the tail end of Spanish rule in the late nineteenth century.[29] Fueled by a classed desire for assimilation (and, later, separation), the ilustrados plumbed European discourses of racial science in search of a glorious past. They took to colonial ethnology in pursuit of ancestry and racial purity, internalizing in the process georacial master narratives that cast the islands as a tabula rasa, an empty stage gradually populated by distinct migrating races, each more civilized than the last.[30] Set within the interpretive space of such narratives and animated by the injuries of racial degradation, the elites' pursuit of origins gave rise, paradoxically, to racist beliefs about how native Filipinos were descended from a Malayan race whose ancient civilization and mild morals made them distinct from the savages who inhabited the mountains. In the bourgeois, protonational imaginary of the colonized elite, a nascent racial order emerged and a literal and figurative distance was carved between the lowlands and the highlands, modern and backward cultures, and between those who had the capacity for (Hispanicized) civilization and those mired in an incontrovertible primitivism.

Think of "Filipino," then, as a name initially grounded on a racist myth. Consider how this myth was mobilized in the service of classed aspirations; how it bolstered claims that the local elites, having come from a people who had once established an ancient civilization, were not unlike the colonial rulers whose own claim to modernity predicated on their status as the last and final arrivals remained unchallenged. Like today's privileged travelers, however, the ilustrados found that their claims to superiority could not be sustained across locations. When the ilustrados journeyed to Madrid, the colonial metropole where they thought they belonged, they found that the class-cum-racial borders they drew between themselves and their internal but externalized others were invisible to the colonial rulers from whom they sought recognition. In 1887, anger broke out among the ilustrados in Madrid when "mountain tribes" from the Philippine islands were brought to the "motherland" to be displayed. The ilustrados resented the fact that "savages" were made to embody the Philippines; they complained that the exposition did not "represent those Islands with dignity or, at least, with decency," that it showed "nothing but the backwardness of the Philippines," and that "everything modern, related to its progress, [had] not been brought to the Exposition."[31] A year before the exhibit, Jose Rizal, the national hero, lamented news that the exhibit would not be "an exposition of the Philippines, but, rather, an exposition of Igorrotes, who will play music, cook, sing, and dance."[32] What Rizal and his ilustrado peers wanted was an industrial exposition that featured Filipino workers and weavers—that is, the *progressive* aspects of the Philippines with which they identified.[33]

At times, the blurring of the imagined lines between the "races" that resided in the Philippine islands prompted gestures of inclusiveness. There were articles written by ilustrados that described the persons on display as "our brothers" and as "compatriots" and "countrymen."[34] More often, however, the collapse of racial and class borders was taken as an affront that required a reassertion of racial difference. In an article that echoes Fanon's painful account of being hailed as a "negro," the ilustrado writer Antonio Luna complained that in Madrid, young women stared at him and muttered, "Jesus! What a hideous sight! It's an Igorot!"[35] For Fanon, the shock of being hailed served as a moment of "discovery," as the instance that precipitated his recognition of the "fact of (his) blackness."[36] For Luna, being named an Igorot did not point to the fact of his racial difference per se but to the ignorance of Madrileños and their failure to make important distinctions: "To these people," he wrote, "Chinese, Igorots, and Filipinos are one and the same."[37] Another ilustrado, Graciano López Jaena, would later cite Luna's article and make the further claim that Filipinos all across Spain were being "shamelessly mortified" with epithets such as "*negros*" and "*igorotes*," names that were used to designate the peoples the ilustrado saw as others.[38]

Here, the instability of the racial categories lodged in the bourgeois imaginary of the ilustrados becomes apparent. Anxiety emerges out of the inability to secure the racial-cum-class boundaries of Filipinoness in the face of encounters with the center's exclusionary racial order. This anxiety, however, was caused by not only the invisibility of the distinctions between the ilustrados and their others but also the persistence of ethnolinguistic and regional differences among the ilustrados in Madrid. There were the somatic differences that came with their disparate mestizo lineages. There were the doubts cast about the very status of Malay as a race. The exact relationship between the multiracial Filipinos and the ancient Malayans was never directly confronted.[39] Rather, the putative racial ancestry of Filipinos was left in the background of protonational imagination and preserved as part of the broad racist logic that allowed the ilustrados to distance themselves from the "savages" of the mountains. At the same time, however, social marginality in the colonial metropolis turned "Filipino" into a catchall name for an emerging collective identity, a rallying point for all those who were thought to possess a capacity for progress but who could not, in fact, be thought of under the classificatory systems of racial science as members of a single race. "Filipino," in other words, emerged during this period as a sign that simultaneously hearkened to a strict racial structure and enabled the erasure of racial difference.

The ambiguity surrounding race and Filipinoness persisted after the end of Spanish colonial rule. At the start of the twentieth century, the Americans took over the task of ordering the racial differences of the Philippines' inhabitants. Technologies such as the census saw the people of the islands split into twenty-five linguistic groups, differentiated according to five skin colors ranging from black to white and distinguished based on types of citizenship and locations of birth.[40] Under the rubric of "benevolent assimilation," systems of American tutelage—of "white love"—were set in place.[41] Close and frequent relations with colonial subjects were seen, not only as a means of "winning hearts and minds," but as a "gift" that could erase the differences that marked the islands and turn the "Filipino" into "a numerous and homogenous English-speaking race, exceeding in intelligence and capacity all other peoples of the tropics."[42] "Filipino" became the name for a race in the making. American (and native) social scientists contended that Filipinos were a people that were "on the move, racially" and that they could one day become Caucasoid or white.[43] The cultural "gifts" of colonization (then indistinguishable from theories of racial transition) were registered in photographs of the natives' inevitable transformation under American tutelage: there were, for instance, "pictures of savages turned into soldiers; prisoners turned into obedient citizens; lazy natives turned into productive laborers; and local elites turned into national politicians already destined for monumentalization by future generations."[44]

The object of elite desire would thus shift. Notions of Hispanicization and racial ancestry receded as bases for claims to civilization and American ideals of democracy, discipline, and secularism rushed in to take their place. Co-opted swiftly into the colonial democracy, the mestizo elites became the privileged recipients of white love, the figures to whom the promise of an independence to come was directly addressed and who stood at the helm of the (re)emerging, administratively unified, and transitioning Filipino nation/race. This shift in the form and face of colonial rule and in the trajectory of imagined movements toward progress was mirrored in the changing direction of actual movements out of Manila and the Philippines. No longer confined to elite journeys to Europe, *transnational* travel increasingly took the form of working-class migration to the United States, particularly to the West Coast.[45] Traveling as U.S. nationals from the 1910s to the 1930s, Filipino workers arrived in states such as California only to discover the harsh discrepancy between the dream of America disseminated through the public school system across the islands and the harsh reality of Filipino reception in America. Indeed, accounts of this period are rife not only with images of disillusionment, homelessness, poverty, murder, beatings, and riots but also again with confusion around the race of Filipinos.[46] In Los Angeles, for instance, where antimiscegenation laws were being crafted in response to panics over the sexuality of migrants, Filipinos were the last set of Asian immigrants to be classified, as the state had difficulty deciding if they were, in fact, part of the "Mongoloid" race.[47]

From independence in 1946 onward, the question of race would lose its prominence in national thought. In the context of newfound sovereignty and in the absence of a colonizers' classificatory gaze, official discourse took on expressly nationalist terms. Internal racial differences were deemphasized, owing in part, no doubt, to American efforts to reconceive the

Filipino as a transitional race homogenously modeled after American whiteness and to the national elite's desire to efface the mestizo heritage that set them apart from the peoples for whom they wished to speak. Attempts to discern the nature, origin, and fissures of the Filipino race all but ceased, even as vestiges of colonial racial politics persisted in the form of systems of privilege and notions of progress, as in the class divides between the descendants of the mestizo landed elite and their workers, the hierarchies that emerged around English language skills, and the persistent desire for American-style modernity. By the end of the twentieth century, references to a Filipino race had largely disappeared from public discourse, though the ambiguity and confusion it signals regarding the relationship of nation and race can still sometimes be readily seen. Every morning, for instance, children in school recite the "Panatang Makabayan" (pledge of allegiance) and profess love not for country or nation (*bayan*) but for "my race" (*aking lahi*).[48]

Meanwhile, the numbers of emigrants continued to swell in the wake of independence. In part, the growth in emigration can be accounted for by structural shifts orchestrated from above, including the Marcos administration's adoption of labor exportation as a dual-purpose policy that simultaneously rid the nation of its excess bodies and ensured a steady stream of foreign currency. There is no doubt, however, that the reasons for the departure of millions cannot be reduced to the cold language of government incentives and legal passage. There are motives for leaving that are harder to pin down and that can only be accessed through individual life narratives, which connect in roundabout ways to postcolonial deprivation and desire, the enshrinement of elsewheres as sites of the good life, and fraught dreams of outward and upward mobility. Whatever form the travels of Filipinos take, however, they are bound together by their origins in a postcolonial nation where race is unnamed. More than just the crossing of national borders, they are movements across the boundaries of racial orders. Indeed, the accounts of misrecognition and the uncertainties about race that were so much a part of travel narratives from eras past are echoed in present-day anecdotes of journeys to distant sites. There are the stories of Filipino travelers not knowing whether to check Asian or Pacific Islander on government forms. There are the countless, incompatible tales of being unexpectedly mistaken for Mexican or Hawaiian, Chinese or Japanese, or even Spanish or Italian. In cities across North America, second-generation migrants negotiate the thorny barriers and links that split and connect "Filipino American" and "Asian American." And on the Internet, Filipinos the world over engage in pop psychology and amateur sociology in attempts to pin down the race of Filipinos.

All the stories of travel and migration, all the casual theorizing about the nature of Filipinoness, offer glimpses into the confusion that surrounds encounters with (and emergence out of) racial orders that are unable to account for the "Filipino." They are, collectively, the fallout of a national history in which notions of race are constructed and abandoned, established then forgotten. How does this history haunt the narratives I am concerned with here, the touristic tales of men bound to a scene steeped in local privilege and faith in a global modernity to come or imagined as already *here*? You might say, in the first instance, that history repeats itself. You might see, in the accounts of disidentification with figures such as domestic workers, vestigial traces of the anger and shame felt by ilustrados who resented having to share a name with those they considered other and whose presence cast doubt on their capacity for progress. Or you could say that colonial racial hierarchies have laid the groundwork for the imaginative and social field in which the men who inhabit the bright lights scene find themselves othered: that the "epidermalization of inferiority" that was an integral element in the logic of colonialism is recapitulated in the microaggressions of everyday racism in the West.[49]

The repetitions of history, however, are always necessarily repetitions in difference. If the mark of race was, for colonial subjects, a category under constant construction, and if, as I have suggested, notions of race did not congeal and were instead put under erasure, then for the mobile elites of whom I speak, encounters with racial difference are encounters with "difference without a concept."[50] Race is, more than anything, a concealed part of social memory, a hidden sign with meanings that interrupt feelings of global belonging and that erupt in unexpected disenchantments that are met with unpredictable responses.

I met Miguel in the summer of 2007. He was in his late twenties, a management consultant working for a large multinational firm. We hit it off from the moment we met, at a bar in Makati's upmarket Legaspi Village. We had much in common and plenty to talk about. He had gone to a private school and private university not unlike those I had attended. He read widely, had an eclectic taste in music, and came from a middle-class family of intellectuals. He was well traveled; he had been to cities I knew well and to many others I had only dreamt of seeing. Perhaps more than anyone I met during the years I was conducting fieldwork, he fit the image of a cosmopolitan.

In Manila, Miguel might be described as *tisoy*, a slang term derived from "mestizo" that is used not as a name that some might claim but as a compliment for those whose bodies have retained traces of foreign blood. His skin was fair, pasty almost; his features were sharp; his hair and eyes were jet black. He could grow a full beard if he wanted to. In primary school plays about the history of the Philippines, he was always given the role of Magellan. He was not part Spanish, though, or at least, like so many Filipinos, he could not trace his personal history back to Spanish roots. He did, however, say once that he had a great-grandfather (or great-grandmother) who was Scottish (or Irish). He did not seem too sure about it. He did not appear to care, either. He said that people did not see him differently, that for others, the question of why he looked the way he did simply did not matter. On websites such as Guys4Men where gay men looked for sex, he marked himself as Asian. Filipinos who ticked "mixed" or "mixed race" in the list of options for "ethnicity," he said, were "trying to make themselves seem better, more . . . white."

Miguel knew, however, that "Asian" evoked an image other than his body. One night, he told me the story of how he learned the painful lesson that bodies must be named, and named accurately. He was twenty-two and in Paris, traveling alone for the first time. He met a local man on a cruising website and they arranged to meet one night. It was, Miguel remembered, the first time he had sought out sex in a foreign country. Afraid of getting lost, he arrived at the place they were supposed to meet half an hour early; he ended up walking nervously around the surrounding blocks, waiting for the time to pass. When the man arrived, however, he did not recognize Miguel from the photograph he shared online. "I'm sorry," he told Miguel. "I thought you were really Asian."

Miguel told me that he could not remember exactly how he reacted to the man's comment. He said that it caught him off guard, that he must have just mumbled something and walked away. He laughed as he said that. I laughed along, even though I knew, as Miguel surely did, that there was nothing particularly funny about the story he had recounted. "You know," he added, "this is the first time I've told anyone about that incident."

I asked him if he arranged to see anyone else he met online after that night. He said he did not but that he discovered the bathhouses. An embarrassed smile then crept onto his face. Whenever he went, he said, he put on a necklace with a silver Chinese pendant.

"Did that do anything?" I asked.

"I don't know," he said. "Maybe. I got some action there."

"What did the pendant say?"

"Beats me," he laughed. "Doesn't matter, does it?"

What mattered for Miguel was that he was legible, that he could be seen for what he was or what he believed himself to be. Rather than risk unintelligibility, he marked his body with a sign that he himself could not read. He entered an economy of desire predicated on a grammar of (racial) difference other than his own. He became "an object in the midst of other objects" and thus potentially (*maybe*) an object of desire. Miguel knew, however, that the space he was trying to occupy—the space reserved for the Asian—was a space of marginality. He saw the signs online ("no Asians") and, in bars, clubs, and bathhouses, he experienced the blatant indifference and subtle rebukes that have become standard fare in Asian accounts of gay life in the West.[51] Alternately too Asian and not Asian enough, he threw himself fully into otherness, even though it meant overwriting, if not forgetting, the privilege inscribed onto his tisoy body at home.

For some, however, the uncertainty that surrounds the race of the Filipino body opens up to modes of self-naming, of making oneself known, that relocate the body from the margin to the center.

Gian was born and raised in Manila but moved to the United States in 2006 to attend business school at a prestigious university in the East Coast. I met him over the holidays one year and made the mistake of casually bringing up a practice I had observed while living and traveling in North America and that I was critical of—namely, that of Filipinos, particularly second-generation migrants, describing themselves as "Filipino and Spanish" regardless of whether or not they could identify a Spanish ancestor.

"Isn't that strange?" I asked, casually. "Do people really think that they're part Spanish?"

The moment the words escaped me, I regretted saying them, for I saw the blush creep onto his face and knew that I had touched a nerve.

"I say that too, sometimes," he admitted, finally filling the air of awkward silence that hung between us. "You have to admit," he said, "it sounds better than just 'Filipino.'"

You might think of this practice, critically as I did, as an attempt to recuperate the colonial past in order to make a claim to whiteness, even to not-quite whiteness, given the position occupied by the "Hispanic" in the racial hierarchies that operate in places like the United States today. You might see in it traces of the enduring power of the mestizo, whose in-betweenness posed a challenge to colonial power but whose inheritance of that power may have, paradoxically, engendered the coding of in-betweenness itself (of being mixed) as something "better."[52] Or you could read the appending of "Spanishness" to "Filipinoness" as the putting on of the "mask" of authority, a rejection of the choice, posited by Fanon, to "turn white or disappear."[53] Gian told me, when I pressed him further about his use of "Filipino and Spanish" as a mode of self-description, that he was not aware that it was a common practice. This practice might be considered then as the unlearned, spontaneous effect of an uncoordinated yet collective will to "camouflage": the result of a desire, informed by anxieties about being *just* Filipino, to become mottled "against a mottled background."[54] However one chooses to read this practice, it remains, first and foremost, an account of oneself addressed to an other. It is a response to a question (i.e., *Where are you from? Who are you?*) and thus a tacit acknowledgment of the legitimacy of the authority of the questioner—that is, of the (white) man who asks and who offers (or withholds) recognition.[55]

A man introduced himself to me at a gay club in Toronto.

"Where are you from?" he asked.

"The Philippines," I replied.

"You don't look Filipino."

"What do I look like?"

"Korean? Chinese? Are you Chinese?"

"No, I'm Filipino."

And then a knowing smile crept onto his lips. "So do you say you're Filipino and Spanish like other Filipinos do?"

I remember this exchange and recall the shock of hearing the man exposing a practice I did not think would be known to him, the shame of being hailed into the folds of not only an othered people but also a people who were trying (and failing) to mask the truth of race. "You only say that you are Filipino and Spanish," I heard the man saying. "You cannot change who you are by changing your name." By phrasing this accusation in the form of a question, the man was able, intentionally or otherwise, to put me in the impossible position of either admitting my own guilt or confirming the guilt of others. *Do you say you're Filipino and Spanish like other Filipinos do?* was, after all, a question that had no right answer. To respond in the affirmative would have been to confess being party to a ruse; to reply with a denial would have been to agree, if tacitly, that Filipinos had no rightful claim to "Spanishness," that we had a proper name, and that our account of our selves had to remain subordinate to the account of those who, like colonizers past, could insist that we be one thing or another, even when faced with the illegibility of our bodies.

Like Miguel, who could not remember how he responded to the man who read his body as "not really Asian," I cannot recall exactly what I said in response to the accusation/question I was faced with in that gay club in Toronto.[56] I might have not said anything at all. I must have felt exposed, felt the blood rushing to my face, and found a way to excuse myself, to avert the gaze of the man who assumed that he knew something of my hidden desires. I remember this moment now as the occasion when the longing to be seen as an object of desire turned into my own longing to be hidden and concealed. It appears as an instance when judgment was passed on the Filipino who was thought to want to be something other than what he was and on me as someone who had confessed and even insisted on his Filipinoness. This brief exchange, predicated on the uncertainties of race, became the "scene of exposure," of shame—that affect that "arises when someone knows, or fears, they have been seen" by what Derrida might have described as the unfathomable gaze of the other who spies "a lapsus, a fall, a failure, a fault, a symptom."[57] Indeed, to paraphrase Derrida, something happened that should not take place during that moment when my body was being read; it was as though at that instant I was going to "admit what cannot be admitted in a symptom" and, thus, wanted to bite my tongue.[58]

Shame appears here as a silencing force. It begins with a look, a knowing smile, a passing of judgment to which I had no response. The shame I remember, however, is not shame at being Filipino per se. It is akin to but not the same as the shame that must have overcome the ilustrados when they saw "savages" on display as representatives of their would-be nation or that which is felt by the privileged Filipinos who come to resent the sight of domestic workers occupying ostensibly transnational sites such as airports. Such instances of shame become occasions for the voicing of disavowal. The ilustrados cried out in protest; they turned to a project that loudly declared "Filipino" as a name that excluded those whom they believed had no capacity for progress. The privileged Filipino traveler, in turn, makes his own distinctions; he creates the OFW, turns her into someone with her own look, her own language, and her own spaces. The very practice of naming oneself as Filipino and Spanish might be considered here as another instance when anxieties about the position occupied by the Filipino in georacial hierarchies engenders the creation of someone other (he who is just Filipino, the pure native). You might consider it alongside other strategies that similarly establish boundaries where none might be readily seen and that obfuscate the mark of Filipinoness. One man, a veteran of the scene, once told me that when people asked him where he was from, he said "Manila" instead of "the Philippines," as though by privileging his urban origins he might sidestep the sense of abjection attached to national belonging. Another time I asked a man who identified as Filipino-Chinese how the people in gay clubs overseas reacted when they learned he was Filipino. "It's not a problem," he said. "I say I'm Chinese."

Strategies such as these need not arise from direct experiences of shaming; they can emerge from the collective memory of the "shame-message" imputed by the colonial past.[59] You might think of these strategies then as preemptive moves adopted to protect the subject from the possibility of being shamed. Still, the threat of failure remains. As the man who asked me whether I said I was Filipino and Spanish like other Filipinos do made clear, strategies can be exposed *as* strategies; a question can level a charge and force someone to feel the shame of being ashamed.[60] Having already established a racial order that set the Filipino as an inferior and having once portrayed Filipinos as a race on the path to whiteness, colonial authority now poses an unanswerable question that says that the colonial other cannot change his position within the hierarchies that have been set in place and that any attempt to move across the boundaries of one's race can be seen, recognized, and mocked. Travel, what might be imagined as the fulfillment of the now centuries-old dream of becoming displaced, becomes paradoxically the occasion when the subject is put in his place. Race, the category in which the history of Philippine colonialism and nationalism has rendered inchoate, is what fixes the Filipino subject in a state of arrest that must be suffered in mute dejection.

A Conspiratorial Silence

In travel, the silence that surrounds race in Manila turns into "the silence of a sudden rupture."[61] The history of uncertainty—of race incited to discourse and erased—accrues and builds up to that moment when the subject finds himself engaged in the sensory labor of attuning to the racial order he finds himself in. There, he presents an account of himself—a deliberate strategy or the voicing of a deeply felt truth or something in between—and awaits, expects, or hopes for recognition, for the return of a desiring gaze. He makes use of the grammars and materials history has given him (a "Spanish" past, a "Chinese" body, an "Asian" imaginary, whatever) in order to make himself known. The moment that follows the giving of this account is the quiet moment of deferral. It is the time before judgment when the "fact" of the subject's "origin" and the meanings attached to his body make their presence felt and appear ready to erupt and wound. *I thought you were really Asian. You don't look Filipino. Are you a nurse? Do you say that you're Filipino and Spanish like other Filipinos do?* In the face of these questions and allegations, silence returns as a modest veil.[62] Talk turns to murmur; the subject's account hangs in the air while the subject sinks into background noise. He mumbles something and averts his gaze. "I slip into corners," says Fanon, "I remain silent, I strive for anonymity, for invisibility. Look, I will accept the lot, as long as no one notices me!"[63]

For the subject bound up in a scene that has already congratulated itself for having "arrived" in the world, what could this moment be but a moment of discovery, the point when the ephemeral dreamspace of gay globality touches matter, enters the subject's line of sight, and is revealed to be guarded by a gate, safe passage through which is predicated on forms of national-cum-racial belonging that cannot be purchased. That this gate exists and that the aspiring transnational subject remains outside it cannot be denied. What Fanon calls "evidence" (the nonwhite body of the subject) is there, unalterable; it torments, pursues, disturbs, and angers.[64] It is reflected back in the insistent, pitiless (or benevolent) gaze of the other from whom recognition is sought and whose eyes mirror "a shame ashamed of itself."[65] Under this gaze, it is difficult to speak, but there remains in the subject a certain disquiet, a mix of anger, confusion, and humiliation, or what Patricia MacCormack, following Serres, called "turbulence within the body."[66] For some, like Fanon, the "noise within," the dissonance that expresses marginality, cannot be contained.[67] *Black Skin, White Masks* is, if anything, a scream, the enunciation of the contradictory forces of desire, resentment, envy, hatred, and self-hatred engendered by the racial orders instituted by colonial authority. For others, the disquiet that arises from the encounter with one's otherness is something that must remain sheathed in silence, like a mark on the body that threatens to recall the injurious lesson learned in travel—that is, the realization that no matter how fast or how far the nonwhite, third-world subject moves, he will remain, like Fanon, "incapable of escaping his race."[68] Indeed, the painful discovery of the "fact" of otherness cannot be revealed, not only because there is no universal discourse on race, but also because this knowledge of difference also registers failure and inadequacy, the sense that something is amiss. It says that desired and imagined elsewheres will remain out of reach even when one is already "there," suggesting a fearful possibility—namely, that the privileged third-world subject, for whom staying "at home" is both a drudgery and a humiliation, can only be global *at home,* away from the gaze of the other who judges, in the third-world city that simultaneously threatens and impels dreams of globalness.[69]

One weeknight in 2008, I was in Makati City's Greenbelt Square, at a bar called "M," a sleek sliver of a bar located between the Ayala Museum and a barely trafficked strip of ultra-high-end designer boutiques such as

Prada and Gucci. On Friday nights, M was usually full. Locals and expatriates crowd the outdoor cocktail tables that were set up just outside the entrance, in front of a bare-bones DJ booth and underneath large spherical lamps that looked, from afar, like a cluster of moons hanging too close to the ground. That night, the place was almost empty. Only three or four tables were occupied, including the one where I was sitting with Arthur, the marketing executive whom I knew as a veteran of the scene and who had just returned from a trip to Cape Town, South Africa, a city I myself had visited a number of years earlier.

"It was so much fun," Arthur was saying. "Very gay friendly. They even give you a pink map at the airport." I did not remember receiving such a map. They must have started handing them out only after my visit. I did remember, however, how gay life in Cape Town had been positioned as something to be seen; how the city was sold aggressively on the Internet as a destination for gay tourists; how it was meant to be "the second San Francisco" and "the gay capital of Africa," a city teeming with trendy restaurants and modern nightspots.[70] Like other privileged parts of Cape Town, however, the city's famed gay village stood on a landscape of contradictions. In my own faded memories, it appears alongside the squalid areas where many impoverished black Cape Townians still live. Indeed, like Manila, and like other third-world cities, Cape Town cannot be imagined as anything but a series of contrasts; and there, perhaps more than anywhere I had been, progress, cosmopolitanism, and wealth were signified by white bodies, by seas of shirtless men crammed into clubs and white dancers posing on bar tops. There, gay globality appeared overwhelmingly white and was materialized, if always partially, in spaces haunted by the absent presence of racialized bodies.

I told Arthur that I too had been to Cape Town, but I did not share with him my own recollections of the city and its gay spaces. I did not want to influence his descriptions with my own account. Wide-eyed and eager to tell me more about his trip, Arthur said that he had gone to the bars, clubs, and one of the best-known bathhouses.

"[The bathhouse] was a really a big place," he said, "not like those tiny, ugly, dingy places here [in Manila]. And the clubs! They were really sophisticated. There were even well-dressed women there with their boyfriends. It was really happening, you know? It was like the center of culture, too. The whole gay district was really nice, upscale. It was like Malate, or the dream of Malate. The bars had courtyards full of people looking nice and enjoying wine."

"That doesn't sound quite like Malate," I said, smiling.

"It's the dream," he said. "The ideal."

Then he began to reminisce about the old Malate, about the brief period during the late 1990s when the intersection of Nakpil and Orosa was filled with fashionable bars and cafés. He said he did not know exactly how all those places died but that one day he, like many other gay men he knew, no longer wanted to go there. "That's how it is here, I guess," he opined. "We get tired of things quickly. It's all about what's new."

"How were the guys in Cape Town?" I asked.

"They were seriously hot."

"Did you hook up with anyone?"

He smiled, and for a moment, I thought I saw a mischievous glint in his eye, a hint that he was about to begin a story of sexual exploit. But then he replied:

"No, I didn't. You know how it is . . ." he trailed. "There's no market for us there . . . I used to look for that [sexual encounters] when I traveled. But that was when I was new. More naïve. Now I just go to look. I try to take it all in [and try to] pick up ideas that I might be able to bring back."

I nodded and dropped the subject. Arthur went on to extol the virtues of Cape Town's gay scene and to compare it favorably to the scene in other cities he had recently visited: Los Angeles, San Francisco, Berlin. We got to talking about the attempts to establish large circuit parties in Manila and the moves to connect "our" scene to the network of gay dance parties already operating across Asia, which took after the long-established chain of parties operating in North America, Europe, and, increasingly, in cities like Cape Town. He said that we had to be patient, that only those who had traveled knew how such parties were supposed to be run, and that we were not "really ready" for a scene akin to those he had observed overseas. Later I wondered whether I should have stopped him then, if I ought to have pushed him further, as I wanted to, on the subject of his lost naïveté. I wondered if I should have denied knowing "how it was" in cities like Cape Town where all "we" could do was look and "take it all in" or if I should have asked him to recount older travel stories, which I "knew" (or expected, at least) would take the form of awkward tales of unmet expectations. I still do not know exactly why I let that topic slide, but I remember the faltering in Arthur's voice during that conversation and the guilty sense that without warning I had wedged a gap in the story he wanted to tell.

We ended up later that night outside Club Government on Makati Avenue. There, I listened to Arthur tell the same stories about Cape Town he had just relayed to me to others who were excited to see him back and eager to hear about his trip. I do not recall exactly how Arthur recounted his trip during the many brief conversations that took place on the street that night or how the details of his account shifted with each retelling. I do remember, however, that his return opened up a narrative space for others to share fragments of their own experiences of travel, mundane accounts of bars, clubs, and parties in distant cities, all shorn of the racial politics that defined them and that could not be assimilated into the casual frame of small talk. The details of those other accounts are lost to me now as well, but I remember imagining all those who relayed their stories not only as *those who knew how it was* or *how things were supposed to run,* as Arthur did, but also as keepers of a shared secret, messengers who had felt that shock of difference that disrupts notions of belonging but which never quite wakes us from the dreamworld of gay globality.[71] A couple I met that night told me that they were planning a trip to Melbourne, where I was living at the time, and asked me about the local gay scene. I gave them a rundown of the more famous bars and clubs and told them to contact me if and when they were coming. I do not know if they ended up going, as I never heard from them again, but sometimes I wonder if they had simply gone without telling me. I wonder if they remember the names of places I rattled off; if they found themselves at the three-story megaclub called "The Market," where, one night, I heard a man standing next to me complain that the club had "too many Asians"; or if they had gone to the Opium Den, a bar that catered to "Asian men and their admirers" and that once staged an amateur strip show featuring two young Asian men writhing on the stage while white men with glass pitchers poured water over them. I wonder now if they witnessed any such spectacle and if it reminded them, as it reminded me, of the images from the history textbooks we grew up with of colonizers arriving on our shores and marking the extension of their empire by way of a christening.

How Whiteness Travels

In chapter 2, I wrote of how dreams of globalness and modernness arrive in the city in the form of signs, how names such as "Global City" index and generate classed desires for someplace else. Like names lodged as signs, stories gathered through travel and that are made to circulate in the third-world city acquire force—not because they maintain a direct correspondence with the places they describe but because they deliver a message: the promise of a condition yet to come. Remember, however, that the messages transmitted by signs can only be heard in silence. Names such as "Fifth Avenue" can only be woven into the barren landscape of the Fort. Contradictory states of being elsewhere and in the third-world city can only be resolved by building *black boxes* around our bodies: a club on a major thoroughfare, cars racing through the city late at night,

Internet portals where traces of otherness are vigilantly exorcised.[72] The third-world city, a landscape of contradictions, is also a "cartography of noises."[73] In order for the bright lights scene to take form, it must emerge from the cacophony of the city as a "black box full of black boxes."[74] As Attali once noted, all sources of disharmony must be "channeled" and "sacrificed" for messages and promises to retain their integrity; dissonances must be eliminated in order to keep noise from spreading.[75]

In travel, however, the source and location of noise becomes less certain. The borders of the scene become dangerously porous; otherness threatens to seep in or, worse, to emerge from within. Indeed, the echoes of colonial history reverberate in foreign yet encompassing racial orders to suggest that what ultimately disrupts the promise of becoming modern and global is not an other that can be disavowed but a part of the subject that must be (but cannot ever be) masked. It would be too simple still, however, to think of racialized difference as a snag on which the dream of gay globality gets caught. Race is, rather, written onto the very fabric of third-world dreams, predicated as they are on the overcoming of the conditions of debasement that defines life in the "periphery"—that is, on the pursuit of universalist ideals signified, under enduring colonial symbolic economies, by the unmarked white body.

Indeed, whiteness has, historically, appeared as part of the message of "progress," as a sign for transcendence toward which colonial subjects were expected to strive.[76] Under Spanish theological rule, whiteness was proclaimed from pulpits as the "spiritual surplus of God, indistinguishable from the white Spaniards who were God's representatives."[77] It stood for the spiritual ideal that would remain forever beyond the reach of the natives who, naked and colored, embodied sinful corporeality. Under U.S. imperialism, the gift of capitalist modernity was part of an offer of "white love," that never-to-be-fulfilled promise that stood hand in hand with the beneficent rereading of the "Filipino race" as a "race on the move," a people transitioning to whiteness.[78] Colonial rule, in other words, established race as "that which must be eschewed in order to approach value"; retroactively, it determined "the meaning of value as that which is not raced (whiteness)."[79]

At once part of the racialized logic of colonial authority and coded as that which is "not raced," whiteness is thus able to exert power and force even in contexts where there is no popular discourse on race. In Tony Perez's gay liberation novella, *Cubao 1980,* for instance, the protagonist, the teenage hustler Tom stumbles onto redemption when he walks by the Araneta Coliseum and catches sight of a sign ("Don Stewart/Charismatic Seminars/ Araneta Miracle Rally") that "something is happening (*me hapening*)." He finds a way into the Coliseum and gets overwhelmed by the noise from the chatter of the crowd, the people calling out to each other, and the yelling of the vendors selling sandwiches, soft drinks, and ice cream. The sounds make him feel small, he says. Then a sound comes from the micro-phone and the American preacher climbs up the stage. The crowd erupts in cheers. Another sound comes from the microphone and the crowd grows quiet, waiting for the preacher to speak. Tom makes one unex-pected, fleeting observation. The preacher, he says, is "so very, very white (*ang puti-puti*)."[80]

In the face of this intense appearance of whiteness, something happens to the crowd. They hear the preacher's message of redemption and deliver-ance; take in his stories about God, the Holy Spirit, man, sin, and eternal life; and begin to clap and shout, to pray and raise their hands, to sing and shake. The preacher tells them to come closer. They start shouting louder and begin to cry. In this ecstatic scene of desire, whiteness throws the crowd into a frenzy; it not only elicits their cries but also cuts through the furor of the crowd to deliver a message, to confer worth and redemp-tion upon Tom. In the face of whiteness, "Tom encounters something in himself that is at once the manifestation of divine presence and the very substance of universal humanness"—that is, that aspect of being that lies beyond worldly determinants of social identity (place, nation, race, sex-uality, etc.)—the "something that is in but not of the body" for which whiteness stands as a privileged sign and which Neferti Tadiar, following Marx, refers to as "value."[81] As Tadiar points out, what Tom beholds in the face of whiteness is not the value of the embodied person (the Ameri-can preacher), nor the value of America (from where the preacher comes), but his own "abdicated and betrayed, but ultimately recuperable, human value."[82] Whiteness, here conferring divine mercy, redeems Tom from the demeaning life of a rent boy; it lifts him from the dire conditions of the third-world city.

The world Tom inhabits and attempts to flee may be nothing like the world of privilege that is the bright lights scene. The desire to be raised from the third-world city, however, is a desire that cuts across the bound-aries of class difference. Indeed, like Tom, the scene recognizes the value of whiteness, or, more accurately, it welcomes the white body as a bearer of value.

When I met Dan in December of 2006, he had only been in Manila for about a month. He was a young photographer from New York who had a grant to document religious rituals in Manila and in some other Philippine provinces for half a year. He had actually known very little about Manila before he arrived, but he had read some things about its Spanish and American colonial past and saw images of its religious rituals. He found them interesting and thought they would make for a good project.

When I met him, he was living in Makati, at a small, overpriced, and inexpensively furnished studio apartment located across Greenbelt. He hardly knew anyone then. His only friend was a young local he had met online who spoke little English and who seemed nervous to see me, a stranger, drinking beer and smoking cigarettes with Dan on the balcony of that little apartment. He made me nervous as well. I thought he looked shifty and I wondered if maybe he was one of those men you sometimes hear about who try to scam foreigners into giving them cash. When he went inside the apartment, to sleep on Dan's bed, I thought about saying something but decided not to. I thought maybe I was letting my class suspicions get the better of me. Besides, Dan did not seem to need warnings. Despite having only been in Manila briefly, he seemed settled and in control, more intrigued than overwhelmed by the unfamiliarity of the city. He also looked tough. He was tall and well built, and his military-style haircut, stubble, and the tattoos on his arms made him appear, despite his boyish face, like someone you did not mess with. He seemed at once rough and angelic, like a too-pretty actor cast to play a thug. "I met him online before I got here," he said, picking up on what must have been my obvious discomfort around the other Filipino man. "He helped me get settled and showed me around. He's nice, really."

I asked him if he had met many other gay men. He said he was beginning to, but that it was difficult to make contact with people before he arrived. He had set up a profile on Guys4Men, but most people refused to believe that his pictures were "real," that he was not just another Filipino with a "fake" profile that used photos of foreign (white) men.

"Why do so many people make fake profiles here?" Dan asked. "I mean, what do they get out of it? It's not like they can meet up with someone and then show up as a completely different person."

"I don't know," I said. "Maybe they think that people won't mind once they get to know them. Or maybe they get people to send them raunchy photos. Or maybe they just want to talk. They probably think more people will listen to them if they looked like they were from someplace else."

"Yeah, I guess," Dan replied. He sounded unconvinced.

I asked him how he finally got around that problem. He said he took a picture of himself in Manila, to show people that he was "really here." He showed me the picture on his laptop. It was taken from the balcony where we were chatting and was shot from a high angle. You could see, behind his face, over the half-obscured cross tattoo on his right shoulder, the soot-stained roofs of shorter buildings, a construction site where a new mall would rise a few years later, the tops of the few trees in that area. It must have been morning when the shot was taken, just before rush hour. The sky was still somewhat grey. Dan, a photographer, made sure to catch the light with his face. It made him stand out against the background, almost as though he were superimposed. I told him it was a nice photograph. I knew that it would be noticed online and that people would respond if he sent them a message.

I did not stay in touch with Dan when I left Manila a few weeks after I met him. A year later, however, I found out that he was still there and that he had never left. I was at Government, the gay club in Makati, and one of my informants was telling me that he had fallen in and out of love with a man from New York, a photographer. I knew right away that it was Dan, but I did not tell my informant that I actually knew the man he was referring to. He said that the man he fell in love with was really intelligent, interesting, and beautiful and that the man was the first person he ever allowed to penetrate him during sex. He said that he thought something was going to happen between them, something serious, but that he was mistaken. The man got bored with him and moved on. It was OK, he said. "Some things just don't work out."

Dan sent me a message when he found out I was in town and invited me to come see him in Makati. He had moved out of the studio apartment on Legaspi Street and was staying at the house of another American, an expatriate with a house in a gated subdivision called San Lorenzo Village. The house was bigger than it looked from the outside. It was grand but modern, sparse but tastefully furnished, the kind of house that might get featured in a magazine. Dan was staying in one of the guest rooms and had a king-sized bed and his own bathroom. We hung out by the pool. Dan was rambling about a number of things: food, movies, and some people he had met. He was tossing around an inflatable dolphin. I could tell he was on something. He said that he was finally heading home in a couple of months but that he would come back six months from then. He was planning on permanently splitting his time between Manila and New York. He had met someone who was doing just that, a guy who spent half of each year taking small jobs in New York and the other half in Manila, living like a king. He did not mention my informant or that man he had been with when he first arrived in Manila. I asked him about that man. *What happened to him? Where was he?* "I don't know," Dan shrugged. "That guy was weird."

A year later, when I returned to Manila for the holidays, I learned that Dan was in the city as well and that he had, in fact, been back for some time. I ran into him by accident at the swankiest bar in the city. I was standing by the bar with one of the owners, who was telling me that they built the bar because they wanted Manila to have something on par with what the best cities in the world had to offer. He was talking about the design of the bar, about the little coves at the back that could be bordered off with hidden panels for additional privacy, when we both saw Dan approaching.

"Dan!" the owner called out. "Bobby, this is Dan. He's the manager . . . Oh, you know each other? Of course you do. It's a small world."

"Yes, it is," I said. "Dan and I met a long time ago."

I did not have much time to talk to Dan that night, but at one point he told me that he had decided not to shuttle between Manila and New York, that he had moved to Manila permanently. There was no point in leaving, he said. Life was better here. Then he saw something from the corner of his eye. He looked annoyed and excused himself. I watched him walk toward one of the security personnel. I could not make out exactly what he was saying, but it seemed clear that he was upset that some people who were in violation of the dress code were being let in.

Later that night, I was talking to a small group of gay men and the subject of Dan came up.

"How did he get this job?" someone was asking. "I don't think he has any experience running a bar."

"Well, you know. He's white," replied another, half-jokingly. "If he says he can run a bar, people will believe him."

"But he's not white," added a third. "He's Latino."

The second man laughed. "Honey, that doesn't mean anything here."

Nowhere to Go

At the beginning of this book, I described Manila's bright lights scene as a world in the making—a pulsing, living, imagined space that one can be "in," a tangle of connections that demarcates, if always haphazardly, the contours of a way of life. This life, I have argued, cannot be disarticulated from the hierarchies, violences, and cultures of domination that operate in the third-world city. It is moved by the force of fantasy, marked by yearnings, and pulled by a trajectory that directs imaginations outward toward the global, forward toward modernity, and upward toward higher states of class privilege.

Forever trying to rise above Manila's urban squalor and disorder, the scene turns mobility into an obligation. It creates a "we" that must find ways to speed through the city, to eke out spaces where elsewheres can thrive, to claim simultaneity with the global present, and to literally fly out and enter global space. All these practices of mobility, however, are anxious and fated to fail, for the city and the abject figures associated with it cannot ever be erased or outpaced. There is always a beggar on a street corner waiting for *our* cars to stop or standing outside a club ready to greet us on our way out. The *bakla* always haunts the scene and never fails to insert the past back into the present. The domestic worker is always already on the airplane and has long occupied *our* place in the global imagination. Indeed, no matter how far or how fast *we* move, there is always a figure that reminds us of *our* time and place. As I argued in chapter 3, there are times, in fact, when abject figures *must* be present, if only so that we may chase it away, keep it out, and thus reinforce the existence of the scene's charged borders.

These borders, in turn, take on many forms. Sometimes they are graphic and readily apparent, as when bars adopt "members only" policies or when entire commercial developments rise on landscapes where traces of disorder are erased. More often, borders are fashioned in surreptitious ways and involve signs that are meaningful and visible only to the *we* of the bright lights scene. A pejorative term such as *jologs,* for instance, cannot be explained even by those who use it and requires a reading of codes that outsiders simply cannot get. Hypervisible or half hidden, the scene's borders are, regardless, palpable and forceful; they make sense to and have an impact on all those who catch sight of them, up close or from a distance.

To speak of borders is to speak in terms of vision, of what is seen or unseen or, better still, of what one desires to see or not to see. Throughout *Under Bright Lights,* I have tried to evoke the feelings of aversion and aspiration that are elicited by the sights we behold from the vantage of the scene. I have, in turn, also tried to describe how the *inside* and *outside* of the scene emerge through visual practices and optical effects. There is the blurring and veiling of the city from behind the tinted window screens of automobiles. There are the circulating images that allow for a kind of optical magnification, for the glimpsing of distant worlds. There is the sight of the city from above; the picture of a prostitution block spied from a hotel suite; soot-stained buildings in the background of a photograph of a "white" man, whose presence in the city had to be seen in order to be believed. Examples such as these point to the way the scene takes form and acquires coherence by reorganizing distance through the crafting of a space between the scene and the sights that surround it.

In the final chapter, however, I also began to describe those things that are excluded as *noise*, as externalities that disrupt the message and promise of gay globality. In a way, you might say, noise offers a more apt metaphor for the interruptions that accompany the worlding of the scene. After all, noise is that which cuts through walls. It renders borders unthinkable, elements inseparable, and forms indistinguishable. Michel Serres writes of noise as turbulence, fury, murmur, the multiple, the sea, thunder and rumbling, a surging swell, the surge of differences.[1] His metaphors are endless, but his point is clear: noise is that from which forms and unities try to violently extract themselves. Noise is what we try to suppress and forget but are never able to.[2] We can shut our eyes, he suggests, but never our ears.

I introduced noise at the end of this book because it is in the context of the encounter with racialization more than anywhere that the scene loses its form. It is, then, that the privileged, third-world gay subject becomes indistinguishable from his others. Indeed, for the privileged subject to discover his race is for him to know that he too stands outside gay globality; for him to be cast out of the world he wishes to enter is for him to be pushed back into the noise of which he was always a part. Earlier I described this moment as the moment when noise turns into a *noise within*. We might think of it now, more accurately still, as the moment when the noise within becomes audible, so loud that it makes it difficult, if not impossible, to speak. Serres calls the moment we hear the din of the body "illness."[3] I have referred to it as "shame." The meanings nesting in these names may be different, but it is worth noting that shame is an affect that others have referred to, not coincidentally, as a "sickness of the self."[4]

To cast the silenced knowledge of racialization as something shrouded in shame is, however, not to dismiss it as something regrettable. Shame opens up to possibilities. It compels a reassessment of the self and of objects of love and interest.[5] It begs questions—"Why am I ashamed? Why can't I speak?"—that spur reevaluations of long-held investments.[6] As Baudrillard once noted, shame is a noble emotion; it can produce an ethics, a "passion of repentance."[7] Here we might think again of complicity and how knowledge of racialization might stir us from the dream of gay globality, how it might mark the beginning of the unmaking of the borders erected within the third-world city. Still, the impact of encounters with racialization is not predictable. Veiled by silence, such encounters can create an impossible situation, wherein the local must be disavowed, even while the global remains forever out of reach, only ever appearing as a willfully amnesiac dream. Put differently, the silenced knowledge of racialization sets the scene in perpetual motion; it keeps *us* jostling in between the impossible locations of *there* and *here* or between the dream of gay globality and full immersion in noise.

At the end of 2009, Typhoon Ondoy (international code name Ketsana) swept through Manila and ravaged the city with floods. I was in Melbourne when Ondoy hit, but images and videos went up quickly on the Internet of spectacular disaster scenes. There were houses fully submerged and people stranded on roofs. There were cars floating through major roads like lightweight rafts. Dead dogs were photographed hanging from wire cables.

There was a video taken from one of the topmost floors of a building in Eastwood City, a dense, walled-in cluster of high-rise condominiums, office towers, and restaurants built along the C-5 highway on the west bank of the Marikina River. I lived in Eastwood City for six months during one of my fieldwork trips. During those months, I spent a few hours each week running on a treadmill in a gym that had something of a reputation as a cruising spot and that had floor-to-ceiling windows that looked directly out onto the river and at the sprawling shantytown that thrived on the opposite bank. I remember those hours as strange hours spent not knowing where to look, time spent in between gay life's play of desiring gazes and the curious view offered by the shantytown. I remember spacing out while staring at life on the other side, at what appeared to me as almost rural scenes of women washing clothes in murky waters, children playing games, a man who was always pushing a wooden cart full of junk through the other side's tall, wild grass.

In the video, you see the river and the shantytown from above. The river looks wide, much wider than I remember it, and it is moving fast, rushing at a pace I did not think it was capable of. A hand, the videographer's, points out all the sites of danger.

"Oh God, Oh God—those shanties! It's going to take those shanties!"

"The shanties are gone! Oh my! Oh my!"

The camera pans. The hand points out all that has been lost to the floods.

"Zero visibility!"

"There was a road over there! Where is the road? Where are the cars?"

"Look! Look! Look at the devastation!"

"Listen! Do you hear that? That's the sound of that house giving in."

Then the camera points down and you see the river break through the walls of Eastwood. The image cuts to the inside of the videographer's car. He is in the basement of the building. He has climbed down sixteen flights to rescue his car from the waters that have broken through Eastwood's borders.

"It's flooding! In the basement!"

He manages to drive his car up to the ground level. On the road, cars are struggling to get through the road in front of the Eastwood Mall and the condominium called One Central Park.

"Oh my! The entire Eastwood is engulfed."

"The river has just broken through the barriers!"

"This is incredible! Inside Eastwood? Are you kidding me?"

"I don't know where to park."

"What is going on?"

Two-and-a-half months after Ondoy struck, I was back in Manila, taking stock of all that I had personally lost in the floods. In my mother's house, which was half submerged for two days, there were piles and piles of destroyed books, files, clothes, and photographs. She kept everything she could that belonged to me. She said she wanted to wait for me to arrive, to see if there was anything I wanted to rescue. I threw out everything but the photographs. There was, however, no one to commiserate with. Everyone I knew had long since moved on from the devastation of Ondoy. Manila was back to normal; I was too late for the mourning.

My reason for coming to Manila, however, was not to assess my losses. I had come to see what had become of the scene, for even before Ondoy struck, I could already sense that the worlds I inhabited in Manila were beginning to fray at the edges. The magazine *Icon,* which had loudly proclaimed that "we" had become "business entities," had ceased publication. The attempts to bring circuit parties to Manila had been deemed "failures" by many. The club Government had closed. Its owner Henry had declared, earlier in 2009, that he had fallen in love with someone from Bangkok and that he was leaving Manila for good. (When I arrived in Manila, people kept telling me that the real reason Government closed was because it had been doing poorly, that there was not enough of a market to keep it afloat.) The other club, Bed, was still open, but it had become, as one of my informants joked, a "miss or miss" destination; it was alternately overcrowded or so empty that they had to close off sections in order to give the illusion that it was full. Three of my key informants had migrated overseas, including Arthur, who had taken a job in Sydney. Another was getting ready to move to Europe. The scene had grown eerily quiet. I wanted to know what was going on.

"Nothing's on," one of my informants told me one Saturday night, when I asked him if there were any events worth checking out while I was in town. "Everything's dead these days. There's nowhere to go."

I asked him about some of the things I had been writing about—all the talk over the years of the scene getting bigger and better, becoming more world class.

"How embarrassing," he said. "We were getting way ahead of ourselves. None of that was ever going to happen."

I remember listening to my informant then and wondering if our world-making had come to an end, if the aspirations, fantasies, and trajectories I was investigating had been swept up by time, and if we had given up the dream of gay globality. I wondered if we had known all along, as my informant suggested, that the dream was doomed to failure and if we had simply gotten ahead of ourselves. I also wondered though about what would come next. How were we going to proceed now that so much of our bordered world had closed and there was "nowhere to go"? What possibilities were open now that the fantasy itself had become embarrassing—*shameful*? During that last trip to Manila, there were few, if any, clues. There were no signs yet of what was coming. Then in February 2010, I received an e-mail invitation for a new event called "Rise," which was being organized by a Filipino man from Sydney, Australia, who had moved back to Manila. The e-mail described the party as "the first in a series of sensational events that will breathe new life into Manila's pink party scene—parties served up at specially handpicked venues around the city that promise to be fun, diverse, and exciting." "You're in for some unforgettable nights that you won't wanna miss," it claimed. "It's a new day and the start of something big. So come RISE—it's time to shine!" Written as both a declaration and an injunction, the invitation served as a promise. It made it clear that shame can be forgotten and that sometimes, when dreams end, they can begin again.

ACKNOWLEDGMENTS

Like many other writers and scholars, I had to leave my hometown in order to write about it. Unlike most, however, I had the great fortune of seeing, remembering, and reimagining Manila, not only from a distance, but also from the vantage of multiple cities. All the places where I found myself working on this book—Toronto, Melbourne, Berlin, Montreal—have, in different ways and to varying degrees, shaped my views on urban life and queer life in the age of mobility and diaspora. I may never be able to fully grasp or articulate the impact these places have had on my writing, but I am grateful for the inspiration they have given me and for the people with whom they put me in contact and who have engaged this project over the years.

At the University of Melbourne, where most of this book was written, I was fortunate to have worked under the guidance of three wonderful mentors. Fran Martin helped shape this project during its early stages, and her unwavering faith and advice over the years have been integral to this book's development. Audrey Yue saw this project through periods of writer's block and had confidence in my writing when I had little or none; for that, I am grateful. Vera Mackie poured more time and energy into this project than I thought reasonable to ask for. I thank her for her generosity, particularly during the final stages of writing my dissertation. Numerous other friends and colleagues in Australia, at the School of Culture and Communication and beyond, have had an effect on this project. I cannot name all of them here, but I would like to thank Steven Angelides, Brett Farmer, Sean Cubitt, and Scott McQuire for reading and commenting on early chapter drafts. I also want to thank my peers—Aren Aizura, Katushiko Suganuma, Sufern Hoe, Leloy Claudio, Romana Byrne, and Fiona Druitt—who offered encouragement, camaraderie, and distraction when I needed them most. Special thanks to Marc Trabsky, who appears in my most meaningful memories of Melbourne.

This book could not have been completed without the support of a postdoctoral fellowship from the ICI Berlin Institute for Cultural Inquiry and I am grateful to its director, Christoph Holzhey, for providing such a unique and lively intellectual environment. At the ICI, I benefitted from the presence of brave and genuine colleagues. Thank you to Sandrine Sanos for her truly indispensible support and friendship; to David Kishik for being a constant (and welcome) source of disagreement and provocation; to Kit Heintzman for "getting" everything that others cannot or do not; to Alice Gavin for sharing my love for scenes of beauty and ruin; to Anaheed al-Hardan and Daniel Barber for echoing my own frustrations and allowing me to speak with no filter; and to Zeynep Bulut, Brigitte Bargetz, Aaron Schuster, Claudia Peppel, and Manuele Gragnolati for their engagement.

This project began (and coincidentally, ends) in the east coast of Canada. In Toronto, Sandra Whitworth, Shannon Bell, and Steven Flusty managed to convince me, perhaps unintentionally, that my ideas about gay culture in Manila were worth committing to paper and pursuing for years to come. This book would not have been possible without their initial encouragement and the influence of the radical scholars and students at York University's Department of Political Science. In Montreal, support for this project has come from the Andrew W. Mellon Foundation, as well as the Department of Art History and Communication Studies and the Institute for Gender, Sexuality, and Feminist Studies at McGill University. I would like to particularly thank Carrie Rentschler and Natalie Oswin for wholeheartedly welcoming me to McGill and Montreal.

Many other colleagues from beyond the places I have called home have generously read, commented, or simply spoken to me about this book or parts of it. I am grateful to Joe Ponce and Chris Berry for their incredibly detailed and thoughtful readings; to Eithne Luibhéid and the editors and anonymous readers of the journals where earlier versions of this book appeared for their help refining my ideas and arguments; to Lisa Duggan for giving me a platform to talk about this project in its final stages; to Kathleen Stewart, whose fearless writing convinced me that it was possible to do more with words; and to Martin Manalansan, without whose pioneering work in Philippine queer studies my own would not be possible and whose advice and support over the years have been invaluable. My expansive gratitude goes out to Roderick Ferguson, whose belief in this project has been humbling, and to Richard Morrison for shepherding it through the publication process.

This project has taken me thousands of miles away from my family in Manila, but their support for my often impossible aspirations has sustained me over the years. I owe them everything. Finally, I would like to thank all the men who shared their stories with me and with whom I spent time during fieldwork. I do not know how to repay them for the memories, trust, and love.

NOTES

Prologue

1. Berlant, "Cruel Optimism," 35.
2. See Stewart, "Machine Dreams," 21–28.
3. All names are pseudonyms.
4. Considine, "Hip-Hopping the Night Away in Manila."
5. I am omitting the URL of Arthur's journal as it would reveal Arthur's real identity.
6. *Ladlad* literally means *unfurled*. The use of this term here comes from the phrase "*paglaladlad ng kapa* [unfurling the cape]," which is used in the gay vernacular, or swardspeak, as similar but not identical to "coming out." See Manalansan, *Global Divas*, 27–28. According to the Commission on Elections (COMELEC), Ladlad's application for accreditation as a party-list organization lacked merit because the group failed to provide proof of nationwide membership. Danton Remoto, the president and founder of Ladlad, complained that the COMELEC did not use the mandatory research fees paid by the organization to properly investigate their membership (see Aning, "Gay Party-List Group Ladlad out of the Race"). Ladlad attempted to gain accreditation again for the 2010 national elections. The COMELEC once again rejected their application, this time on explicitly homophobic grounds. Referencing the teachings of American Bible scholar Lehman Strauss, the COMELEC resolution claimed that the group "tolerates immorality" and that granting the petition would mean "exposing our youth to an environment that does not conform to the teachings of our faith." The Supreme Court ultimately ordered the COMELEC to put Ladlad back on the ballot. Ladlad, however, did not win any seats.
7. The program of Ladlad consists of an antidiscrimination bill (targeted primarily at workplaces such as schools, hospitals, restaurants, hotels, entertainment centers, and government offices), microfinance and livelihood projects for poor and handicapped LGBT Filipinos, and the establishment of centers for old and abandoned LGBT Filipinos, as well as for homeless LGBT youth.

8. Stewart, "Atmospheric Attunements," 447.

9. *Matapobre* is a term used to describe those who look down on the poor. It is a conjunction of the words *mata* (eye) and *pobre* (poor).

10. Lingis, *Abuses,* 148.

Introduction

1. On "third world places in first world drag," see Tadiar, *Fantasy-Production,* 2. On "falling upwards," see Virilio, *Open Sky,* 67–68.

2. As Steven Connor, following Michel Serres, has argued, "Topology is not concerned with exact measurement . . . but rather with spatial relations, such as continuity, neighborhood, insideness and outsideness, disjunction and connection." See Connor, "Topologies," 106.

3. Hénaff, "Of Stones, Angels, and Humans," 59.

4. See Virilio, *The Lost Dimension,* 71; Morrison, *Tar Baby,* 286.

5. Tadiar, *Things Fall Away,* 148.

6. Though the term *third world* has fallen out of fashion in both academic and popular writing, I use it here to retain the material and visceral experience of poverty and global marginality it evokes and that is largely lost in euphemisms such as *developing, underdeveloped,* and *global South.*

7. As Deleuze has argued, "Every diagram is intersocial and constantly evolving. It never functions in order to represent a persisting world but produces a new kind of reality, a new model of truth . . . [T]he diagram is the map of relations between forces." See Deleuze, *Foucault,* 35–36.

8. Taussig, *The Nervous System.*

9. Stewart, "Weak Theory in an Unfinished World," 72.

10. Ibid., 74.

11. See Virilio, "The Overexposed City," 15–31.

12. Straw, "Cultural Scenes," 412–13 and "Scenes and Sensibilities."

13. Williams, *Politics and Letters,* 159; Stewart, "Arresting Images," 431; Serres, *The Parasite,* 224–25.

14. Wilson, "Afterword: Worlding as Future Tactic," 212.

15. Ahmed, *The Cultural Politics of Emotion,* 156; Puar, *Terrorist Assemblages,* 22.

16. Sedgwick, *Tendencies,* viii.

17. Wiegman, "Object Lessons," 382.

18. Warner, "Introduction," xvii.

19. Jack Halberstam has noted that queer studies has been especially invested in the movement of queer subjects from rural to urban settings. This book echoes Halberstam's critique of "metronormativity," or the tendency in queer studies to privilege the city as a site of queerness. However, rather than drawing attention to nonurban environments (as Halberstam does), my aim here is to draw attention

to the material and psychogeographical divisions that make the city itself unthinkable as a coherent unit in which queer radicality might be located. See Halberstam, *In a Queer Time and Place*, 36–37; see also Tongson, *Relocations*, 5–7.

20. It is, in part, due to the necessarily mobile and transgressive connotations of *queer* that I choose not to use the term here beyond referencing ideas such as *queer space* that are part of the existing literature on nonnormative sexualities. Further, the term *queer*, which continues to circulate as an umbrella term for forms of nonnormative sexual subjectivity, fails to capture the fact that the scene I describe is imagined and produced as a decidedly gay male space. Indeed, as I discuss in the chapter on the *bakla*, the scene maintains a complicated relationship to transwomen and transfemininity and has almost no contact with the worlds inhabited by lesbians, transmen, and other sexual minorities.

21. Virilio, *The Lost Dimension*, 15.

22. Virilio, *Open Sky*, 91.

23. Following Edward Said, Derek Gregory defines "imaginative geographies" as "imaginations given substance" or "fabrications," a word, he reminds us, that "usefully combines 'something fictionalised' and 'something made real.'" See Gregory, *The Colonial Present*, 17–19.

24. Virilio, "The Last Vehicle," 106–19. See also McQuire, "Blinded by the (Speed of) Light."

25. See Virilio, *The Aesthetics of Disappearance*, and Abbas, *Hong Kong*, 8–12.

26. LiPuma and Koelble, "Cultures of Circulation and the Urban Imaginary," 157.

27. Ibid., 155; see also Read, "The Urban Image," 48–65.

28. See McQuire, "The Politics of Public Space."

29. See Siegert, *Relays*, 108–10.

30. See Himpele, *Circuits of Culture*, 14.

31. Straw, "The Circulatory Turn"; Gaonkar and Povinelli, "Technologies of Public Forms," 385–97.

32. Gaonkar and Povinelli, "Technologies of Public Forms," 391–92.

33. Ibid.

34. Lee and LiPuma, "Cultures of Circulation," 191–213.

35. Read, "The Urban Image," 49. The term *polyrhythmical* derives from Lefebvre's work on the "rhythms" of cities—that is, the different paces, negotiations, and encounters of everyday urban life. See Lefebvre, *Rhythmanalysis*.

36. Mbembé, "Aesthetics of Superfluity," 398.

37. Gaonkar and Povinelli, "Technologies of Public Forms," 394–95.

38. Gregory, *The Colonial Present*, 17; Puar, *Terrorist Assemblages*, 39.

39. Read, "The Urban Image," 48–50.

40. Gaonkar and Povinelli, "Technologies of Public Forms," 395.

41. Baudrillard, *America*, 27–28.

42. Stewart, "The Perfectly Ordinary Life."

43. As Gibson-Graham has argued elsewhere, class is "a process without an essence." "Class processes have no core or condition of existence that governs their development more closely than any other and to which they can ultimately be reduced." See Gibson-Graham, *The End of Capitalism (as We Knew It)*, 55.

44. Frow, *Cultural Studies and Cultural Value*, 111.

45. The term *queer space* was developed first by cultural geographers to designate disruptions of spaces that are naturalized as "heterosexual" through the repetitive performances of heterosexuality. For representative examples, see Bell and Valentine, *Mapping Desires*; Ingram, Bouthillette, and Retter, *Queers in Space*; Duncan, *Body Space*. For a recent revisiting of this work, see Browne, Lim, and Brown, *Geographies of Sexualities*.

46. Duggan, *The Twilight of Equality*, 43–66.

47. See, for instance, Manalansan, "Race, Violence, and Neoliberal Spatial Politics in the Global City," 141–55; Bell and Binnie, "Authenticating Queer Space," 1807–20; Casey, "The Queer Unwanted and Their Undesirable 'Otherness,'" 125–36; Rushbrook, "Cities, Queer Space, and the Cosmopolitan Tourist," 183–206; Giorgi, "Madrid *en Tránsito*," 57–79; Puar, "A Transnational Feminist Critique of Queer Tourism," 935–46. The interest in the relationship of gay life to the market goes back further, to at least the publication of John D'Emilio's classic essay, "Capitalism and Gay Identity."

48. See Oswin, "Critical Geographies and the Uses of Sexuality," 89–103.

49. See Luibhéid, "Queer/Migration," 169–90. The most explicit statement on complicity and gay white male subjects arguably comes from Heidi Nast, who contended that "certain EuroWhite-identified gay men—relatively youthful, of some means, and typically childless—are well positioned to take advantage of key avenues of exploitation and profiteering in postindustrial world orders." It should be noted that Nast acknowledges that her critique relates more directly to the (market-driven) image of gay white men rather than "real live" men, though she also insists that this image speaks to hegemonic desires and cannot be dismissed as nonrepresentative of "the ideals and practices in which 'real' people invest." See Nast, "Queer Patriarchies, Queer Racisms, International."

50. Natalie Oswin also makes the case against "faith (being) placed in women and queers of color as still radical subjects" and notes that the "politics of normalization are not limited to gay white males." See Oswin, "Critical Geographies and the Uses of Sexuality," 96.

51. As Zygmunt Bauman argues, "Mobility climbs to the rank of the uppermost among the coveted values—and the freedom to move, perpetually a scarce and unequally distributed commodity, fast becomes the main stratifying factor of our late-modern or postmodern times." See Bauman, *Globalization*, 2.

52. Amin and Thrift note that "objects of passion" concerned with representation (e.g., films, texts, and other images) not only portray life but "make life run" and "become the world" because people respond or "act to" them. See Amin and Thrift, *Cities*, 88; see also Latour, "The Politics of Explanation," 127.

53. On "speed classes" and "mobile classes," see Virilio, *The Art of the Motor,* 79; George, "Fast Castes," 115–18; and Bauman, *Liquid Modernity,* 151–52.

54. See Najmabadi, "Interview with Gayatri Spivak"; see also Tsing, *Friction,* 1, 6–8.

55. Benjamin, "The Work of Art in the Age of Mechanical Reproduction," 217–51.

56. Nostalgia here designates the longing to return to the pattern of exchange (between subject and object) that preceded mechanical reproduction. See Lichtenstein, *Behind Closed Doors,* 148–50; Benjamin, "The Work of Art in the Age of Mechanical Reproduction," 222–24.

57. Stewart, "Machine Dreams," 22. On attachments to unattainable "objects of desire," see also Berlant, *Cruel Optimism,* 23–28.

58. Ibid.; see also Latour, *We Have Never Been Modern.* On being "gay/modern," see Giorgi, "Madrid *en Tránsito,*" 62.

59. In this way, this book is also informed by phenomenology and, in particular, explorations of how postures are effected by relationships to objects. See Amin and Thrift, *Cities,* 78–104; Lingis, *The Imperative*; and (on orientations) Ahmed, *Queer Phenomenology.*

60. The idea of "meshwork" is borrowed from De Landa, *A Thousand Years of Nonlinear History,* 32, 69. On "distributed agency," see Ansell-Pearson, *Germinal Life,* 171.

61. Read, "The Urban Image," 60.

62. From the mid-1990s on, much of the literature on queer sexualities outside the West has taken on the terms set out by broader debates on cultural globalization and has been positioned as a corrective to works that emphasize the "homogenizing power of gayness gone global." In particular, the work of Dennis Altman and his deployment of the terms "global queering" and "global gay" have been the subject of much debate. While Altman has been careful not to claim that there exists an essential gay identity that operates transnationally, the questions he raises about whether the forces of globalization have produced a "common consciousness and identity based on homosexuality" has largely been read as a suggestion that the globalization of modernity has led to the emergence of a universal gay identity. Subsequent work on queer globalization has, correspondingly, involved the explication of specific practices that demonstrate the "localization of globally mobile understandings of sexuality." See Berry, Martin, and Yue, "Introduction," 6–7. For representative examples, see the following collections: Manderson and Jolly, *Sites of Desire, Economies of Pleasure*; Povinelli and Chauncey, "Thinking Sexuality Transnationally"; Cruz-Malavé and Manalansan, *Queer Globalizations*; and Welker and Kam, "Of Queer Import(s)." See also Altman, "Rupture or Continuity? The Internationalization of Gay Identities"; "On Global Queering"; "Global Gaze/Global Gays"; and *Global Sex.* For notable summaries, see Oswin, "Decentering Queer Globalization"; and Jackson, "Capitalism and Global Queering."

63. On "appropriating the materials of modernity," see Appadurai, *Modernity at Large,* 17. Appadurai's work has been deeply influential in this literature. See Berry, Martin, and Yue, "Introduction," 4–7.

64. Blackwood, "Transnational Discourses and Circuits of Queer Knowledge in Indonesia," 501. See Boellstorff, *The Gay Archipelago* and *A Coincidence of Desires.*

65. Rofel, *Desiring China,* 88, 110.

66. Sánchez-Eppeler and Patton, "Introduction: With a Passport out of Eden," 3.

67. Garcia, "Villa, Montano, Perez," 176–77.

68. Baytan, "*Bading na Bading,*" 182 (emphasis in the original).

69. Collins, "Identity, Mobility, and Urban Place-Making," 181.

70. Jackson, "Capitalism and Global Queering," 359. On modernity as an experience of "creative adaptation," see Gaonkar, "On Alternative Modernities," 1–18.

71. Here I echo Tom Boellstorff's observation about the "implicit theories of agency that underlie many descriptions of mass-mediated erotics, desire, and pleasure in Asia (and elsewhere)." "Again and again," he says, "a presocial, erotic, desiring self is granted an assumed ontological priority . . . Notice the verbs: queer Asians are said to 'appropriate', 'resist', and 'struggle'. The tone is triumphant, the mood confident, the good and bad sides clearly drawn, and the teleologies linear, marching resolutely toward global freedom" (Boellstorff, "I Knew It Was Me," 23).

72. Bagas, "Priding the Party," 10.

73. For a critique of the uses of irony in globalization theory, especially in Appadurai's work, see Tadiar, *Fantasy-Production,* 1–24.

74. Tadiar, *Things Fall Away,* 153.

75. Ibid.; on "gay modernity," see Giorgi, "Madrid *en Tránsito,*" 57–60.

76. Stewart, "Still Life," 410; Stewart, *A Space on the Side of the Road,* 48. My reference here to postcolonial desire is informed by recent correctives within postcolonial theory, particularly critiques of hybridity. Simon Gikandi, for instance, has noted that often what postcolonial subjects desire is neither "cultural hybridity nor ontological difference" but "a modern life in the European sense of the word." Similarly, Revathi Krishnaswamy notes that the articulations of "alternative" modernities problematically elide the fact that the question of modernity is subject to intense internal debate even within particular spaces. She points out, for instance, that claims about the alternative modernity offered by Indian cricket or secularism can only be sustained by occluding their gendered and casteist character. Similarly, I would suggest that to hold up and celebrate the hybridity of the bright lights scene as still another example of an alternative modernity runs the risk of ignoring the scene's role in the reproduction of inequalities. See Gikandi, "Globalization and the Claims of Postcoloniality"; and Krishnaswamy, "Postcolonial and Globalization Studies."

77. Bauman, *Globalization,* 92.

78. Stewart, "Weak Theory in an Unfinished World," 73.

79. Tsing, *Friction*, 1–12.

80. Valentine, *Imagining Transgender*, 27.

81. Stewart, "The Perfectly Ordinary Life"; Stewart, *Ordinary Affects*, 3–4.

82. On the shape of the ethnographic text, see Thornton, "The Rhetoric of Ethnographic Holism."

83. See Norris, *The Contest of Faculties*; and Lepselter, "The Flight of the Ordinary," 18–19.

84. On average, the interviews lasted two and a half hours.

85. See Armstrong, "On the Possibility of Spectral Ethnography," 243–45.

86. Autoethnography has been most thoroughly adopted at the intersection of sociology and communication studies. In anthropology, it is far less common and has received a less enthusiastic welcome. See Bochner and Ellis, *Ethnographically Speaking;* and Reed-Danahay, *Auto/Ethnography*. For an incisive and comprehensive critique, see Buzard, "On Auto-Ethnographic Authority." It is important to note that the uses of autoethnography remain highly varied. Most famously, Mary Louise Pratt forwarded an explicitly anticolonial version of autoethnography in *Imperial Eyes*. In her formulation, autoethnographic texts are seen, not as "authentic or autochthonous forms of self-representations" but as "collaboration(s) with and appropriation of the idioms of the conqueror." James Clifford, reviewing *Imperial Eyes*, found in Pratt's deployment of autoethnography something akin to the multivocal ethnography he was trying to sketch out during the 1980s, describing it as a means of redressing the picture of natives as "perpetually on the receiving (or resisting) end of descriptions, stories, and stereotypes." See Pratt, *Imperial Eyes,* 7; Clifford, "No Innocent Eyes," 4. In some ways, this book is more informed by this version of autoethnography than the work of Bochner, Ellis, and Reed-Danahay, which focus on the personal experiences of authors and are largely divorced from the politics of post- and neocolonialism.

87. Lionnet, "Autoethnography," 100.

88. See Leibing and McLean, "Learn to Value Your Shadow!," 10–11. See also Clifford, "On Ethnographic Authority," 34–38.

89. Stewart, "The Perfectly Ordinary Life."

90. Stewart, *A Space on the Side of the Road*, 21.

91. Stewart, "Weak Theory in an Unfinished World," 77.

1. Automobility and the Gay Cityscape

1. For a more detailed discussion of Malate, see Collins, "Identity, Mobility, and Urban Place-Making," 180–98.

2. In his discussion of driving, Virilio foregrounds the distorting effect of automobile speed on vision. He speaks of objects being hurled against the windshield, the displaying of inanimate objects as if they were animated by a violent

movement, or what he calls "dromoscopy." He writes, "Accelerated traversal is linked with a certain problem of perception . . . [T]he function of high-speed vehicles consists less in transporting the passenger than in causing physical reality to slide by . . . to modify . . . the surfaces of visual experience" (Virilio, *Negative Horizon*, 113).

3. It was the Futurists who first welcomed the "aesthetic of speed." As F. T. Marinetti writes, "We say that the world's magnificence has been enriched by a new beauty; the beauty of speed . . . We cooperate with mechanics in destroying the old property of distance and wild solitudes, the exquisite nostalgia of parting, for which we substitute the tragic lyricism of ubiquity and omnipresent speed" (Marinetti, "The Founding and Manifesto of Futurism," 41).

4. On the car–automobile as a unit or assemblage, see Dant, "The Driver-Car."

5. Eye contact, says Georg Simmel, "represents the most perfect reciprocity in the whole field of human relationship" (See Simmel, "Sociology of the Senses: Visual Interaction," 358).

6. Simmel, "The Stranger," 402.

7. I am thinking here of the reciprocal sexual desire established by eye contact in practices such as cruising or what Henning Bech called "gaze(s) . . . combined with . . . mobility." As Roland Barthes, recalling his fondness for hustlers, likewise notes, "Mere eye contact . . . eroticizes." See Bech, *When Men Meet*, 106; Barthes, *Incidents*, s9.

8. Over a century ago, Marx noted the importance of speed to the development of capitalist economies. "Capital," he wrote, "must strive to tear down every spatial barrier to intercourse, i.e. to exchange, and conquer the whole earth for its market . . . it strives . . . to annihilate this space with time" (Marx, *Grundrisse*, 539). While Marx was referring, specifically, to the establishment of a global capitalist economy, the idea of speed, of unobstructed circulation, has since emerged as the prime quotient of modern social relations. As Scott McQuire has noted, "Modernization has become synonymous with acceleration across all areas of social life. Speed has been the mechanical soul of modernity." This has become the case, not only for industrialists, but for all those who imagine themselves as "apostles of progress," for whom speed is not only a means for capital expansion, but an aesthetic, its own end. See McQuire, "Pure Speed—from Transport to Teleport," 26.

9. It was Le Corbusier who dreamt up ineffable space, transcendent space, and the "fourth dimension." "The fourth dimension," he writes, "is the moment of limitless escape evoked by exceptionally just consonance" (Le Corbusier, *New World of Space*, 7–8). On the attachment of gay subjectivity to travel, see Knopp, "Ontologies of Place, Placelessness, and Movement."

10. Baudrillard, *America*, 9.

11. See Tadiar, "Manila's New Metropolitan Form"; and Tadiar, "Manila's Assaults," 9–20.

12. Tadiar, "Manila's New Metropolitan Form," 155.

13. Baudrillard, *America,* 56.

14. CNN, "Claire Danes No Thrilla for Manila."

15. As Heidegger argues, a sense of nearness or proximity is possible only because humans occupy a space of intelligibility. Nearness is a function of familiarity or immediacy; one is near whatever one finds immediate, regardless of how measurably close or far away it may be (Heidegger, "Language," 196). See also Casey, *The Fate of Place,* 280–84.

16. See Ahmed, *Queer Phenomenology,* 56–58.

17. Husserl, "The World of the Living Present and the Constitution of the Surrounding World that Is Outside the Flesh," 149.

18. See Husserl, *Ideas Pertaining to a Pure Phenomenology and to a Phenomenological Philosophy: Second Book;* Merleau-Ponty, *The Primacy of Perception,* 5; and Ahmed, *Queer Phenomenology,* 51–56.

19. Tadiar, "Manila's New Metropolitan Form," 154.

20. Ibid.

21. *Sosyal* is a term used in Manila to refer to people, things, and places that are upper class. This reputation was ultimately short lived. A few years after research for this book was concluded, Government closed down purportedly due to financial difficulties. Bed, in turn, regained popularity, though it would come to face competition from a new club called O-Bar, which opened its first branch in the mid-2000s but did not rise to prominence until after Government shut down.

22. Virilio, *A Landscape of Events,* xi. The road is a non-place here only for those who occupy it in passing. For others, such as those who work there as beggars or perhaps live along its alleys, it might take on the character of "anthropological place," a place ascribed with meaning, history, and identity (Augé, *Nonplaces,* 51–53).

23. See Collins, "Identity, Mobility, and Urban Place-Making," 185–88.

24. In Manila, *callboy* is used to refer to all male prostitutes.

25. For a reading of performances in male strip clubs in Manila, see Tolentino, "Macho Dancing, the Feminization of Labor, and Neoliberalism in the Philippines."

26. Virilio, *Popular Defense and Ecological Struggles,* 98–99.

27. Virilio, *A Landscape of Events,* 40.

28. Ibid., 38, emphases added.

29. Ibid., emphasis in the original. I am reminded here of Blanchot's *étrangeté,* which he associates with the "immense pleasure" of experiencing the world as though through a plane of glass: "Whoever has disappeared completely and is suddenly there before you behind a pane of glass, becomes a sovereign figure." The "phenomenon of the window-pane" functions here as a play of presence and absence. "It inscribes within a scene or an event a difference that suspends or neutralizes them, strips them of presence" (quoted and translated in Hill, *Blanchot,* 155). In Manila, we might say, the difference that is neutralized is the violence of class difference. The underclass, the figures of abjection and fear, become, quite literally,

objects on display. They can be perused, judged, and discussed as though they had no presence. In other parts of Manila, there are also massage parlors where one can select "therapists" from a glass room. Managers often stand outside those rooms with clients offering recommendations.

30. Prostitution is illegal in the Philippines. It is, however, widespread and laws against it are seldom enforced.

31. de Certeau, *The Practice of Everyday Life,* 91–92.

32. See Le Corbusier, *Aircraft.* On the parallels between Le Corbusier and the character of Howard Roark in Ayn Rand's *The Fountainhead,* see Vidler, "Bodies in Space/Subjects in the City."

33. We rarely see nature as actually occupying space, preferring instead to see it as part of the blank canvas of any given landscape. In speaking of the relationship of space being occupied by nature, I take my cue from Michel Serres, who, for altogether different reasons, speaks of feeling "claustrophobic outside." See Serres, *Detachment,* 4.

34. As Serres notes, "That's what it is to be an object, a thing of this world . . . a light captured, seized" (Serres, *Rome,* 59).

2. Elsewhere, between Palawan and the Global City

1. Smith, "Road Kill," 21.

2. Stewart, "Machine Dreams," 21–27.

3. Hénaff, "Of Stones, Angels and Humans," 61. See also Serres, *Angels: A Modern Myth.*

4. Hénaff, "Of Stones, Angels and Humans," 69.

5. Rabasa, "Elsewheres," 73.

6. Derrida, *Without Alibi,* xxxii.

7. "Derrida's Elsewhere."

8. Stewart, *A Space on the Side of the Road,* 144.

9. "Stones" represent, in Serres's thought, a kind of built environment or the actual thickness of the material world through which signs (and thought) passes. He discusses this, most poignantly, through the figure of Rome: "(Rome) gives flesh to the word; it builds. Rome incarnates itself; it is construction. Rome is not of the word, like Athens; it is not of the book, of breath, or of writing, like Jerusalem . . . Rome is hard and dumb as stone, black as the depths of stone." See Serres, *Rome,* 57–58.

10. Godzich, "The Semiotics of Semiotics," 445.

11. Saskia Sassen first identified London, New York, and Tokyo as global cities based on their concentrations of capital flows. While indicators for global cities have since been expanded to include both political and cultural yardsticks (for instance, in the work of the Global and World Cities Study Group and Network or GaWC), the idea remains that globalness can be assessed by measuring the density of different

forms of traffic. See Sassen, *The Global City*. For work from GaWC, see Taylor, "Leading World Cities."

12. Pynchon, "The Secret Integration," 150.

13. In *America,* Baudrillard links social desertification to the "real" deserts of the United States: "The inhumanity of our ulterior, asocial, superficial world," he says, "immediately finds its aesthetic form here, its ecstatic form. For the desert is simply that: an ecstatic critique of culture, an ecstatic form of disappearance" (Baudrillard, *America,* 6).

14. It is worth noting that deserts have long been understood as empty spaces, particularly in colonial thought. The emptiness of deserts is often merely the product of imagination and desire rather than a description of fact (as in the case of previously occupied African lands). The Fort, it should be pointed out, achieves emptiness only through substantial effort—for instance, through continued efforts to keep out vendors, public transportation, squatters, and the like. See Atkinson, "Myths of the Desert as Empty Space," 107–22.

15. Bonifacio High Street is, in fact, not a street at all, but a strip mall bordered on two sides by open-air parking lots and split in the middle by a narrow lawn.

16. Derrida and Cixous, "From the Word to Life," 2.

17. Stewart, *A Space on the Side of the Road,* 146.

18. Augé, *Non-places,* 95.

19. Ibid.; see also Silverman, *Inscriptions,* 178.

20. Stewart, *A Space on the Side of the Road,* 146.

21. Ibid.

22. See, for example, Tan, "More than Meets the Eye."

23. Virilio, "The Last Vehicle," 108.

24. The NBC (Nation Broadcasting Corporation) Tent is a large, air-conditioned tent leased out for special events.

25. Stewart, *A Space on the Side of the Road,* 140.

26. Tsing, *Friction,* 5–6.

27. Virilio, *Open Sky,* 35–45.

28. Ibid., 26.

29. See Castells, *The Rise of the Network Society: The Information Age.*

30. See McQuire, "Immaterial Architectures."

31. This is how Serres discusses the shape produced by the imbrication of "localized, pocketed life" and "de-localized, global matter-information." See Connor, "Topologies," 113; see also Serres, *Atlas,* 61–85.

32. While the "annihilation of space by time" was posited by Marx in the *Grundrisse* as a consequence of the logic of capital, the phrase appears in various forms across discussions of both modernity and globalization. Marinetti famously declared in the Futurist Manifesto that "time and space died yesterday"; Le Corbusier, in *City of Tomorrow,* described technologies like telephones and cables as "apparatus(es) for abolishing time and space"; and Marshall McLuhan spoke

of how the "global embrace" of media had begun to abolish space and time. See Marx, *Grundrisse,* 538–39; Apollonio, *The Futurist,* 22; Le Corbusier, *The City of Tomorrow and Its Planning,* 187; McLuhan, *Understanding Media,* 24.

33. In this way, Virilio very much remains a pupil of Merleau-Ponty. Virilio himself discusses this relationship briefly during an interview. See Armitage, "From Modernism to Hypermodernism and Beyond," 18.

34. Virilio, *Open Sky,* 22, 26.

35. On vision and driving, see Virilio, *Negative Horizon,* 105–19; on airplanes and cinema, Virilio, *The Vision Machine,* 3; on the perspective of real space, see Virilio, *Open Sky,* 26, 36.

36. Virilio, *Open Sky,* 37 (emphases in the original).

37. The concept of "time-lag" is used by Homi Bhabha to refer to that moment of delay—"a contingent moment in the signification of closure"—which, for him, marks a space of relative autonomy for postcolonial subjects. Bhabha, *The Location of Culture,* 180–87.

38. Virilio, *Negative Horizon,* 38; also, *Open Sky,* 125.

39. Virilio, *Open Sky,* 37.

40. Virilio, "The Overexposed City," 20–23.

41. Ibid., 18.

42. Stewart, *A Space on the Side of the Road,* 146. See also Peirce, *Collected Papers, vols. 1 and 2.*

43. Rabasa, "Elsewheres," 74.

44. The U.K. version of *Queer as Folk* ran from 1999 to 2000 and was aired by Channel 4. The American adaptation ran from 2000 to 2005 and was shown on the cable network Showtime. Much controversy was spurred by both versions' explicit depiction of gay sex and by what some saw as its unabashed celebration of commercial gay male culture. Despite or precisely because of this, *Queer as Folk* not only rated well in the United Kingdom and in North America, it also earned a global following. Unsurprisingly, the U.S. version (which was actually filmed in Toronto, Canada) became more popular worldwide, despite earning a less enthusiastic response from critics. See, for example, Martel, "An End to Notches on the Headboard."

45. In the United States, *Queer as Folk* parties were also held at various clubs. These were, however, part of official tours meant to promote the launch of individual seasons. Correspondingly, hundreds of thousands of dollars were spent to re-create Babylon in different settings. In 2004, for instance, five hundred thousand dollars was budgeted to transform 2,000–3,000 capacity clubs all over the United States to effect a futuristic version of Babylon (Paoletta, "'Queer as Folk' Tour Gives Babylon Club a Twist").

46. In studies of postcolonial sexualities, the absence of coming out as a common metaphor and narrative in non-Western settings is often taken as an indication of the persistence of (geography-based) difference. The notion of "*paglaladlad*

ng kapa" or "unfurling the cape" used by some Filipino gay men is often cited as an example of how gay subjectivity is understood as an ongoing change rather than a one-time process of identification. While this metaphor is still used by some Filipino gay men, it is worth noting that it has little to no resonance among my informants, some of whom had never heard of the metaphor and all of whom came equipped with their own coming-out narratives. On "unfurling the cape," see Garcia, *Philippine Gay Culture*, 117–18; Boellstorff, *A Coincidence of Desires*, 199–200; and Manalansan, *Global Divas*, 27–35.

47. These quotes were published in an online journal. I am omitting the URL here in order to protect my informant's identity.

48. Tadiar, "The Dream-Work of Modernity," 144.

49. Tadiar, *Fantasy-Production*, 6.

50. See Buck-Morss, *The Dialectics of Seeing*, 252–86; Benjamin, *The Arcades Project*, 435, 907–908.

51. Tadiar, *Fantasy-Production*, 6.

52. Žižek, "The Real in Ideology," 264.

53. Stewart, "Machine Dreams," 22; Tadiar, "The Dream-Work of Modernity," 143–82.

54. Toward the end of my fieldwork, however, Cubao was also starting to gain prominence as a creative hub, largely due to the influx of artists. Parts of Cubao became major hangouts for another subset of gay men, particularly those attached to independent fashion, music, and art scenes.

55. My translation from Tagalog. All subsequent translations are my own. Original Tagalog: "Kasi, iyong Cubao, karaniwan lang daw kung tingnan—parang pusang local . . . Pakainin mo ng basura, puwede. Natutulog sa tabi ng kalsada, bihirang nagkakasakit. Sipain mo, ihagis sa kanal, hindi sumusurender, buhay. Ku' minsan, kakaripas ng takbo—ku' minsan, lalaban. Siyam iyong anino sa sikat nung araw. Ganyan iyong Cubao.

Ganyan iyong Cubao, kung araw.

Kung gabi naman—'tanong mo ke Butch, sasabihin no'n—kung gabi, libog na libog iyong pusang Cubao. Kumikisap iyong mata sa dilim, ang daming ilaw, ang lahat gumagalaw. 'Punta kang Ali, Superstor, Piesta Carnival, Parmers'. Pusang nag-iinit, ngumangawngaw sa lakas nung mga tugtugin, gumugulong sa simento, namimilipit, naghahanap, ang daming aliw" (Perez, *Cubao 1980*, 3–4).

56. Tadiar, "In the Face of Whiteness as Value," 167.

57. The values that Perez espouses throughout the collection, most notably in the poem "Manipesto," are summarized in the foreword to *Cubao 1980*. For a more extensive discussion, see Manalansan, *Global Divas*, 36; Garcia, *Philippine Gay Culture*, 297–344; and Tadiar, "In the Face of Whiteness as Value," 143–82.

58. While HIV/AIDS panic emerged in Manila in the eighties and early nineties, it was largely absent during my fieldwork. This was, however, not because of

increased education about the disease nor because of declining rates of infection but, to my mind, because of poor data collection and testing practices. Indeed, though I was not collecting data on HIV/AIDS or safe-sex and testing practices as part of my research, it became clear to me, through both anecdotes and interviews, that only a small number of gay men in Manila had ever been tested for HIV. Many, in fact, did not know where to get tested and routinely engaged in high-risk sexual practices. Reports since my fieldwork ended reveal alarming infection rates. In 2013, a new HIV case was being reported every three hours (as opposed to every three days in 2003), making the Philippines one of only nine countries in the world with rising transmission rates. See Trivedi, "Every Three Hours Someone in the Philippines Gets HIV"; and Tan, "AIDS, Medicine, and Moral Panic in the Philippines."

59. Colt 45 is a local strong beer marketed primarily to lower-class consumers.

60. This is the same Bernard whom I write about in the previous chapter.

61. Such geographical imaginations trouble the metronormative reading of the city as a homogenous site that allows for "the full expression of the sexual self." Here, however, the devalued site is not the rural setting often constructed as the other of a queer-friendly urban world but a district: a part of the city that allows for expressions of nonnormative sexuality that are not endorsed by the prevailing class order. See Halberstam, *In a Queer Time and Place*, 36–37.

62. Bhabha, *The Location of Culture*, 9.

63. Tadiar, *Fantasy-Production*, 7.

64. Appadurai, *Modernity at Large*, 29–31.

65. Garcia, "Villa, Montano, Perez," 176.

66. On the equation of agency and "resistance," see Mahmood, *The Politics of Piety*, 9.

67. Tadiar, *Fantasy-Production*, 3.

68. Ibid., 2.

69. Ibid.

70. Ibid.

71. Ibid., 6.

72. Ibid., 2.

3. The Specter of *Kabaklaan*

1. Buse and Stott, *Ghosts*, 14.

2. Derrida, *Specters of Marx*, xix; see also Davis, "*Ét at Présent*: Hauntology, Specters, and Phantoms." Derrida coins the term *hantologie* as a pun on ontology, supplanting the focus of the latter on being and presence with the indefinite position of the ghost.

3. Virilio makes reference to the "transapparent horizon" or the "final horizon of indirect visibility" spawned by telecommunications technologies. See Virilio, *Open Sky*, 25.

4. The struggles of queer migrants, their exclusion from commercial and political spaces, and the various strategies they employ to negotiate their displacement have spawned critical discussions of the intersections of migration and sexuality. See Patton and Sánchez-Eppler, *Queer Diasporas*; Luibhéid, "Queer/ Migration"; Luibhéid and Cantú, *Queer Migrations*; Cruz-Malavé and Manalansan, *Queer Globalizations*; and Gopinath, *Impossible Desires*.

5. For Derrida, the revenant is based on "originary iteration." It represents an absolute memory or a memory that is not relative to the present. The "revenant is a past that has never been present, an immemorial or eternal past." Lawlor, *Derrida and Husserl*, 217–25. See Derrida, *Specters of Marx*, 10.

6. Derrida, *Specters of Marx*, 125–26.

7. For a more detailed discussion of incarnation and the body in Derrida's work on spectrality, see Cheah, *Spectral Nationality*, 384–90.

8. On imaginative geographies, see Gregory, "Connective Dissonance," 197–214.

9. Flusty, *De-Coca-Colonization*, 47.

10. See Tan, "From *Bakla* to Gay"; and Garcia, "Peformativity, the *Bakla*, and the Orientalizing Gaze."

11. See Johnson, *Beauty and Power*; and Cannell, *Power and Intimacy in the Christian Philippines*.

12. See Manalansan, *Global Divas*, 12, 24. For a brief review of these texts and other works on the bakla, see Manalansan, *Global Divas*, 35–44.

13. It is worth noting that figures likened to the *bakla*, most notably, the Thai *kathoey* and the Indonesian *waria*, are also constantly being reconceptualized, despite their popular imaging as coherent local sexual formations. See Jackson, "Gay Adaptation, Tom-Dee Resistance, and *Kathoey* Indifference"; Jackson and Sullivan, *Lady Boys, Tom Boys, Rent Boys*; Blackwood, *Falling into the Lesbi World*; and Boellstorff, *A Coincidence of Desires*, 78–113.

14. The term *swardspeak* comes from *sward*, which means homosexual or *sissy* in the Cebuano dialect. See Manalansan, *Global Divas*, 46.

15. Manalansan, *Global Divas*, 46–47.

16. Ibid., 48.

17. While discussing the decline in the use of swardspeak among gay men, I was told by one informant that it continued to thrive in call centers, where a large number of gay men worked. Among my informants, it was taken for granted that the call center industry contained a disproportionately high number of gay men. The reasons for this were not entirely clear, though casual conversations about this phenomenon often led to the suggestion that gay men were attracted to or required the higher salaries offered by call centers, which allowed them to live separately from their families and hence sustain sexual and romantic relationships. One informant who worked in a call center, for instance, was kicked out of his family's house while still in college. Call centers were the only places he could secure a

relatively high-paying job given his lack of a college degree and his superior English language skills. Still, the concentration of gay men in call centers does not explain why swardspeak remains popular there or why some of the gay men who use swardspeak while at their call center jobs choose not to do so while in other places. To explain this phenomenon, it would be necessary to conduct more detailed research on gay life and call centers in Manila. The informant who first informed me about the prevalence of swardspeak in call centers, however, did suggest that it was used as a means of establishing "in groups." Another suggested that it had to do with the large numbers of lower-class men and *jologs* in call centers. I suspect, however, that it also has to do with the specific role of language in call centers— that is, the way they spur language play through the adoption of fake (American) accents, for instance. Swardspeak, itself a hodgepodge of languages, appears to fit in perfectly in a context that requires people to constantly shift linguistic codes. It is worth noting, additionally, that in call centers, swardspeak is spoken not only exclusively by gay men but also by the straight women who hang out with them.

18. Manalansan, *Global Divas*, 75.

19. *Benta* literally means "to sell" or something that will sell easily. In the years after my fieldwork was completed, swardspeak appeared to regain popularity among the general public, particularly through its new inception as *bekimon*. It is unclear, however, whether the same shift can be observed in upmarket gay bars and clubs.

20. Manalansan, *Global Divas*, 32.

21. Ibid., 115–16, 97.

22. Ibid., 97 (Manalansan's translation).

23. Johnson, *Beauty and Power*, 55.

24. Cannell, *Power and Intimacy in the Christian Philippines*, 206.

25. The close articulation of Filipino and American culture is discussed by Manalansan in an earlier article. He argues that this articulation has produced a border culture without territorial contiguity, sustained primarily by the widespread use of the English language and American popular culture. See Manalansan, "(Re)locating the Gay Filipino."

26. Agoncillo, "Circuit Meister," 55.

27. Bagas, "Priding the Party," 10.

28. While the example discussed here is New York, others have demonstrated how Filipinos (among other Asians) are excluded through the tightly structured (racial) hierarchies that operate in gay scenes in countries most often associated with global gayness. See, for example, Jackson, "That's What Rice Queens Study! White Gay Desire and Representing Asian Homosexualities."

29. Villarin, "Editor's Note," 6.

30. It is also worth noting that the bakla's own struggles, particularly against familial homophobia, are often depicted in capitalist terms. The standard narrative suggests that the bakla are ultimately accepted by their families because they are

"hard workers" with no dependents and thus are able to financially support and take care of ageing parents. See Garcia, *Philippine Gay Culture*, 354.

31. On occasion, for instance, parties are held in celebration of releases from pop artists such as Madonna, Kylie Minogue, Rihanna, and Justin Timberlake, among others.

32. CircuitAsia, "Testimonials," http://www.circuitasia.com, accessed October 16, 2006.

33. Indeed, the promotional materials of circuit parties make no claims about Asia; instead, they boast of the repertoire of DJs in the city system of gay globality and declare that "the entire world is (now) our venue" (CircuitAsia, "Testimonials"). Within the Philippines, there are only nascent references to a regional imaginary, mostly confined to foreign policy texts. I suspect that this has to do with the archipelago's peculiar Spanish-American colonial history, which has produced a contemporary culture that struggles to find commonalities with the rest of Asia and that tends to look to the United States for both cultural and political models. One could argue, however, that a sense of *Asian-ness* is growing, given increased consumption of East Asian popular culture in the mid-2000s.

34. Giorgi, "Madrid *en Tránsito*," 62.

35. Generation Pink, "About."

36. Crookshank, "And Everything Turns White."

37. Derrida, *Specters of Marx*, 49.

38. Bhabha, *The Location of Culture*, 244; see also Giorgi, "Madrid *en Tránsito*," 59.

39. Giorgi, "Madrid *en Tránsito*," 59.

40. Derrida, *Specters of Marx*, 99. On the *parlorista* as comic relief, see Baytan, "*Bading na Bading*: Evolving Identities in Philippine Cinema."

41. Giorgi, "Madrid *en Tránsito*," 60–64.

42. Late in 2008, Guys4Men was bought by and subsumed under another gay personal ads website, Planet Romeo (http://www.planetromeo.com).

43. Phil Anderson, e-mail message to the author, October 16, 2006. Anderson was the webmaster of Guys4Men.com during the time of correspondence. He also confirmed that the majority of members from Manila joined between 2004 and 2006.

44. These quotes were taken from publicly posted profiles on http://www.guys4men.com, accessed October 20, 2006.

45. Many others have pointed to the privilege afforded to masculinity and hypermasculinity by gay men. Jack Halberstam, for instance, has argued that gay men work through shame by "producing normative masculinities and presenting themselves as uncastrated, muscular, whole"; Halberstam, "Shame and White Gay Masculinity," 228. See also Connell, *Masculinities*, 143–63; Ward, "Queer Sexism"; Duncan, "Out of the Closet and into the Gym"; Bergling, *Sissyphobia*; and Ridge, Plummer, and Peasley, "Remaking the Masculine Self and Coping in

the Liminal World of the 'Gay Scene.'" On gay masculinity and Internet use, see Dowsett, Williams, Ventuneac, and Carballo-Diéguez, "'Taking It Like a Man': Masculinity and Barebacking Online"; and Payne, "Str8acting."

46. Butler, *Gender Trouble*, 174.

47. The feminization of Asian men in general and gay Asian men in particular is well documented. In the classic essay "Looking for My Penis," Richard Fung notes how, in gay pornography, Asian men are portrayed as vulnerable, exposed, and ready to be penetrated; Fung, "Looking for My Penis." David Eng discusses this phenomenon more thoroughly as "racial castration." See Eng, *Racial Castration*; see also the following collections: Leong, *Asian American Sexualities*; Eng and Hom, *Q&A: Queer in Asian America*; and Jackson and Sullivan, *Multicultural Queer*.

48. In some ways, however, such sentiments were short lived and cyclical. Between 2006 and 2009, there were periods when these house parties seemed to disappear and people were once again excited to visit the clubs.

49. For instance, it seemed unproblematic for the scene to valorize individuals such as Bryanboy, the globally famous Filipino socialite blogger whose practice of cross-dressing has been rearticulated with his "new-moneyed obsession" with luxury items and, consequently, functions as a form of cultural capital "visible" in modern gay culture. See http://www.bryanboy.com.

50. Manalansan, *Global Divas*, 24–26.

51. See the forum "TransGENDER vs. TRANSsexuals," http://www.guys 4men.com, accessed October 16, 2006.

52. Gomez, "R-E-S-P-E-C-T: A Personal Essay on the Filipino Transgendered Experience."

53. Note that in the quote from the article, I have retained the term *bakla,* whereas Gomez provides a bracketed translation of *bakla* as "gay." This again demonstrates the uncertainties regarding both terms and their relationship with one another.

54. On the differences between Western gender variant subjectivities and kabaklaan, see Garcia, "Performativity, the *Bakla,* and the Orientalizing Gaze."

55. It is worth noting that the colonial and racial politics of the globalization of "trans" identities has become an important area of critique within trans studies. See Valentine, *Imagining Transgender*; Stryker, "We Who Are Sexy: Christine Jorgensen's Transsexual Whiteness in the Postcolonial Philippines"; and Aizura, "Travelers across the Boundaries of Sex: Travel, Transnationality, and Trans Subjectivity."

56. Derrida, *Specters of Marx,* 41.

57. Ibid., 100.

58. Gordon, *Ghostly Matters*, 16.

59. Giorgi, "Madrid *en Tránsito*," 59.

60. Derrida, *Specters of Marx,* 65.

61. Bhabha, *The Location of Culture*, 45.

62. Derrida, *Specters of Marx,* 64.

63. Ibid., 79, 54.

64. Virilio, *The Art of the Motor,* 7.

65. Virilio, "The Last Vehicle."

66. Derrida, *Specters of Marx,* 140.

67. Bauman, *Globalization,* 94.

68. Derrida, *Specters of Marx,* 133.

4. Transnational Transit and the Circuits of Privilege

1. The size and scale of modern airports have led to the emergence of so-called airport cities or cities of the air. As John Thackera notes, "Both cities and airports cover large areas; both are a complex of intersecting transport systems, economies, buildings, and people" (Thackera, "Lost in Space," 60–69).

2. Indeed, one of the characteristic traits of airports is that they are, in Martha Rosler's terms, "tremendous colonizers, turning the land they occupy and the surrounding areas into wasteland." Rosler writes, "As a city effaces the ground on which it stands, the airport bulldozes and flattens out the spaces of nature. It brings the land as close as possible to a condition of perfection in which geometry has conquered diversity or incident" (Rosler, "In the Place of the Public," 73).

3. The Marcos dictatorship, which was in power from 1965 until the EDSA Revolution in 1986, was well known for its edifice complex. This was particularly associated with the former First Lady, Imelda Marcos, who, as both governor of Metro Manila and minister of Human Settlements, championed and oversaw the construction of iconic buildings. Foremost among these are the main theater of the Cultural Center of the Philippines or CCP (1969) and the Manila Film Center (1981). The Film Center, dubbed "the Parthenon," speaks most directly to the violence and Imeldific excess involved in the architectural dreams of the conjugal dictatorship. Built at a breakneck pace, a section of the scaffolding collapsed during construction and buried some 169 workers. According to reports, Imelda Marcos insisted that the bodies simply be paved over in order to finish construction in time for the Manila Film Festival. See Lico, *Edifice Complex*; Tadiar, "Manila's Assaults"; Tadiar, "Manila's New Metropolitan Form"; and Benedicto, "Queer Space in the Ruins of Dictatorship Architecture."

4. It was Imelda who dreamt of transforming Metro Manila into the "City of Man": "an environment within which man can develop his full potential, where any man can live fully, happily, and with dignity." See Nells-Lim, "Metro Manila in the 1980s," 63 (quoted in Lico, *Edifice Complex,* 52).

5. The original airport that serviced Manila was the Manila International Air Terminal, which was built on Nielson Field, now Ayala Avenue, the main artery of the Makati CBD. It was moved in 1948 to Nichols Field, in what is now the site of Terminal 2. In 1972, a fire destroyed the terminal. The government replaced it

with a smaller terminal, which serviced the city until the present-day Terminal 1 was completed in 1981. Terminal 1 was originally named the Manila International Airport. It was renamed the Ninoy Aquino International Airport in 1987, after the slain, anti-Marcos opposition leader whose death prompted the revolution against Marcos and whose wife, Corazon Aquino, assumed the presidency at the end of the dictatorship. Note that my description of NAIA here refers exclusively to Terminal 1, which remains the main international terminal.

6. Leandro Locsin was Imelda Marcos's most favored architect. It is notable that Locsin's architecture drew explicitly from ideas of national evolution, mapping a movement from local forms like the nipa hut toward a reinterpretation of those forms within a vision of stark modernity, celebrating, for instance, the plasticity of concrete. The synergy between Imelda and Locsin (reportedly stemming from a conversation at a party in her honor) appears to be grounded in a similar concern with making the nation speak a modernist vocabulary, a concern that persists in the privileged pursuit of "newness." Locsin once said, for example, that he believed "that one would do well to look back once in a while to see what we had, not in order to return to it, but to make use of it to create something new" (quoted in Gadi-Baltazar, "Locsin: Innovator and Architect," 76). See also Lico, *Edifice Complex,* 74–75.

7. When Manuel Castells defined the "space of flows," he described flows as "purposeful, repetitive, programmable sequences of exchange and interaction." In a sense, the absence in NAIA of the recognizable elements of airports might be seen as an interruption in the sequences of interaction, making the airport at once a glitch in the flow of bodies and an integral part of its infrastructural support. See Castells, *The Rise of the Network Society: The Information Age,* 412. Similarly, Marc Augé refers to the airport as the prototypical "non-place" or a space of "circulation, communication and consumption, where solitudes coexist without creating any social bond or even a social emotion." For Augé, however, non-places do not exist in pure form. "Place and non-place are rather like opposed polarities: the first is never completely erased, the second never totally completed; they are like palimpsests on which the scrambled game of identity and relations is ceaselessly rewritten." The overwhelming presence of Manila *in* NAIA might, in this sense, be taken as a challenge to the very placelessness of NAIA. See Augé, *Non-places,* 78–79; and "Paris and the Ethnography of the Contemporary World," 178.

8. Augé notes that what makes non-places distinct from "anthropological places" is that they do not integrate earlier places, instead listing, classifying, and promoting them to "the status of places of memory." See Augé, *Non-places,* 78.

9. Stewart, *A Space on the Side of the Road,* 51.

10. Ballard, "The Ultimate Departure Lounge," 121.

11. See Cresswell, *On the Move,* 219–58.

12. Non-places, says Augé, are produced by "supermodernity," which is characterized by three figures of excess: "an excess of simultaneous events" (the

acceleration of history or the speeding up of information flows), "excess space" (the shrinking of the planet), and, more important here, "excess individualism," which refers to how supermodernity works to "fold the individual back on himself, close her off, constituting him or her as a witness of rather than an actor in contemporary life." See Augé, *Non-places*, 1–6; also Augé, *A Sense for the Other*, 103–5.

13. The word *balikbayan* is a conjunction of *balik* (return) and *bayan* (nation). It is commonly used as a noun that refers to return migrants. The balikbayan box is the cardboard box used by many Filipinos when traveling. Many wealthy Filipinos often frown upon balikbayan boxes, which are often associated with what are perceived to be common Filipino practices like overpacking and refusing to abide by baggage restrictions. Balikbayan boxes are, moreover, seen as both cheaper and lighter alternatives to luggage.

14. On labor migrants as "human excess," see Tadiar, *Fantasy-Production*, 113–49. In 2007 alone, 1,077,623 OFWs were deployed, over 95 percent of whom exited through NAIA. Deployment rates have been consistent for the past decade, showing only a growth rate of 1.4 percent from 1998 to 2007. The majority of OFWs remain headed to other Asian countries, the Middle East, and Europe, though it is worth noting that the 2007 data also show that there are now OFWs in over 150 countries and territories. See Philippines Overseas Employment Administration, *Overseas Employment Statistics 2007* (http://www.poea.gov.ph).

15. I am reminded here of the distinction Zygmunt Bauman makes between two paradigmatic experiences of travel: that of the tourist and that of the vagabond. "Tourists," says Bauman, "become wanderers and put the bitter-sweet dreams of homesickness above the comforts of home—because they want to; either because they consider it the most reasonable life-strategy 'under the circumstances', or because they have been seduced by the true imaginary pleasures of a sensation-gatherer's life." Vagabonds "are on the move because they have been pushed from behind—having first been spiritually uprooted from the place that holds no promise, by a force of seduction or propulsion too powerful, and often too mysterious, to resist." Bauman rightly notes, however, that "there is a large part, arguably a substantial majority of the society of consumers/travelers, who cannot be quite sure where do they stand at the moment and even less can be sure that their present standing will see the light of the next day" (Bauman, *Globalization*, 92).

16. Stewart, *A Space on the Side of the Road*, 67.

17. On Filipino seafarers, see Fajardo, *Filipino Crosscurrents*.

18. By referring to OFWs as "labor commodities," I am extending the argument raised by Tadiar, who once described overseas domestic work as the "objectification of social relations of dispossession (the domestic helper not possessing her body inasmuch as it is sold on behalf of and to others . . .)." This core logic of objectification applies to all OFWs, though it is clear that domestic helpers, whose

bodies and work are so evidently gendered and racialized, occupy a markedly pronounced case of labor-power being "at the disposal of employers/owners" (Tadiar, *Fantasy-Production*, 117).

19. In the following sections, I borrow a strategy from Kathleen Stewart, who employs imperatives ("picture," "imagine") in order to "catch [her readers] up in the dialogic provisionality" of the ethnographic spaces she "re-presents" (Stewart, *A Space on the Side of the Road*, 9–10).

20. "Mrs. M" is a reference to Imelda Marcos. Perhaps unsurprisingly, Imelda Marcos has been readily adopted within the gay community as an icon, as a symbol of excess, fabulousness, and so on (Benedicto, "Queer Space in the Ruins of Dictatorship Architecture").

21. I remember, for instance, that one such shantytown emerged seemingly overnight next to the gated village where my family once lived and that its sudden appearance raised fears among the homeowners, who hired construction workers (perhaps from that shantytown itself) to raise the walls around the village and crown them with barbed wire and broken glass. I remember that one day, a fire broke out in that shantytown and that the moment the black smoke started to spill into the sky over our village and the fires began rushing to the walls, our neighbor whose house was most in danger ran quickly to his garage to move his vintage Mercedes out of harm's way. For more on gated communities, see Blakely and Snyder, *Fortress America*; and Coy and Pöhler, "Gated Communities in Latin American Megacities."

22. See Dickey, "Permeable Homes"; and Sun, *Maid in China*.

23. Augé writes, "Alone, but one of many, the user of a non-place is in contractual relations with it (or with the powers that govern it). He is reminded, when necessary, that the contract exists . . . The contract always relates to the individual identity of the contracting party . . . [P]roof that the contract has been respected comes at the immigration desk, with simultaneous presentation of the boarding pass and an identity document: different countries have different requirements in this area (identity card, passport, passport and visa), and checks are made at departure time to ensure that these will be properly fulfilled. So the passenger accedes to his anonymity only when he has given proof of his identity; when he has countersigned (so to speak) the contract . . . In a way, the user of the non-place is always required to prove his innocence" (Augé, *Non-places*, 101–2).

24. Rafael, *White Love*, 213. The more general term *OFW* has largely supplanted *OCW* or *Overseas Contract Worker*, which refers to laborers such as construction workers, seafarers, and domestic helpers employed on a contractual basis, in both official and popular discourses. Though the term OFW technically covers most labor migrants, it retains the undesirable meanings of OCW. For instance, many Filipino professionals working in corporations overseas jokingly refer to themselves as OCWs. They may, in fact, technically be OCWs and be governed by the same institutions and regulations as contracted labor. The joke lies in the shared

knowledge that they remain distinct (from the laborers associated with the term OCW) due to the nature of their work, class background, and social status.

25. Fernandez, "From Boracay to Greece."

26. Stewart, *A Space on the Side of the Road,* 120.

27. Fernandez, "From Boracay to Greece," 31.

28. See Classen, "The Odor of the Other."

29. Geronimo Sy, a columnist at the *Manila Times,* had this to say about Fernandez: "She flaunted political correctness when she dared to be true to herself and called OFWs for who they are: A noisy lot intruding into personal space sacred to others in small places like economy seats." Another columnist adds, "I think Malu was simply writing what she thought and sensed. That's freedom of the press. And what she wrote was just the truth. Everybody knows that." And even in the blogosphere, where the most violent protestations were aired, at least one OFW agreed: "I'm not defending Malu Fernandez nor her recent article. I'm not the one who would belittle my fellow OFWs. But what Malu Fernandez wrote is her opinion . . . The truth is that Malu Fernandez wrote something true. Something existing in our daily lives. Something that is perceived common by a lot of other people, not just Filipinos but the whole world." See Sy, "Malu Fernandez: Hate Ugly Filipinos"; Jurado, "Educating Migrants"; and Poypogi, "The Price of Being Yourself," *Poypogi* (blog), August 24, 2007, poypogi.wordpress.com, accessed October 28, 2008.

30. Lopez, "Who Is Malu Fernandez," *Betty Lopez* (blog), August 18, 2007, bettytlopez.i.ph, accessed October 28, 2008.

31. Yan, "Malu Fernandez: What's Economy Class?," *Fuba Genre* (blog), August 18, 2007, http://www.fubargenre.com, accessed October 28, 2008.

32. Comment on "BIG ot Malu Fernandez," *Myepinoy* (blog), August 23, 2007, myepinoy.wordpress.com, accessed October 28, 2008.

33. Comment on "The Pinoy Press Top 10: Great Quotes from Malu Fernandez," *The Pinoy Press* (blog), August 24, 2007, http://www.pinoypress.net, accessed October 28, 2008.

34. The charge against Fernandez's "tactlessness" was, in fact, further articulated in numerous responses that conceded her points but claimed that they were not to be aired in "polite society." For instance, see Sunny C., "We Are Snobs," *BlogHer,* September 2, 2007, http://www.blogher.com, accessed October 28, 2008.

35. Bryanboy, "Malu Fernandez Rides Economy Class," *Bryanboy* (blog), August 17, 2007, http://www.bryanboy.com, accessed October 28, 2008.

36. As Catherine Choy has noted, nurse migration from the Philippines is, in fact, not new. In 1979, a World Health Organization report already observed that among nurse-sending countries, "the largest outflow of nurses 'by far' was from the Philippines." The initial emergence of the Philippines as a nurse-sending country can be credited (in part, at least) to American systems of education, infrastructure, and public health. The subsequent growth in numbers is far more difficult to explain. Choy contends, for instance, that part of the explanation lies in

the "culture of migration" or the ways in which narratives about the promise of immigration shape Filipino nurses' desire to migrate abroad and also in the "institutionalization of nurse migration"—that is, the aggressive collaboration between recruitment agencies, foreign hospitals, and governments. See Choy, *Empire of Care*, 1–5. As if to demonstrate the emergence of the nurse as a key representative of Filipino labor migration, a *New York Times Sunday Magazine* special report on OFWs featured on its cover a lone Filipino nurse standing in medical scrubs on an empty beach. Recent data shows that of the New York area's 215,000 Filipinos, 3 out of 10 are nurses or other health care practitioners. See Deparle, "A Good Provider Is One Who Leaves"; and Berger, "Filipino Nurses, Healers in Trouble."

37. Commenting on the separate phenomena of nurse migration and domestic worker migration (as well as migration into overseas entertainment and sex industries) from the Philippines, Choy notes that "while these different groups of overseas workers need to be studied on their own terms, the feminization, racialization, and commodification of these laborers as well as the degrading stereotypes that often accompany these processes bind them together in the new millennium" (Choy, *Empire of Care*, 189). Similarly, Martin Manalansan prefers to use the term "global care industry," pointing to the common gendering and racializing processes that underpin different forms of migrant work coded as "domestic," from professional nursing to "unskilled" domestic carework, such as tending to the elderly. See Manalansan, "Queer Intersections"; see also Parreñas, *Servants of Globalization*, 65.

38. Estrella, "Nursing Schools Peddle Dreams."

39. The rise in nursing schools has been so dramatic that the presence of "substandard" nursing schools has become a matter of concern for the national government, with the Commission on Higher Education threatening in 2009 to shut down some 177 schools that failed to pass a single graduate in the nursing licensure exams; see "Failed Schools' Closure to Address Nurses' Glut."

40. "In recent years," notes Manalansan, "it has become apparent that the Filipino or Filipina woman as the global careworker par excellence exists hand in hand with the male migrant careworker, specifically gay Filipino men, who are becoming the new figure of foreign careworkers" (Manalansan, "Queer Intersections," 249–50).

41. Tadiar, *Fantasy-Production*, 122–25; Rafael, *White Love*, 212–27.

42. Tadiar, *Fantasy-Production*, 127.

43. Rafael, *White Love*, 217–23.

44. Ibid., 213.

45. Jurado, "Educating Migrants."

46. Aguilar, "The Dialectics of Transnational Shame and National Identity," 118–25.

47. Tadiar, *Fantasy-Production*, 129. It is worth noting here that the focus on domestic workers in discussions of the image of Filipinos abroad has to do with

not only their ubiquity but also the nature and geography of their work. Male OFWs, often associated with either construction work in underpopulated parts of the Middle East or seafaring, are traditionally out of sight.

48. Aguilar, "The Dialectics of Transnational Shame and National Identity," 120–21.

5. White Noise and the Shock of Racial Shame

1. Fanon, *Black Skin, White Masks,* 109.

2. Michael Taussig refers to the "tense stasis of shock itself, a phase of compressed nothingness in which memory, space, and time all coagulate and then reconfigure past and present" (Taussig, *My Cocaine Museum,* 235).

3. Fanon, *Black Skin, White Masks,* 109; Manalansan, *Global Divas,* 65.

4. Taussig, *My Cocaine Museum,* 248.

5. See Probyn, *Blush,* 2; Taussig, *The Magic of the State,* 162.

6. Taussig, *The Magic of the State,* 162.

7. To link shame to queer complicity is, I would suggest, to reject reinvestments in gay shame as a counterpoint to gay pride. As Jack Halberstam has very rightly noted, the rubric of gay shame can and often does operate as a universalizing framework that works to rebuild "the (white gay male) self that shame dismantled" by projecting shame onto racialized and feminized bodies. My interest here, following Halberstam, is in using shame as part of a "tactic in the struggle to make privilege . . . visible" (Halberstam, "Shame and White Gay Masculinity").

8. Serres, *Hermes,* 66–70.

9. Attali, *Noise,* 26.

10. For Serres, the primary source of noise is within the body. He writes of the "subliminal murmur our proprioceptive ear sometimes strains to hear: billions of cells dedicated to biochemical reactions, the likes of which should have us all fainting from the pressure of their collective hum." When this noise becomes audible, he says, we call it "illness." We are only healed when we are able to silence our organs. See Serres, *The Five Senses,* 106–7.

11. See, for example, the following: Caluya, "The Rice Steamer"; Buckland, *Impossible Dance,* 128–58; Manalansan, "Race, Violence, and Neoliberal Spatial Politics in the Global City"; Armstrong, *Forging Gay Identities,* 134–53; and Gosine, "Blonde to Brown at Gay.Com."

12. Manalansan, "Race, Violence, and Neoliberal Spatial Politics in the Global City," 144.

13. Makalani, "Introduction," 2. See also Mills, *The Racial Contract.*

14. Makalani, "Introduction," 3–4.

15. Saldanha, "Reontologizing Race," 19. See also Saldanha, *Psychedelic White.*

16. Saldanha, "Reontologizing Race," 19.

17. Ibid., 18.

18. Ibid.

19. Ibid., 20.

20. Fanon, *Black Skin, White Masks,* 109.

21. The absence of a well-developed discourse on race in the Philippines has only recently earned sustained academic attention. See, in particular, Aguilar, "Tracing Origins"; Rodriguez, *Suspended Apocalypse*; Ponce, *Beyond the Nation,* esp. chapter 6; Isaac, *American Tropics*; and Pisares, "Do You Mis(recognize) Me?"

22. On constructions of the Moros (the Islamic peoples of Mindanao), see Abinales, *Making Mindanao,* 45–68. On the racial politics of colonial agriculture in the Philippines, see Aguilar, *Clash of Spirits,* 156–88.

23. Aguilar, "Tracing Origins," 629–32.

24. See Holt, *Colonizing Filipinas,* 120–29. See also Hilsdon, *Madonnas and Martyrs,* 39, 103–4.

25. The Philippines has long maintained a complicated and ambivalent relationship with Asia. In Manila, it is typical to hear remarks about how the Philippines is more akin to Latin American countries given its history of Spanish and American colonial rule. People also routinely mention that the Philippines is the only predominantly Christian nation in the region. This distanced relationship to the region is reflected in different areas of social and political life. For instance, unlike other Southeast Asian countries, there is rarely any mention in the news media of the Association of Southeast Asian Nations (ASEAN).

26. Aguilar, "Tracing Origins," 611–20.

27. The Philippine film, television, and fashion industries are full of foreign-born Filipinos. In fact, a popular Internet-circulated joke list called "You Know You Are a Second Generation Pinoy If" includes an entry that states, "You actually believe that you could become a Filipino movie star back home because you think you're better looking than the Filipinos back home."

28. Rondilla, "Filipinos and the Color Complex."

29. Rafael, *White Love,* 7.

30. Aguilar, "Tracing Origins," 612–20.

31. López Jaena, *Discursos y Artículos Varios (Selected Speeches and Articles),* 151–52, quoted in Aguilar, "Tracing Origins," 614.

32. Rizal, *The Rizal-Blumentritt Correspondence,* 22, quoted in Aguilar, "Tracing Origins," 614. *Igorrotes* or Igorots was a name used to refer to mountain tribes allegedly descended from a wave of migrating Malays who intermarried with the black-skinned Negritos who arrived before them.

33. Aguilar, "Tracing Origins," 615.

34. Ibid., 615–16.

35. Fores-Ganzon, *La Solidaridad,* vol. 1, 444.

36. Fanon, *Black Skin, White Masks,* 111–12.

37. Fores-Ganzon, *La Solidaridad,* vol. 1, 444–45.

38. López Jaena, *Discursos y Artículos Varios,* 171.

39. Aguilar, "Tracing Origins," 629.

40. Rafael, *White Love,* 32.

41. Ibid., 23.

42. U.S. Bureau of the Census, *Census of the Philippine Islands,* vol. 1, 40, quoted in Rafael, *White Love,* 32.

43. In 1930, the sociologist Emory Bogardus published an article, titled "What Race Are Filipinos?," where he argued that "there is no Filipino race, but a Filipino race in the making . . . The Filipinos are daily becoming more like Caucasians. They are a people on the move racially, from Mongoloid toward Caucasoid" (Bogardus, "What Race Are Filipinos?"). Further, as Ariela Julie Gross has pointed out, "Liberal advocates of Filipino rights sought to distinguish the Filipinos from other groups who were the targets of prejudice and discrimination—'Mongolians' in particular—but also to assert that both racial and cultural identities could change with assimilation and that Filipinos . . . were undergoing a transformation and could even become white" (Gross, *What Blood Won't Tell,* 247).

44. Rafael, *White Love,* 81–83.

45. The U.S. National Origins Act effectively banned all immigration from Asia by the late 1920s. Filipinos, then recognized as U.S. nationals, were the only group that could get around the ban. Often directly targeted by recruitment agencies in search of cheap labor, the number of Filipinos in the United States rose from under 3,000 in 1910 to almost 110,000 in 1930. See Bonus, *Locating Filipino Americans,* 35–37.

46. See also Espiritu, *Filipino American Lives* and *Home Bound,* 23–45.

47. Gross, *What Blood Won't Tell,* 246–52.

48. The interchangeability of *bayan* and *lahi* here marks a difference from the English-speaking world, where nationality and race were beginning to be disarticulated by as early as the mid-nineteenth century. See Banton, *Racial and Ethnic Competition.*

49. Fanon, *Black Skin, White Masks,* 11.

50. Deleuze, *Difference and Repetition,* 23–25.

51. See, for example, Eng and Hom, *Q&A: Queer in Asian America*; and Jackson and Sullivan, *Multicultural Queer.*

52. On the privilege afforded to "Eurasian" subjects, see Matthews, "Eurasian Persuasions"; and Haritaworn, *The Biopolitics of Mixing.*

53. Fanon, *Black Skin, White Masks,* 63.

54. Lacan, *The Four Fundamental Concepts of Psycho-analysis,* 99.

55. See Butler, *Giving an Account of Oneself,* 12.

56. It is worth noting here that, in contrast to Miguel, I was being accused of being "Asian" (Korean or Chinese); this is what the man wanted to read me as and stands in opposition to what he assumed I would call myself (part Spanish). In other words, he wanted to see me as an Asian who wanted to be European. He

was saying, "You look Asian, therefore I assume you don't want to be seen that way." He was, in this way, interpellating me as racially ashamed.

57. Rose, *On Not Being Able to Sleep,* 1; Derrida, "The Animal That Therefore I Am," 373; Leys, *From Guilt to Shame,* 126. For a discussion of the relationship of shame and vision, see Munt, *Queer Attachments,* 9–10.

58. Derrida, "The Animal That Therefore I Am," 373.

59. Wilce, *Crying Shame,* 121.

60. On the shame of being ashamed, see Probyn, *Blush,* 2.

61. Bhabha, "Remembering Fanon," ix.

62. Serres, *The Five Senses,* 86.

63. Fanon, *Black Skin, White Masks,* 116.

64. Ibid., 117.

65. Derrida, "The Animal That Therefore I Am," 372–73.

66. MacCormack, *Cinesexuality,* 76; Serres, *The Five Senses,* 106.

67. Serres, *The Five Senses,* 106; Attali, *Noise,* 29.

68. Fanon, *Black Skin, White Masks,* 67.

69. As Sara Ahmed writes, "Shame may be restorative only when the shamed other can 'show' that its failure to measure up to a social ideal is temporary." The permanent failure of the racialized third-world subject to become "global" is precisely what makes it impossible to recuperate shame as a basis for identity. See Ahmed, *The Cultural Politics of Emotion,* 107.

70. For discussions of gay culture in Cape Town, see Visser, "Gay Men, Tourism, and Urban Space"; Elder, "Love for Sale"; and Oswin, "Researching 'Gay Cape Town.'"

71. Stewart, "Conspiracy Theory's Worlds," 13.

72. Serres, *The Five Senses,* 106.

73. Attali, *Noise,* 22.

74. Serres, *The Five Senses,* 106.

75. Attali, *Noise,* 22.

76. Tadiar, "In the Face of Whiteness as Value," 148.

77. Ibid.

78. Rafael, *White Love,* 19–51.

79. Tadiar, "In the Face of Whiteness as Value," 149.

80. For a fuller reader of this pivotal moment in the novella, see Tadiar, "In the Face of Whiteness as Value," 143–45.

81. Dyer, *White,* 14; Tadiar, "In the Face of Whiteness as Value," 146–50.

82. Tadiar, "In the Face of Whiteness as Value," 145.

Coda

1. See Serres, *Genesis.*
2. Ibid., 49–57.
3. Serres, *The Five Senses,* 106.
4. Probyn, *Blush,* 3.
5. Ibid., xii–xiii.
6. Ibid., xii.
7. Baudrillard, *Cool Memories IV,* 27.

Abbas, Ackbar. *Hong Kong: Culture and the Politics of Disappearance.* Minneapolis: University of Minnesota Press, 1997.

Abinales, Patricio N. *Making Mindanao: Cotabato and Davao in the Formation of the Philippine Nation-State.* Quezon City: Ateneo de Manila University Press, 2000.

Agoncillo, Paul. "Circuit Meister." *Icon Magazine,* July–September 2005.

Aguilar, Filomeno V. *Clash of Spirits: The History of Power and Sugar Planter Hegemony on a Visayan Island.* Honolulu: University of Hawaii Press, 1998.

———. "The Dialectics of Transnational Shame and National Identity." *Philippine Sociological Review* 44, nos. 1–4 (1996): 101–36.

———. "Tracing Origins: *Ilustrado* Nationalism and the Racial Science of Migration Waves." *Journal of Asian Studies* 64 (2005): 605–37.

Ahmed, Sara. *The Cultural Politics of Emotion.* New York: Routledge, 2004.

———. *Queer Phenomenology: Orientations, Objects, Others.* Durham, N.C.: Duke University Press, 2006.

Aizura, Aren Z. "Travelers across the Boundaries of Sex: Travel, Transnationality, and Trans Subjectivity." PhD diss., University of Melbourne, 2009.

Altman, Dennis. "Global Gaze/Global Gays." *GLQ: A Journal of Lesbian and Gay Studies* 3, no. 4 (1997): 417–36.

———. *Global Sex.* Crows Nest, New South Wales: Allen and Unwin, 2001.

———. "On Global Queering." *Australian Humanities Review* 2 (1996). Accessed September 7, 2009. http://www.lib.latrobe.edu.au/AHR/archive/Issue-July 1996/altman.html.

———. "Rupture or Continuity? The Internationalization of Gay Identities." *Social Text* 14 (1996): 77–94.

Amin, Ash, and Nigel Thrift. *Cities: Reimagining the Urban.* Cambridge, U.K.: Wiley-Blackwell, 2002.

Aning, Jerome. "Gay Party-List Group Ladlad Out of Race." *Philippine Daily Inquirer,* March 1, 2007.

Ansell-Pearson, Keith. *Germinal Life: The Difference and Repetition of Deleuze.* London: Routledge, 1999.

Apollonio, Umbro, ed. *The Futurist Manifestos*. New York: Viking Press, 1973.

Appadurai, Arjun. *Modernity at Large: Cultural Dimensions of Globalization*. Minneapolis: University of Minnesota Press, 1996.

Armitage, John. "From Modernism to Hypermodernism and Beyond: An Interview with Paul Virilio." In *Virilio Live*, edited by John Armitage, 25–56. London: Sage, 2001.

Armstrong, Elizabeth A. *Forging Gay Identities: Organizing Sexuality in San Francisco, 1950–1994*. Chicago: University of Chicago Press, 2002.

Armstrong, Justin. "On the Possibility of Spectral Ethnography." *Cultural Studies, Critical Methodologies* 10 (2010): 243–50.

Atkinson, David. "Myths of the Desert as Empty Space: Enduring European Imaginaries of North Africa and the Challenges of Material Geographies." In *Libia Oggi*, edited by Paola Gandolfi, 107–22. Bologna: Il Ponte, 2005.

Attali, Jacques. *Noise: The Political Economy of Music*. Translated by Brian Massumi. Minneapolis: University of Minnesota Press, 1985.

Augé, Marc. *Non-places: Introduction to an Anthropology of Supermodernity*. Translated by John Howe. London: Verso, 1995.

———. "Paris and the Ethnography of the Contemporary World." In *Parisian Fields*, edited by Michael Sherringham, 175–79. London: Reaktion, 1996.

———. *A Sense for the Other*. Stanford, Calif.: Stanford University Press, 1998.

Bagas, Jonas. "Priding the Party." *Icon Magazine*, July–September 2005.

Ballard, J. G. "The Ultimate Departure Lounge." In *Airport*, edited by Steven Bode and Jeremy Millar, 118–21. London: The Photographers' Gallery, 1997.

Banton, Michael. *Racial and Ethnic Competition*. Cambridge, U.K.: Cambridge University Press, 1983.

Barthes, Roland. *Incidents*. Translated by Richard Howard. Berkeley: University of California Press, 1992.

Baudrillard, Jean. *America*. Translated by Chris Turner. London: Verso, 1998.

———. *Cool Memories IV: 1995–2000*. Translated by Chris Turner. New York: Verso, 2003.

Bauman, Zygmunt. *Globalization: The Human Consequences*. Cambridge, U.K.: Polity Press, 1998.

———. *Liquid Modernity*. Cambridge, U.K.: Polity Press, 2000.

Baytan, Ronald. "*Bading na Bading*: Evolving Identities in Philippine Cinema." In *AsiaPacifiQueer: Rethinking Genders and Sexualities*, edited by Fran Martin, Peter A. Jackson, Mark McLelland, and Audrey Yue, 181–96. Urbana: University of Illinois Press, 2008.

Bech, Henning. *When Men Meet: Homosexuality and Modernity*. Chicago: University of Chicago Press, 1997.

Bell, David, and Jon Binnie. "Authenticating Queer Space: Citizenship, Urbanism and Governance." *Urban Studies* 41 (2004): 1807–20.

Bell, David, and Gill Valentine, eds. *Mapping Desires: Geographies of Sexualities.* New York: Routledge, 1995.

Benedicto, Bobby. "Queer Space in the Ruins of Dictatorship Architecture." *Social Text* 117 (2013): 25–47.

Benjamin, Walter. *The Arcades Project.* Translated by Howard Eiland and Kevin McLaughlin. Cambridge, Mass.: Harvard University Press, 1999.

———."The Work of Art in the Age of Mechanical Reproduction." In *Illuminations,* translated by Harry Zohn, 217–51. New York: Schocken Books, 1969.

Berger, Joseph. "Filipino Nurses, Healers in Trouble." *New York Times,* January 27, 2008.

Bergling, Tim. *Sissyphobia: Gay Men and Effeminate Behavior.* Binghamton: Haworth Press, 2001.

Berlant, Lauren. "Cruel Optimism." *differences: A Journal of Feminist Cultural Studies* 17, no. 3 (2006): 20–36.

———. *Cruel Optimism.* Durham, N.C.: Duke University Press, 2011.

Berry, Chris, Fran Martin, and Audrey Yue. "Introduction: Beep-Click-Link." In *Mobile Cultures: New Media in Queer Asia,* edited by Chris Berry, Fran Martin, and Audrey Yue, 1–20. Durham, N.C.: Duke University Press, 2003.

Bhabha, Homi K. *The Location of Culture.* New York: Routledge, 1994.

Blackwood, Evelyn. *Falling into the Lesbi World: Desire and Difference in Indonesia.* Honolulu: University of Hawaii Press, 2010.

———. "Transnational Discourses and Circuits of Queer Knowledge in Indonesia." *GLQ: A Journal of Lesbian and Gay Studies* 14, no. 4 (2008): 481–507.

Blakely, Edward J., and Mary Gail Snyder. *Fortress America: Gated Communities in the United States.* Washington, D.C.: Brookings Institution Press, 1997.

Bochner, Arthur P., and Carolyn Ellis, eds. *Ethnographically Speaking: Autoethnography, Literature, and Aesthetics.* Walnut Creek, Calif.: Alta Mira Press, 2002.

Boellstorff, Tom. "I Knew It Was Me: Mass Media, 'Globalization,' and Lesbian and Gay Indonesians." In *Mobile Cultures: New Media in Queer Asia,* edited by Chris Berry, Fran Martin, and Audrey Yue, 21–51. Durham, N.C.: Duke University Press, 2003.

———. *The Gay Archipelago: Sexuality and Nation in Indonesia.* Princeton, N.J.: Princeton University Press, 2005.

———. *A Coincidence of Desires: Anthropology, Queer Studies, Indonesia.* Durham, N.C.: Duke University Press, 2007.

Bogardus, Emory S. "What Race Are Filipinos?" *Sociology and Social Research* 16 (1931–32): 274–79.

Bonus, Rick. *Locating Filipino Americans: Ethnicity and the Cultural Politics of Space.* Philadelphia: Temple University Press, 2000.

Browne, Kath, Jason Lim, and Gavin Brown, eds. *Geographies of Sexualities: Theory, Practices and Politics.* Aldershot, U.K.: Ashgate, 2007.

Buckland, Fiona. *Impossible Dance: Club Culture and Queer World-Making*. Middletown, Conn.: Wesleyan University Press, 2002.

Buck-Morss, Susan. *The Dialectics of Seeing: Walter Benjamin and the Arcades Project*. Cambridge, Mass.: MIT Press, 1991.

Buse, Peter, and Andrew Stott. *Ghosts: Deconstruction, Psychoanalysis, History*. Basingstoke: Macmillan, 1999.

Butler, Judith. *Gender Trouble: Feminism and the Subversion of Identity*. New York: Routledge, 1990.

———. *Giving an Account of Oneself*. New York: Fordham University Press, 2005.

Buzard, James. "On Auto-ethnographic Authority." *Yale Journal of Criticism* 16, no. 1 (2003): 61–91.

Caluya, Gilbert. "The Rice Steamer: Race, Desire, and Affect in Sydney's Gay Scene." *Australian Geographer* 39, no. 3 (2008): 283–92.

Cannell, Fenella. *Power and Intimacy in the Christian Philippines*. Cambridge, U.K.: Cambridge University Press, 1999.

Casey, Edward S. *The Fate of Place: A Philosophical History*. Berkeley: University of California Press, 1998.

Casey, Mark E. "The Queer Unwanted and Their Undesirable 'Otherness.'" In *Geographies of Sexualities: Theory, Practices and Politics*, edited by Kath Browne, Jason Lim, and Gavin Brown, 125–36. Aldershot, U.K.: Ashgate, 2007.

Castells, Manuel. *The Rise of the Network Society: The Information Age. Economy, Society and Culture Vol. 1*. Oxford: Blackwell, 1996.

Cheah, Pheng. *Spectral Nationality: Passages of Freedom from Kant to Postcolonial Literatures of Liberation*. New York: Columbia University Press, 2003.

Choy, Catherine Ceniza. *Empire of Care: Nursing and Migration in Filipino American History*. Durham, N.C.: Duke University Press, 2003.

"Claire Danes No Thrilla for Manila." *CNN*, September 23, 1998. Accessed December 29, 2007. http://edition.cnn.com/SHOWBIZ/News/9809/23/showbuzz.

Classen, Constance. "The Odor of the Other: Olfactory Symbolism and Cultural Categories." *Ethos* 20, no. 2 (1992): 133–66.

Clifford, James. "No Innocent Eyes." Review of *Imperial Eyes*, by Mary Louise Pratt. *Times Literary Supplement*, September 11, 1992.

———. "On Ethnographic Authority." In *The Predicament of Culture: Twentieth Century Ethnography, Literature, and Art*, 21–54. Cambridge, Mass.: Harvard University Press, 1988.

Collins, Dana. "Identity, Mobility, and Urban Place-Making: Exploring Gay Life in Manila." *Gender and Society* 19, no. 2 (2005): 180–98.

Connell, R. W. *Masculinities*. Cambridge, U.K.: Polity Press, 1995.

Connor, Steven. "Topologies: Michel Serres and the Shapes of Thought." *Anglistik* 15 (2004): 105–17.

Considine, Austin. "Hip-Hopping the Night Away in Manila." *New York Times,*
June 4, 2006.

Coy, Martin, and Martin Pöhler. "Gated Communities in Latin American Megacities: Case Studies in Brazil and Argentina." *Environment and Planning B: Planning and Design* 29 (2002): 355–70.

Cresswell, Tim. *On the Move: Mobility in the Modern Western World.* New York:
Routledge, 2006.

Crookshank. "And Everything Turns White." *Generation Pink Online Exclusive.*
Accessed October 16, 2006. http://www.generationpink.com/4_whiteparty.asp.

Cruz-Malavé, Arnaldo, and Martin F. Manalansan IV, eds. *Queer Globalizations:
Citizenship and the Afterlife of Colonialism.* New York: New York University
Press, 2002.

Dant, Tim. "The Driver-Car." In *Automobilities,* edited by Mike Featherstone, Nigel Thrift, and John Urry, 61–80. London: Sage, 2005.

Davis, Colin. "*Ét at Présent*: Hauntology, Specters and Phantoms." *French Studies*
59, no. 3 (2005): 373–79.

de Certeau, Michel. *The Practice of Everyday Life.* Translated by Steven Rendall.
Berkeley: University of California Press, 1984.

De Landa, Manuel. *A Thousand Years of Nonlinear History.* New York: Zone
Books, 1997.

Deleuze, Gilles. *Difference and Repetition.* Translated by Paul Patton. London:
Athlone Press, 1994.

———. *Foucault.* Translated by Séan Hand. London: Athlone Press, 1986.

D'Emilio, John. "Capitalism and Gay Identity." In *Powers of Desire: The Politics
of Sexuality,* edited by Ann Snitow, Christine Stansell, and Sharan Thompson,
100–113. New York: Monthly Review Press, 1983.

Deparle, Jason. "A Good Provider Is One Who Leaves." *New York Times Sunday
Magazine,* April 22, 2007.

Derrida, Jacques. "The Animal That Therefore I Am (More to Follow)." *Critical
Inquiry* 28 (2002): 369–418.

———. *Spectres of Marx: The State of the Debt, the Work of Mourning, and the
New International.* Translated by Peggy Kamuf. New York: Routledge, 1994.

———. *Without Alibi.* Translated and edited by Peggy Kamuf. Stanford, Calif.:
Stanford University Press, 2002.

Derrida, Jacques, and Hélène Cixous, with Armell Aliette. "From the Word to Life:
A Dialogue between Jacques Derrida and Hélène Cixous." Translated by Ash-
ley Thompson. *New Literary History: A Journal of Theory and Interpretation*
31, no. 1 (2006): 1–13.

"Derrida's Elsewhere." Transcript of documentary film by Safaa Fathy. Accessed
October 1, 2005. http://www.lrc.edu/eng/Derrida/Elsewhere.htm.

Dickey, Sara. "Permeable Homes: Domestic Service, Household Space, and the Vulnerability of Class Boundaries in Urban India." *American Ethnologist* 27 (2000): 462–89.

Dowsett, Gary W., Herukhuti Williams, Ana Ventuneac, and Alex Carballo-Diéguez. "'Taking It Like a Man': Masculinity and Barebacking Online." *Sexualities* 1, nos. 1–2 (2008): 121–41.

Duggan, Lisa. *The Twilight of Equality: Neoliberalism, Cultural Politics, and the Attack on Democracy.* Boston: Beacon Press, 2003.

Duncan, Duane. "Out of the Closet and into the Gym: Gay Men and Body Image in Melbourne, Australia." *Journal of Men's Studies* 15, no. 3 (2007): 331–47.

Duncan, Nancy, ed. *Body Space: Destabilizing Geographies of Gender and Sexuality.* London: Routledge, 1996.

Dyer, Richard. *White.* London: Routledge, 1997.

Elder, Glen. "Love for Sale: Marketing Gay Male P/leisure Space in Contemporary Cape Town, South Africa." In *A Companion to Feminist Geography,* edited by Lise Nelson and Joni Seager, 578–89. Malden, Mass.: Blackwell, 2004.

Eng, David L. *Racial Castration: Managing Masculinity in Asian America.* Durham, N.C.: Duke University Press, 2001.

Eng, David L., and Alice Y. Hom, eds. *Q&A: Queer in Asian America.* Philadelphia: Temple University Press, 1998.

Espiritu, Yen Le, ed. *Filipino American Lives.* Philadelphia: Temple University Press, 1995.

———. *Home Bound: Filipino American Lives across Cultures, Communities, and Countries.* Berkeley: University of California Press, 2003.

Estrella, Chit. "Nursing Schools Peddle Dreams." *Manila Times,* March 22, 2005.

"Failed Schools' Closure to Address Nurses' Glut." *Philippine Daily Inquirer,* October 26, 2009.

Fajardo, Kale Bantigue. *Filipino Crosscurrents: Oceanographies of Seafaring, Masculinities, and Globalization.* Minneapolis: University of Minnesota Press, 2011.

Fanon, Frantz. *Black Skin, White Masks.* Translated by Charles Lam Markmann. New York: Grove Press, 1967.

Fernandez, Malu. "From Boracay to Greece!" *People Asia,* June 2007.

Flusty, Steven. *De-Coca-Colonization: Making the Globe from the Inside Out.* New York: Routledge, 2005.

Fores-Ganzon, Guadalupe, trans. *La Solidaridad* [Solidarity], vol. 1, 1889. Pasig City, Philippines: Fundación Santiago, 1996.

Frantz, Fannon. "Remembering Fanon." Foreword to *Black Skin, White Masks,* by Homi K. Bhabha, vii–xxv. Translated by Charles Lam Markmann. London: Pluto Press, 1986.

Frow, John. *Cultural Studies and Cultural Value.* Oxford: Clarendon Press, 1995.

Fung, Richard. "Looking for My Penis: The Eroticized Asian in Gay Porn Video." In *Q&A: Queer in Asian America,* edited by David L. Eng and Alice Y. Hom, 115–34. Philadelphia: Temple University Press, 1998.

Gadi-Baltazar, Rita. "Locsin: Innovator and Architect." *Solidarity* 2, no. 6 (1967): 69–78.

Gaonkar, Dilip Parameshwar. "On Alternative Modernities." *Public Culture* 11 (1999): 1–18.

Gaonkar, Dilip Parameshwar, and Elizabeth A. Povinelli. "Technologies of Public Forms: Circulation, Transfiguration, Recognition." *Public Culture* 15 (2003): 385–97.

Garcia, J. Neil C. "Performativity, the *Bakla* and the Orientalizing Gaze." *Inter-Asia Cultural Studies* 1, no. 2 (2000): 265–81.

———. *Philippine Gay Culture: The Last Thirty Years, Binabae to Bakla to Silahis to MSM.* Quezon City: University of the Philippines Press, 1996.

———. "Villa, Montano, Perez: Postcoloniality and Gay Liberation in the Philippines." In *AsiaPacifiQueer: Rethinking Genders and Sexualities,* edited by Fran Martin, Peter A. Jackson, Mark McLelland, and Audrey Yue, 163–80. Urbana: University of Illinois Press, 2008.

Generation Pink. "About." Accessed October 16, 2006. http://www.generation-pink.com.

George, Susan. "Fast Castes." In *Speed: Visions of an Accelerated Age,* edited by Jeremy Millar and Michael Schwartz, 115–18. London: The Photographers' Gallery, 1998.

Gibson-Graham, J. K. *The End of Capitalism (as We Knew It): A Feminist Critique of Political Economy.* Oxford: Blackwell, 1996.

Gikandi, Simon. "Globalization and the Claims of Postcoloniality." *South Atlantic Quarterly* 100, no. 3 (2001): 627–58.

Giorgi, Gabriel. "Madrid *en Tránsito*: Travelers, Visibility and Gay Identity." *GLQ: A Journal of Lesbian and Gay Studies* 8, nos. 1–2 (2002): 57–79.

Godzich, Wlad. "The Semiotics of Semiotics." In *On Signs,* edited by Marshall Blonsky, 421–47. Baltimore: Johns Hopkins University Press, 1985.

Gomez, Francis. "R-E-S-P-E-C-T: A Personal Essay on the Filipino Transgendered Experience." *Manila Times,* June 25, 2006.

Gopinath, Gayatri. *Impossible Desires: Queer Diasporas and South Asian Public Cultures.* Durham, N.C.: Duke University Press, 2005.

Gordon, Avery F. *Ghostly Matters: Haunting and the Sociological Imagination.* Minneapolis: University of Minnesota Press, 1997.

Gosine, Andil. "Blonde to Brown at Gay.Com: Passing White in Queer Cyberspace." In *Queer Online: Media, Technology and Sexuality,* edited by Kate O'Riordan and David J. Phillips, 139–54. New York: Peter Lang, 2007.

Gregory, Derek. *The Colonial Present: Afghanistan, Palestine, Iraq.* Oxford: Blackwell, 2004.

———. "Connective Dissonance: Imaginative Geographies and the Colonial Present." In *Space Odysseys: Spatiality and Social Relations in the 21st Century,* edited by Jørgen Ole Bærenholdt and Kirsten Simonsen, 197–214. Aldershot, U.K.: Ashgate, 2004.

Gross, Ariela Julie. *What Blood Won't Tell: A History of Race on Trial in America.* Cambridge, Mass.: Harvard University Press, 2008.

Halberstam, Judith. *In a Queer Time and Place: Transgender Bodies, Subcultural Lives.* New York: New York University Press, 2005.

———. "Shame and White Gay Masculinity." *Social Text* 23, nos. 3–4 (2005): 219–33.

Haritaworn, Jinthana. *The Biopolitics of Mixing: Thai Multiracialities and Haunted Ascendancies.* Farnham, U.K.: Ashgate, 2012.

Heidegger, Martin. "Language." In *Poetry, Language, Thought,* translated by Alfred Hofstadter, 185–208. New York: Harper and Row, 1971.

Hénaff, Marcel. "Of Stones, Angels and Humans: Michel Serres and the Global City." *SubStance* 26, no. 2 (1997): 59–80.

Hill, Leslie. *Blanchot: Extreme Contemporary.* New York: Routledge, 1997.

Hilsdon, Anne-Marie. *Madonnas and Martyrs: Militarism and Violence in the Philippines.* Quezon City: Ateneo de Manila University Press, 1995.

Himpele, Jeff D. *Circuits of Culture: Media, Politics, and Indigenous Identity in the Andes.* Minneapolis: University of Minnesota Press, 2008.

Holt, Elizabeth Mary. *Colonizing Filipinas: Nineteenth-Century Representations of the Philippines in Western Historiography.* Quezon City: Ateneo de Manila University Press, 2002.

Husserl, Edmund. *Ideas Pertaining to a Pure Phenomenology and to a Phenomenological Philosophy: Second Book.* Translated by Richard Rojcewicz and André Schuwer. Dordrecht: Kluwer Academic Publishers, 1989.

———. "The World of the Living Present and the Constitution of the Surrounding World That Is Outside the Flesh." In *Husserl at the Limits of Phenomenology,* edited by Leonard Lawlor and Bettina Bergo, 132–54. Evanston, Ill.: Northwestern University Press, 2002.

Ingram, Gordon Brent, Anne-Marie Bouthillette, and Yolanda Retter, eds. *Queers in Space: Communities/Public Places/Sites of Resistance.* Seattle: Bay, 1997.

Isaac, Allan Punzalan. *American Tropcis: Articulating Filipino America.* Minneapolis: University of Minnesota Press, 2006.

Jackson, Peter A. "Capitalism and Global Queering: National Markets, Parallels among Sexual Cultures, and Multiple Queer Modernities." *GLQ: A Journal of Lesbian and Gay Studies* 15, no. 3 (2009): 357–95.

———. "Gay Adaptation, Tom-Dee Resistance, and Kathoey Indifference: Thailand's Gender/Sex Minorities and the Episodic Allure of Queer English." In *Speaking in Queer Tongues: Globalization and Gay Desire,* edited by William L. Leap and Tom Boellstorff, 202–30. Urbana: University of Illinois Press, 2004.

———. "That's What Rice Queens Study! White Gay Desire and Representing Asian Homosexualities." *Journal of Australian Studies* 65 (2000): 181–89.

Jackson, Peter A., and Gerard Sullivan, eds. *Lady Boys, Tom Boys, Rent Boys: Male and Female Homosexualities in Contemporary Thailand.* New York: Haworth, 1999.

———. *Multicultural Queer: Australian Narratives.* Binghamton: Haworth Press, 1999.

Johnson, Mark. *Beauty and Power: Transgendering and Cultural Transformation in the Southern Philippines.* Oxford: Berg, 1997.

Jurado, Emil. "Educating Migrants." *Manila Standard Today,* August 31, 2007.

Knopp, Larry. "Ontologies of Place, Placelessness, and Movement: Queer Quests for Identity and Their Impact on Contemporary Geographic Thought." *Gender, Place and Culture* 11, no. 1 (2004): 121–34.

Krishnaswamy, Revathi. "Postcolonial and Globalization Studies: Connections, Conflicts, Complicities." In *The Postcolonial and the Global,* edited by Revathi Krishnaswamy and John C. Hawley, 2–21. Minneapolis: University of Minnesota Press, 2007.

Lacan, Jacques. *The Four Fundamental Concepts of Psycho-analysis.* Edited by Jacques-Alain Miller and translated by Alan Sheridan. New York: Norton, 1978.

Latour, Bruno. "The Politics of Explanation: An Alternative." In *Knowledge and Reflexivity,* edited by Steve Woolgar, 155–77. London: Sage, 1988.

———. *We Have Never Been Modern.* New York: Harvester Wheatsheaf, 1991.

Lawlor, Leonard. *Derrida and Husserl: The Basic Problem of Phenomenology.* Bloomington: Indiana University Press, 2002.

Le Corbusier. *Aircraft.* London: Studio Publications, 1935.

———. *The City of Tomorrow and Its Planning.* Translated by Frederick Etchells. London: Architectural Press, 1971.

———. *New World of Space.* New York: Reynal and Hitchcock, 1948.

Lee, Benjamin, and Edward LiPuma. "Cultures of Circulation: The Imaginations of Modernity." *Public Culture* 14 (2002): 191–213.

Lefebvre, Henri. *Rhythmanalysis: Space, Time and Everyday Life.* New York: Continuum, 2004.

Leibing, Annette, and Athen McLean. "'Learn to Value Your Shadow!': An Introduction to the Margins of Fieldwork." In *The Shadow Side of Fieldwork: Exploring the Blurred Borders between Ethnography and Life,* edited by Athena McLean and Annette Leibing, 1–28. Oxford: Blackwell, 2007.

Leong, Russell, ed. *Asian American Sexualities: Dimensions of the Gay and Lesbian Experience.* New York: Routledge, 1996.

Lepselter, Susan Claudia. "The Flight of the Ordinary: Narrative, Poetics, Power and UFOs in the American Uncanny." PhD diss., University of Texas at Austin, 2005.

Leys, Ruth. *From Guilt to Shame: Auschwitz and After.* Princeton, N.J.: Princeton University Press, 2007.

Lichtenstein, Thérèse. *Behind Closed Doors.* Berkeley: University of California Press, 2001.

Lico, Gerard. *Edifice Complex: Power, Myth, and Marcos State Architecture.* Quezon City: Ateneo de Manila University Press, 2003.

Lingis, Alphonso. *Abuses.* Berkeley: University of California Press, 1994.

———. *The Imperative.* Bloomington: Indiana University Press, 1998.

Lionnet, Françoise. "Autoethnography: The An-archic Style of *Dust Tracks on a Road.*" In *Autobiographical Voices: Race, Gender, Self-Portraiture,* 97–129. Ithaca: Cornell University Press, 1989.

LiPuma, Edward, and Thomas Koelble. "Cultures of Circulation and the Urban Imaginary: Miami as Example and Exemplar." *Public Culture* 17 (2005): 153–79.

López Jaena, Graciano. *Discursos y Artículos Varios (Selected Speeches and Articles), with Notes and Commentaries by Jaime C. de Veyra.* Manila: Bureau of Printing, 1951.

Luibhéid, Eithne. "Queer/Migration: An Unruly Body of Scholarship." *GLQ: A Journal of Lesbian and Gay Studies* 14, nos. 2–3 (2008): 169–90.

———, ed. "Queer/Migration." A special issue of *GLQ: A Journal of Lesbian and Gay Studies* 14, nos. 2–3 (2008).

Luibhéid, Eithne, and Lionel Cantú, eds. *Queer Migrations: Sexuality, U.S. Citizenship, and Border Crossings.* Minneapolis: University of Minnesota Press, 2005.

MacCormack, Patricia. *Cinesexuality.* Aldershot, U.K.: Ashgate, 2008.

Mahmood, Saba. *The Politics of Piety: The Islamic Revival and the Feminist Subject.* Princeton, N.J.: Princeton University Press, 2005.

Makalani, Minkah. "Introduction: Diaspora and the Localities of Race." *Social Text* 27, no. 1 (2009): 1–10.

Manalansan, Martin F., IV. *Global Divas: Filipino Gay Men in the Diaspora.* Durham, N.C.: Duke University Press, 2003.

———. "Queer Intersections: Sexuality and Gender in Migration Studies." *International Migration Review* 40, no. 1 (2006): 239–40.

———. "Race, Violence, and Neoliberal Spatial Politics in the Global City." *Social Text* 23, nos. 3–4 (2005): 141–55.

———. "(Re)Locating the Gay Filipino." *Journal of Homosexuality* 26, nos. 2/3 (1993): 53–72.

Manderson, Lenore, and Margaret Jolly, eds. *Sites of Desire, Economies of Pleasure: Sexualities in Asia and the Pacific.* Chicago: University of Chicago Press, 1997.

Marinetti, F. T. "The Founding and Manifesto of Futurism." In *Marinetti: Selected Writings*, edited by R. W. Flint and translated by R. W. Flint and Arthur A. Coppotelli, 39–44. New York: Farrar, Straus and Giroux, 1971.

Martel, Ned. "An End to Notches on the Headboard." *New York Times*, August 6, 2005.

Marx, Karl. *Grundrisse: Foundations of the Critique of Political Economy*. Translated by Martin Nicolaus. London: Allen Lane/NLR, 1973.

Matthews, Julie. "Eurasian Persuasions: Mixed Race, Performativity and Cosmopolitanism." *Journal of Intercultural Studies* 28, no. 1 (2007): 41–54.

Mbembé, Achille. "Aesthetics of Superfluity." *Public Culture* 16 (2004): 373–405.

McLuhan, Marshall. *Understanding Media: The Extensions of Man*. London: Abacus, 1964.

McQuire, Scott. "Blinded by the (Speed of) Light." *Theory, Culture and Society* 16, nos. 5–6 (1999): 143–59.

———. "Immaterial Architectures." *Space and Culture* 8, no. 2 (2005): 126–40.

———. "The Politics of Public Space in the Media City." *First Monday*. Accessed February 10, 2010. http://uncommonculture.org/ojs/index.php/fm/article/view/1544/1459.

———. "Pure Speed—from Transport to Teleport." In *Speed: Visions of an Accelerated Age*, edited by Jeremy Millar and Michiel Schwartz, 26–31. London: The Photographers' Gallery, 1998.

———. "Urban Screens: Discovering the Potential of Outdoor Screens for Urban Society." *First Monday*. (2006). Accessed February 10, 2010. http://firstmonday.org/issue/view/217.

Merleau-Ponty, Maurice. *The Primacy of Perception*. Translated by James M. Edie. Evanston, Ill.: Northwestern University Press, 1964.

Mills, Charles W. *The Racial Contract*. Ithaca: Cornell University Press, 1997.

Morrison, Toni. *Tar Baby*. London: Chatto and Windus, 1981.

Munt, Sally. *Queer Attachments: The Cultural Politics of Shame*. Aldershot, U.K.: Ashgate, 2007.

Najmabadi, Afsaneh. "Interview with Gayatri Spivak." *Social Text* 9, no. 3 (1991): 122–34.

Nast, Heidi. "Queer Patriarchies, Queer Racisms, International." *Antipode* 34 (2002): 874–909.

Nells-Lim, J. "Metro Manila in the 1980s." *Manila Magazine*, June 1981.

Norris, Christopher. *The Contest of Faculties: Philosophy and Theory after Deconstruction*. London: Routledge, 1986.

Oswin, Natalie. "Critical Geographies and the Uses of Sexuality: Deconstructing Queer Space." *Progress in Human Geography* 32, no. 1 (2008): 89–103.

———. "Decentering Queer Globalization: Diffusion and the 'Global Gay.'" *Environment and Planning D: Society and Space* 24 (2006): 777–90.

————. "Researching 'Gay Cape Town': Finding Value-Added Queerness." *Social and Cultural Geography* 6, no. 4 (2005): 567–86.

Paoletta, Michael. "'Queer as Folk' Tour Gives Babylon Club a Twist." *Billboard,* March 13, 2004.

Parreñas, Rhaçel Salazar. *Servants of Globalization: Women, Migration, and Domestic Work.* Stanford, Calif.: Stanford University Press, 2001.

Patton, Cindy, and Benigno Sánchez-Eppler, eds. *Queer Diasporas.* Durham, N.C.: Duke University Press, 2000.

Payne, Robert. "Str8acting." *Social Semiotics* 17, no. 4 (2007): 525–38.

Peirce, Charles S. *Collected Papers, vols. 1 and 2.* Edited by Charles Hartshorne and Paul Weiss. Cambridge, Mass.: Harvard University Press, 1974.

Perez, Tony. *Cubao 1980 at Iba Pang Mga Katha: Unang Sigaw ng Gay Liberation Movement sa Pilipinas* [Cubao 1980 and Other Works: The First Cry of the Gay Liberation Movement in the Philippines]. Manila: Cacho Publishing House, 1992.

Pisares, Elizabeth H. "Do You Mis(recognize) Me? Filipina Americans in Popular Music and the Problem of Invisibility." In *Positively No Filipinos Allowed: Building Communities and Discourse,* edited by Antonio Tiongson, Ricardo Gutierrez, and Edgardo Gutierrez, 172–98. Philadelphia: Temple University Press, 2006.

Ponce, Martin Joseph. *Beyond the Nation: Diasporic Filipino Literature and Queer Reading.* New York: New York University Press, 2012.

Povinelli, Elizabeth A., and George Chauncey, eds. "Thinking Sexuality Transnationally." A special issue of *GLQ: A Journal of Lesbian and Gay Studies* 5, no. 4 (1999).

Pratt, Mary Louise. *Imperial Eyes: Travel Writing and Transculturation.* London: Routledge, 1992.

Probyn, Elspeth. *Blush: Faces of Shame.* Minneapolis: University of Minnesota Press, 2005.

Puar, Jasbir K. *Terrorist Assemblages: Homonationalism in Queer Times.* Durham, N.C.: Duke University Press, 2007.

————. "A Transnational Feminist Critique of Queer Tourism." *Antipode* 34 (2002): 935–46.

Pynchon, Thomas. "The Secret Integration." In *Slow Learner: Early Stories.* Boston: Little, Brown, 1985.

Rabasa, José. "Elsewheres: Radical Relativism and the Frontiers of Empire." *Qui Parle* 16, no. 1 (2006): 71–94.

Rafael, Vicente L. *White Love and Other Events in Filipino History.* Durham, N.C.: Duke University Press, 2000.

Read, Stephen. "The Urban Image: Becoming Visible." In *The Body in Architecture,* edited by Deborah Hauptmann, 48–65. Rotterdam: 010 Publishers, 2006.

Reed-Danahay, Deborah. *Auto/Ethnography: Rewriting the Self and the Social.* Oxford: Berg, 1997.

Ridge, Damien, David Plummer, and David Peasley. "Remaking the Masculine Self and Coping in the Liminal World of the 'Gay Scene.'" *Culture, Health and Sexuality* 8, no. 6 (2006): 501–14.

Rizal, Jose. *The Rizal-Blumentritt Correspondence.* Manila: Jose Rizal National Centennial Commission, 1961.

Rodriguez, Dylan. *Suspended Apocalypse: White Supremacy, Genocide, and the Filipino Condition.* Minneapolis: University of Minnesota Press, 2010.

Rofel, Lisa. *Desiring China: Experiments in Neoliberalism, Sexuality and Public Culture.* Durham, N.C.: Duke University Press, 2007.

Rondilla, Joanne L. "Filipinos and the Color Complex: Ideal Asian Beauty." In *Shades of Difference: Why Skin Color Matters,* edited by Evelyn Nakano Glenn, 63–80. Stanford, Calif.: Stanford University Press, 2009.

Rose, Jacqueline. *On Not Being Able to Sleep: Psychoanalysis and the Modern World.* London: Chatto and Windus, 2003.

Rosler, Martha. "In the Place of the Public: Observations of a Frequent Flyer." *Assemblage* 25 (1994): 61–79.

Rushbrook, Dereka. "Cities, Queer Space, and the Cosmopolitan Tourist." *GLQ: A Journal of Lesbian and Gay Studies* 8, nos. 1–2 (2002): 183–206.

Saldanha, Arun. *Psychedelic White: Goa Trance and the Viscosity of Race.* Minneapolis: University of Minnesota Press, 2007.

———. "Reontologizing Race: The Machinic Geography of Phenotype." *Environment and Planning D: Society and Space* 24 (2006): 9–24.

Sánchez-Eppeler, Benigno, and Cindy Patton. "Introduction: With a Passport out of Eden." In *Queer Diasporas,* edited by Benigno Sánchez-Eppeler and Cindy Patton, 1–14. Durham, N.C.: Duke University Press, 2007.

Sassen, Saskia. *The Global City: New York, London, Tokyo.* Princeton, N.J.: Princeton University Press, 1991.

Sedgwick, Eve Kosofsky. *Tendencies.* Durham, N.C.: Duke University Press, 1993.

Serres, Michel. *Angels: A Modern Myth.* Translated by Francis Cowper. Edited by Philippa Hurd. New York: Flammarion, 1995.

———. *Atlas.* Paris: Editions Julliard, 1994.

———. *Detachment.* Translated by Genevieve James and Raymond Federman. Athens: Ohio University Press, 1989.

———. *The Five Senses: A Philosophy of Mingled Bodies.* Translated by Margaret Sankey and Peter Cowley. London: Continuum, 2008.

———. *Genesis.* Translated by Geneviève James and James Nielson. Ann Arbor: University of Michigan Press, 1995.

———. *Hermes: Literature, Science, Philosophy.* Edited by Josué V. Harari and David F. Bell. Baltimore: Johns Hopkins University Press, 1982.

———. *The Parasite.* Translated by Lawrence R. Schehr. Baltimore: Johns Hopkins University Press, 1982.

———. *Rome, the Book of Foundations.* Translated by Felicia McCarren. Stanford, Calif.: Stanford University Press, 1991.

Siegert, Bernhard. *Relays: Literature as an Epoch of the Postal System.* Translated by Kevin Repp. Stanford, Calif.: Stanford University Press, 1999.

Silverman, Hugh J. *Inscriptions: Between Phenomenology and Structuralism.* New York: Routledge, 1987.

Simmel, Georg. "Sociology of the Senses: Visual Interaction." In *Introduction to the Science of Sociology,* edited by Robert E. Park and Ernest W. Burgess, 356–61. Chicago: University of Chicago Press, 1969.

———. "The Stranger." In *The Sociology of Georg Simmel,* translated and edited by Kurt Wolff, 402–8. New York: Free Press, 1950.

Smith, Mick. "Road Kill: Remembering What Is Left of Our Encounters with Animals." In *Emotion, Place and Culture,* edited by Mick Smith, Joyce Davidson, Laura Cameron, and Liz Bondi, 21–34. Burlington: Ashgate, 2009.

Stewart, Kathleen. "Arresting Images." In *Aesthetic Subjects,* edited by Pamela R. Matthews and David McWhirter, 431–38. Minneapolis: University of Minnesota Press, 2003.

———. "Atmospheric Attunements." *Environment and Planning D: Society and Space* 29 (2011): 445–53.

———. "Conspiracy Theory's Worlds." In *Paranoia within Reason: A Casebook on Conspiracy as Explanation,* edited by George E. Marcus, 13–20. Chicago: University of Chicago Press, 1999.

———. "Machine Dreams." In *Modernism, Inc.: Body, Memory, Capital,* edited by Jani Scandura and Michael Thurston, 21–28. New York: New York University Press, 2001.

———. *Ordinary Affects.* Durham, N.C.: Duke University Press, 2007.

———. "The Perfectly Ordinary Life." *The Scholar and Feminist Online* 2, no. 1 (2003). Accessed November 29, 2009. http://www.barnard.edu/sfonline/ps/stewart.htm.

———. *A Space on the Side of the Road: Cultural Poetics in an Other America.* Princeton, N.J.: Princeton University Press, 1996.

———. "Still Life." In *Intimacy,* edited by Lauren Berlant, 405–20. Chicago: University of Chicago Press, 2000.

———. "Weak Theory in an Unfinished World." *Journal of Folklore Research* 45, no. 1 (2008): 71–82.

Straw, Will. "The Circulatory Turn." In *The Wireless Spectrum: The Politics, Practices and Poetics of Mobile Media,* edited by Barbara Crow, Michael Longford, and Kim Sawchuk, 17–28. Toronto: University of Toronto Press, 2010.

———. "Cultural Scenes." *Loisir et Société/Society and Leisure* 27, no. 2 (2004): 411–22.

———. "Scenes and Sensibilities." *Public* 22/23 (2002): 245–57.

Stryker, Susan. "We Who Are Sexy: Christine Jorgensen's Transsexual Whiteness in the Postcolonial Philippines." *Social Semiotics* 19, no. 1 (2009): 79–91.

Sun, Wanning. *Maid in China: Media, Mobility, and a New Semiotic of Power.* New York: Routledge, 2009.

Sy, Geronimo. "Malu Fernandez: Hate Ugly Filipinos." *Manila Times,* August 30, 2007.

Tadiar, Neferti Xina M. "The Dream-Work of Modernity: The Sentimental Education of Imperial France." *boundary 2* 22, no. 1 (1995): 143–83.

———. *Fantasy-Production: Sexual Economies and Other Philippine Consequences for the New World Order.* Hong Kong: Hong Kong University Press, 2004.

———. "In the Face of Whiteness as Value: Fall-Out of Metropolitan Humanness." *Qui Parle* 13, no. 2 (2003): 143–82.

———. "Manila's Assaults." *Polygraph* 8/9 (1996): 9–20.

———. "Manila's New Metropolitan Form." *differences: A Journal of Feminist Cultural Studies* 5, no. 3 (1993): 154–78.

———. *Things Fall Away: Philippine Historical Experience and the Makings of Globalization.* Durham, N.C.: Duke University Press, 2009.

Tan, Kiki. "More than Meets the Eye." *Outrage Magazine,* no. 2 (2009). Accessed April 10, 2009. http://www.outragemag.com.

Tan, Michael L. "AIDS, Medicine, and Moral Panic in the Philippines." In *Framing the Sexual Subject: The Politics of Gender, Sexuality, and Power,* edited by Richard Parker, Regina Maria Barbosa, and Peter Aggleton, 143–64. Berkeley: University of California Press, 2000.

———. "From *Bakla* to Gay: Shifting Gender Identities and Sexual Behaviors in the Philippines." In *Conceiving Sexuality: Approaches to Sex Research in a Postmodern World,* edited by Richard G. Parker and John H. Gagnon, 85–96. New York: Routledge, 1995.

Taussig, Michael. *The Magic of the State.* New York: Routledge, 1997.

———. *My Cocaine Museum.* Chicago: University of Chicago Press, 2004.

———. *The Nervous System.* New York: Routledge, 1992.

Taylor, Peter J. "Leading World Cities: Empirical Evaluations of Urban Nodes in Multiple Networks." *Urban Studies* 42 (2005): 1593–1608.

Thackera, John. "Lost in Space: A Traveller's Tale." In *Airport,* edited by Steven Bode and Jeremy Millar, 60–69. London: The Photographers' Gallery, 1997.

Thornton, Robert. "The Rhetoric of Ethnographic Holism." *Cultural Anthropology* 3 (1988): 285–303.

Tolentino, Rolando B. "Macho Dancing, the Feminization of Labor, and Neoliberalism in the Philippines." *TDR: The Drama Review* 53, no. 2 (2009): 77–89.

Tongson, Karen. *Relocations: Queer Suburban Imaginaries.* New York: New York University Press, 2011.

Trivedi, Anjani. "Every Three Hours Someone in the Philippines Gets HIV." *Time,* July 24, 2013.

Tsing, Anna L. *Friction: An Ethnography of Global Connection.* Princeton, N.J.: Princeton University Press, 2005.

Valentine, David. *Imagining Transgender: An Ethnography of a Category.* Durham, N.C.: Duke University Press, 2007.

Vidler, Anthony. "Bodies in Space/Subjects in the City: Psychopathologies of Modern Urbanism." *differences: A Journal of Feminist Cultural Studies* 5, no. 3 (1993): 31–51.

Villarin, Richie. "Editor's Note." *Icon Magazine,* January/February/March 2005.

Virilio, Paul. *The Aesthetics of Disappearance.* Translated by Philip Beitchman. New York: Semiotext(e), 1991.

———. *The Art of the Motor.* Translated by Julie Rose. Minneapolis: University of Minnesota Press, 1995.

———. *A Landscape of Events.* Translated by Julie Rose. Cambridge, Mass.: MIT Press, 2000.

———. "The Last Vehicle." In *Looking Back on the End of the World,* edited by Dietmar Kamper and Christoph Wulf, 106–19. New York: Semiotext(e), 1989.

———. *The Lost Dimension.* Translated by Daniel Moshenberg. New York: Semiotext(e), 1991.

———. *Negative Horizon: An Essay on Dromology.* Translated by Michael Degener. London: Continuum, 2005.

———. *Open Sky.* Translated by Julie Rose. London: Verso, 1997.

———. "The Overexposed City." *Zone* 1/2 (1987): 15–31.

———. *Popular Defense and Ecological Struggles.* Translated by Mark Plizzotti. New York: Semiotext(e), 1990.

———. *The Vision Machine.* Translated by Julie Rose. Bloomington: Indiana University Press, 1994.

Visser, Gustav. "Gay Men, Tourism, and Urban Space: Reflections on Africa's 'Gay Capital.'" *Tourism Geographies* 5, no. 2 (2003): 168–89.

Ward, Jane. "Queer Sexism: Rethinking Gay Men and Masculinity." In *Gay Masculinities,* edited by Peter M. Nardi, 152–75. London: Sage, 2000.

Warner, Michael. "Introduction." In *Fear of a Queer Planet: Queer Politics and Social Theory,* edited by Michael Warner, vii–xxxi. Minneapolis: University of Minnesota Press, 1993.

Welker, James, and Lucetta Kam, eds. "Of Queer Import(s): Sexualities, Genders, and Rights in Asia." A special issue of *Intersections: Gender, History, and Culture in the Asian Context* 14 (2006).

Wiegman, Robyn. "Object Lessons: Men, Masculinity, and the Sign *Women.*" *Signs: Journal of Women in Culture and Society* 26, no. 2 (2001): 79–105.

Wilce, James M. *Crying Shame: Metaculture, Modernity, and the Exaggerated Death of Lament.* Oxford: Wiley-Blackwell, 2009.

Williams, Raymond. *Politics and Letters: Interviews with the New Left Review.* London: New Left Books, 1979.

Wilson, Rob. "Afterword: Worlding as Future Tactic." In *The Worlding Project: Doing Cultural Studies in the Era of Globalization,* edited by Rob Wilson and Christopher Leigh Connery, 209–23. Santa Cruz, CA: New Pacific Press, 2007.

Žižek, Slavoj. "The Real in Ideology." *PsychCritique* 2, no. 3 (1987): 255–70.

All locations are in Manila, Philippines, unless otherwise specified.

Bobby Benedicto is an Andrew W. Mellon postdoctoral fellow in the humanities at McGill University.